There was a blinding flash as an enemy round hit our parapet. That was all I remember from the knockdown round. Dan Phillips fared no better than I. How long we lay on the floor of the pit is anyone's guess. I heard Dan groan before I reached up to feel my ears. My hand came back red. Phillips groaned again before I spoke. "My ears are bleeding, and I can't hear a thing, Dan."

"My eyes are bleeding, and I can't see a thing!"

I think we had both been out of it for some time. S.Sgt. Arthur Brooks leaped into the pit with a wet rag in each hand. When he began washing Phillips's face, we repeated our statements. Judging from his answer, Brooks had heard the remarks before.

"Don't worry about it guys. One of you can see, and the other one can hear, so stick together. I've got to get back to my weapon before we get ate up. . . ."

By William T. Craig
Published by Ivy Books:

SCARE TIME
LIFER! From Infantry to Special Forces
TEAM SERGEANT: A Special Forces NCO at Lang Vei and
   Beyond

TEAM SERGEANT

A Special Forces NCO at Lang Vei and Beyond

William T. Craig

IVY BOOKS • NEW YORK

An Ivy Book
Published by The Ballantine Publishing Group
Copyright © 1998 by William T. Craig

http://www.randomhouse.com

Library of Congress Catalog Card Number: 97-93916

ISBN 0-8041-1714-4

Manufactured in the United States of America

First Edition: April 1998

10 9 8 7 6 5 4 3 2 1

This book is humbly dedicated to:

Editor Owen Lock, who planted the seeds into the hard ground.

All the officers and enlisted personnel who paid the ultimate price in the wars that have preserved our entity and self-respect. Especially the following, mentioned in this text, who paid that ultimate price for you and me.

Ashley, Eugene	Vietnam
Badaloti, Huston	Vietnam
Burke, Earl	Vietnam
Card, William R.	Thailand
Combs, Al	Vietnam
Delong, Chuck	Laos
Hamilton, Gilbert L.	Vietnam
Hoagland, George	Vietnam
Holt, James	Vietnam (MIA)
Lindewald, Charles	Vietnam (MIA)
Moreland, James	Vietnam (MIA)
Pegram, Richard E. Jr.	Vietnam
Phillips, Daniel	Vietnam (MIA)
Quamo, George	Laos
Terry, Ronald	Vietnam
Torres, Estevan	Vietnam

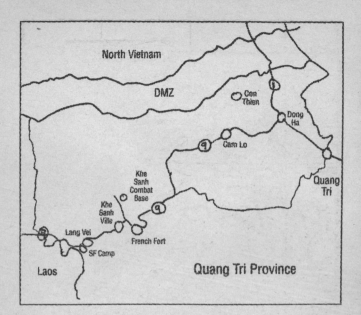

North Vietnam

DMZ

Con Thien

Dong Ha

Cam Lo

Khe Sanh Combat Base

Khe Sanh Ville

French Fort

Lang Vei

SF Camp

Quang Tri

Laos

Quang Tri Province

CHAPTER 1

In September of 1964, I was stationed on Okinawa with Company A, 1st Special Forces Group (Airborne). A sergeant first class (E7) with fourteen years in the Army, an authorized Okinawan wife, and a three-month-old son, I was now drawing $350 a month base pay, $55 jump pay, $22.50 overseas pay, and $114.90 quarters allowance. I had money coming outta my Corcoran jump boots. I was also on Temporary Duty (TDY) orders for Vietnam for the second time in a one-year span. No mean feat for a five-eleven, 162 pound, reddish-brown-headed, thirty-seven-year-old youngster from the foothills of Oklahoma.

I was assigned as an assistant operations sergeant to a master sergeant (E8) on control detachment B-130 for 180 days or less; so the orders read. My administrative duties concerning my new family would take up the fifteen remaining days on island.

The A-132 detachment commander for whom I'd worked on the last venture to "war-torn," would be of great assistance in the aftermath of my marriage to Miss Hatsuko Ago. Now employed at 1st SF Group Headquarters at Bishagawa, Major Victor Hugo made sure that Mrs. Craig's military ID card was issued promptly. He also speeded up the part I thought might be a stumbling block in my latest miniwar with United States government red tape—a U.S. birth certificate for James J. Craig.

Once again Major Hugo was an asset—the U.S. State

1

Department issued the certificate before Detachment B-130 embarked. James Joseph was now a bona fide foreign-born U.S. citizen. The only restriction he would ever encounter would be his bar to the office of president of the United States. The restriction clearly states that the president must be born on U.S. soil, regardless of the status of his parents, apparently. Here was a law that has outlived the times, made before the U.S. ever had multitudes of GIs and their families stationed in foreign lands. The United States doesn't change its rules and regulations to adjust to world changes.

I mulled that over many times before we departed for Can Tho, deep in the heart of the Delta, in IV Corps of South Vietnam. Finally, I concluded: that (1) our forefathers never meant for us to be the leaders of the free world; (2) most Americans are still isolationist, and (3) WWII didn't teach them zilch.

Regardless, Hatsuko and James were in good enough shape to survive the six months without a husband or father. Company A, 1st SF Group (Airborne) placed the icing on the cake with the appointment of a sponsor. S.Sgt. Frank Fowler, now officially James's godfather, and his wife, Suzie, would look after them in my absence. With its sponsor program, Special Forces was, again, ten years ahead of the rest of the U.S. Army. It is now an official program throughout the world wherever U.S. forces are stationed with dependents.

I spent some of my time in briefings concerning IV Corps and the Civilian Irregular Defense Group (CIDG) camps that the B-detachment would be servicing. Frankly, I didn't look forward to the boring interlude of six months on a control detachment.

A C-130 transport aircraft departed with twenty-three TDY souls on or about September 12, 1964. Two days more of mundane briefings in our Command Headquarters at Nha Trang, that of the 5th Special Forces Group (Abn), and we were off to the IV Corps Headquarters city of Can Tho.

The B-detachment's facilities were conveniently located next to the Can Tho airstrip. The runway could accommodate landings by C-130 four-engine cargo aircraft, so the smaller two-engine Caribou and C-123 cargo planes would present no problems.

The permanent buildings were one story and arranged in a square-shaped perimeter. The approximate 100-by-100-yard layout consisted of a headquarters section for administrative offices, sleeping quarters, a canteen and bar (naturally), and an S-4 (Supply) office. This setup would keep the twenty-three-man B-detachment busy supplying the five A-detachments with supplies, payrolls, and admin help. As usual, nothing is ever as smooth as it may seem on paper. There were some built-in problems as well.

Despite our being subordinate to the 5th SF Group for Command & Control, the Military Advisory and Assistance Group (MAAG) of Vietnam had to pretend they were in charge of something, and we therefore had to pass on everything we did to their headquarters. An HQ that could, and would, do nothing to help us accomplish our mission. Being a nonconformist in a group of peers, my first, and last, dispute with MAAG came quicker than anyone expected.

In a week, I had flown to all A-detachments and discussed what type of support we could assist with, as well as what we could not. Rations for CIDG troops and other goods were obtained in Vietnam through local procurement. We maintained a five-day emergency stock of ammunition and medical supplies. Over nine thousand line items of supplies were handled. In 1964 a monthly average of approximately 311 tons of supplies was delivered by the B-detachment's support facilities at Can Tho, practically all of it by air transportation. I scheduled all supply and personnel flights to all A camps and would accompany supply flights when necessary. This part of the job was old hat to me, due to my experience in the B-detachment in Da Nang in 1962. It was additional duties assigned by Sergeant Major Avery that would be my undoing.

I am speaking in the main of reports to MAAG that justified

our existence as well as part of theirs. Weekly reports that I made out about A- and B-detachment activities were sent forward each week. It was, frankly, a pain in the ass to me, but I knew I couldn't change the U.S. Army, at least not in a month or two. However, when a captain came into our headquarters one day, Sergeant Major Avery escorted him to my desk. After he was seated, the session began.

"You make out the weekly progress reports, Sergeant First Class Craig?"

"Yes sir, Captain Duane. I collect the information from Operations, Supply, and the A-detachments, then compile and forward it to your headquarters, sir. Are you having a problem with them?"

"Oh no, Sergeant, in fact, they are more than satisfactory. I'm here about a tag-on report that is due—like yesterday."

"I'm unaware of any tag-on report, sir," I answered, truthfully.

"So I understand, after talking to Sergeant Major Avery. You must also forward a monthly report in addition to your weeklies!" Duane stated.

My blood pressure zoomed and my face reddened, but before I could stick my size 8W in my mouth, Duane arose. "I'll expect the monthly on my desk the second or third day of each month, Sergeant."

I closed my open mouth, but my brain was churning. Fourteen years in the Army and I'm back to being a friggin' clerk, I thought. Screw them leg assholes and the horses they rode in on. Just because they are so useless they can't combine the weeklies, I have to do it for them? It ain't gonna happen, GI!

The door had barely hit Captain Duane in the ass before Avery called me in to his tiny office. "Don't feel bad, Bill, we were unaware of the requirement as well," he said.

"I feel nothing but pure disgust, Sergeant Major," I told him. "All they have to do is combine the weeklies every month and they're home free. I don't feel like I should do it for the leg bastards! I'm an Air Operations sergeant, not a damn company clerk!" There, I had gotten it off my chest in a military manner.

Avery's complexion was almost as red as his hair before he managed to retort. "We don't always have to like what we do, Sergeant. Just do it!"

"I'm just gonna be too busy, Sergeant Major. You have clerks, let them do it. I think MAAG ought to do it, and if you'll let me, I'll tell that dumb captain just that."

I knew Avery had his twenty years in for retirement, so why I made the last statement was beyond me. "I'll pass on your idea to the executive officer and see if he can swing it. You're dismissed, Sergeant Craig!"

"Right, Top," I said under my breath, "the first chance I get, I'm gone. If I'd wanted to work for MAAG, I'd have gotten out of SF and started screwin' off like the rest of the leg bastards."

I did nothing on the report the next week, as I was preoccupied with flying to the camps, which were the sole reason for our existence. Two things happened that week that changed my status a tad. A radio operator showed me a request from Nha Trang and the 5th SF Group asking for volunteers for Delta Project. Berry then relayed a message from MAAG to me, to the effect that I was to get the report in on time and to quit being insubordinate. I wouldn't comply with either of MAAG's requests. The radio operator forwarded my name to 5th SF Group Headquarters as a volunteer; my name, rank, and cigarettes went forward without the knowledge of anyone but the 05B.4S (SF radio operator) and myself.

Much to the amazement of Major Fixit and the disgust of Avery, in three days I was ordered to the China Sea city of Nha Trang and Delta Project. Of course, I knew that support detachments were a necessity, but they just weren't my cup of tea. I had lasted only one month with B-130. No one, least of all Avery, shed any tears upon my departure.

The 5th Special Forces Group Command was located next to the modern Air Force base of Nha Trang. Other units near the strip were helicopter units and the 8th Field Army Hospital. Halfway between Saigon and Da Nang lay the resort city where I would be stationed for the rest of my TDY tour.

The permanent change of station (PCS) 5th Special Forces Group Headquarters facilities were built in a square configuration of one-story buildings. Surrounding the permanent wooden structures were large squad tents with board floorings. Delta Project, called B-52 for administrative reasons, was living in the squad tents. This allowed the PCS people to quarter in the air-cooled structures. Considering they had twelve-month tours and ours were six months, it was only fair.

I was greeted by the NCO in command of the project at the 5th SF Group Headquarters and jeeped to a tent, duffel bag and all. After arranging my personal equipment in one of the tents, I was moved to a briefing room in the complex. I was overjoyed to discover many TDY people from Okinawa among the personnel I would be serving with. Pat Cotter, NCO-in-charge Tony Duarte, Lloyd Fisher, Ron Terry, Paul Tracy, and Chuck Delong were among the capable noncommissioned officers then with Delta Project.

The briefing was not long nor drawn out. Captain Richardson, a PCS victim, got to the heart of the matter. "B-52, or Delta Project, will eventually be a country-wide reconnaissance unit that will be deployed in recon teams of from six to eight men. Our relief force, or Mike Force, will be the First Vietnamese Ranger Company, who are at this time a few miles down the road. Our H-34 helicopters are assigned by the Vietnamese and are flown by real live local yokels."

Before I could open my big mouth, Richardson continued. "These pilots are the best in the business, and almost all of them graduated from helicopter school when it first came into being at Fort Sill, Oklahoma. I would hate to have to count the flying hours they have compiled since they qualified!

"Now let's talk about the personnel that will be involved in this endeavor groundwise. Each recon team will have two

American SF people. These personnel, such as yourself, will be TDY from Okinawa and PCS from the 5th Special Forces Group. Some of these people are at present training their eight to ten natives for their teams. Some are further along than others.

"Your team and your assistants are now ready to begin training. You'll have a few days to prepare for the task. We want them ready to go in a month or so. Here is a copy of your schedule, study it! You and your assistant, Staff Sergeant Charles Delong, will use the permanent classroom buildings for your indoor training and the area behind you for your outdoor exercise. Camp Dong Ba Thin will be used for your four-day jump school.

"We've already done it for four teams so it's time enough, Sergeant Craig. Your team will then be ready for their five-day graduating exercise. This consists of a night jump from a fixed-wing aircraft, probably a U.S. Army Caribou or an Air Force C-123. The jump altitude will be six hundred feet or less." Richardson must have been attempting to keep me wide-awake.

"Once on the ground, you will recon the denied area, to be named later, for five days and nights. Once you have been evacuated, the fun and games of training will be over and you will be playing for keeps. Any questions, Sergeant Craig?"

I noted Master Sergeant (M.Sgt.) Duarte smiling at the stupid look on my face, but I bravely answered. "Sir," I said slowly, "if jumping from six hundred feet at night is fun, I'm happy I've been a deprived soldier for lo these many airborne years. Seriously, what ethnic group will Delong and I be training, sir?"

Duarte took up the slack: "We have twenty Montagnards from the Central Highlands, and they will train together. When you've finished, the ones who live through the training will belong to you and Delong. Anything else, Bill?"

"I should have covered that, Sarge," Richardson said. "It's a problem that we have. These people have had basic training, so patrolling, scouting, communications, rappelling from helicopters, and, of course, jump school, will be your mainstay of instruction. The Yards understand enough Vietnamese, so you'll have to go with a Vietnamese interpreter. He'll stay with your recon team after training."

"The Yards are great hunters, and language will not be a problem," I said. "But map reading and that four-day jump school? I can only say, we'll try sir! We'll be ready come Monday morning."

I met S.Sgt. (E5) Charles Delong after supper that night in our makeshift dining facility, and we agreed to attempt to get our act together the next day. I knew Delong only socially, from the bars and clubs on the coral rock of Okinawa. The lanky six-feet-two-inch soldier with brown hair and almond eyes packed 175 pounds of muscle on his twenty-eight-year-old frame.

Staff Sergeant Delong didn't have the instructional experience that I did, so I agreed to teach most classroom material. The hands-on training in the field, where an interpreter was not so vital, I deferred to the younger soldier boy. Our training duo was ready to get it on come Monday morning. To the surprise of no one, the physical training was omitted from the hurry-up training schedule. Special Forces people, most of them at least, knew the importance of physical conditioning and practiced it routinely, and entirely on their own time.

Monday morning in a tented classroom that featured an elevated instructor's platform, we met our interpreter and students for the first time. Ho Chin was a lowland ethnic Vietnamese raised in Saigon and he looked it—Vietnamese, that is. Small in stature at five-two, the slender interpreter had Chinese facial features and was dressed in camouflage fatigues, the same as us and the Montagnards. Ho Chin's only real disadvantage was that he would be despised by the Yards because of their upbringing. Having to listen to classes in Vietnamese would do little to improve the relationship with the mountain folk. From experience, I knew that the

Yards and Americans would learn enough of each other's lingo to make Chin obsolete ASAP.

The Montagnards, Vietnam's answer to the American Indian, wore camouflage fatigues and were dark-skinned, with long black-as-coal hair that hung down to their rear ends in some cases. At five feet six inches or so, they were taller than the low-land Vietnamese. They scowled at Chin, then grinned broadly when we stepped onto the stage in our duty uniforms. Their teeth were white, probably due to some Special Forces medic having introduced them to the toothbrush. Along with the new piece of machinery came "open your mouth" inspections and care and cleaning classes. When they were seated, through Chin I introduced everyone in sight.

Course orientation was quick to follow. I had thought the "Jumping from Big Bird" training would cause some heads to come up and look all around, but mention of the four-day jump school caused not a murmur.

The map reading portion that would be presented in the classroom was difficult for the instructor(s), and it took both of us for several reasons. The Yards came from the highlands and knew the area like the proverbial "book." So who needs a book . . . er, map? you might say. But to be able to properly inform your evacuation source, normally a helicopter, you must be able to give the aircraft the proper coordinates (usually six or eight digits). This could be very difficult even for seasoned map readers. Because the missions were to be in denied or enemy areas, that task was critical to survival for all concerned. Delong, Chin, and I therefore had to teach the class how to count to ten before we progressed into the very basics.

The last day of map reading was spent in the boonies that abound near Nha Trang. How we got them through it all in one piece is beyond me. Three weeks of ten-hour days went swiftly for not only Delong and myself, but for the students as well. Then we were ready for "Jumping from Big Bird" training.

The four-day jump school was now trying to stare us down.

The subject matter really boiled down to only a few subjects despite the fact that the "real" jump school, at Fort Benning, Georgia, took three weeks to teach them. These subjects were: fitting and wearing of the T-10 personnel parachute; parachute landing falls; emergency procedures (films only); and miscellaneous subjects such as guiding the parachute, chute storage, and aircraft procedures. In addition to omitting many minor Fort Benning subjects, there would be no punishment, such as push-ups, for training mistakes. We had no time for it. If the instructors at Bragg, Benning, and Fort Campbell jump schools had heard that, at least in my day, many of them would probably have resigned. Some people get their cookies off on that sort of thing.

One procedure Delong and I concocted was one I thought was brilliant for two mere senior jumpers: except during breaks, the parachutes would be worn by the trainees at all times. That would mean they were putting the chute on and taking it off sixteen to twenty times in one ten-hour day. Good training for a bunch of newbies.

The film on emergency procedures was also a great time-saving device, having all the pictures that the cliché says are worth a thousand words; at least in relation to the use of the reserve parachute basics: when, where, and how to activate. The film also demonstrated how to exit from an aircraft and how the T-10 personnel chute deploys. Delong and I showed that jewel every time we were presented an opportunity.

Dong Ba Thin, located only a few miles from Nha Trang, was the drop zone location that would prove or disprove the worth of our instruction. We qualified all of our students without any injuries to speak of. The training was invaluable to me, and later in my Special Forces career, I would use many of the lessons learned.

CHAPTER 2

The squad tent classroom on the outskirts of the 5th Special Forces Headquarters area set the scene for the training exercise briefing that would qualify the Yards as real-life recon people.

I knew in my heart that no one, and I mean no one, in that room had ever jumped a fixed-wing aircraft at six hundred actual feet above terra firma. I responded quickly so Master Sergeant Duarte and Captain Richardson would not think I was content with the arrangements.

"It's against the regulations, sir," I said. "Twelve hundred feet for training jumps, Captain."

"This will qualify as a combat jump, Sergeant Craig. However, you will wear reserves!" Richardson thought I would complain, but he was wrong this time. I had, apparently, given in and up. We had a combination of deskbound heroes and observers running the show.

But Delong surprised everyone. "At six hundred feet a reserve parachute is excess baggage, sir," my partner said. "If your main chute has a complete malfunction, by the time your reserve parachute deploys you'll be splattered all over hell." The wording of Richardson's answer proved it wasn't his idea.

"It's good training, Staff Sergeant Delong." Delong threw in the towel as well.

Cam Ranh Bay would be a staging area of no small dimension once the buildup of American troops began in 1965, but just then it was a fairly insignificant stategic military location.

Located thirty-five kilometers from Nha Trang, the Catholic mission and church and a platoon of misguided Viet Cong awaited our early morning arrival. The weather forecast for that Wednesday morning was cool, overcast, and visibility of practically zilch. I would inspect equipment and brief our people at 1700 Tuesday. I did not worry about the Yards keeping their mouths shut, because their very existence depended upon it.

I briefed Staff Sergeant Delong over three beers in a secluded area of the Special Forces Club that very night after supper. "I'll lead the stick because we need no hesitating in the door, the drop zone not being that huge, Chuck." Delong only nodded, so I carried on. "Bring up the rear and push 'em! Make sure they know to throw that static line out and away from the door when they make their turn to exit."

"Why, Bill?" he asked.

It had never dawned on me that Delong had not jumped the WWII-era C-47 "Gooney Bird." I proceeded to brief him after a refill and concluded with: "The static line cable extends from the top of the back of the aircraft to the bottom of the aircraft by the door. If you don't throw the static line down and out before you exit, it may wrap around your neck. That could ruin your whole day. Got it?"

"Okay, William, I dig it," Delong came back. "How about a gold star for our wings? Hell, it's a combat jump."

I wasn't ready for that, but I shoulda been. I did the best I could with it only after mulling it over in my mind. Then I began my longest speech of the evening. "Young soldier boy, you still have things to learn about the U.S. Army. On the positive side, a gold star on our wings and a dime would buy us a cup of coffee and set us apart from most of our peers. To an enlisted swine, medals, stars, etcetera, are useless. They are viewed, at least by me, as a means of officers getting on the promotion list to the next highest grade. Until the entire officers corps has a shot at them, you can forget medals and most decorations. For instance, at this time in the Army, they are a no-no for MAAG and SF advisers. Army politics won't allow it yet. I am just concerned at this time that we don't get a static line wrapped around our troops' necks during the jump."

To further emphasize my point about medals and decorations, I related the story of SFC Bob Pronier leading a charge up a hill against the NVA, or VC, at Buon Mi Ga only months before, and receiving only the Bronze star with a V device. "Now that I think about it, he was lucky he got anything but a bullet up his ass!" I said.

Delong indicated that he was following my train of thought.

Wednesday morning at thirty minutes after midnight, eight Montagnard warriors, a Vietnamese interpreter, Delong, and I were almost ready. We had both rigger-checked the Yards, Chin, and ourselves by the dim light available in an aircraft hangar. Besides the T-10 personnel chute, we toted weapons, web gear, and rucksacks. This was topped with the steel helmet the Army was so fond of. That noisemaker would be left on the drop zone (DZ) with the chutes and other used or useless equipment. The Vietnamese Cowboy and his H-34 helicopter people could take out the leftovers come Wednesday at 0700.

Because we were scheduled to leave the Nha Trang Air Force Base at 0100 and not drop until 0200, my mind began the search for some answers. Where in the hell were the Vietnamese C-47 pilots gonna fly for damn near one hour? It would only take ten minutes to be in a jump attitude over the drop zone at Cam Ranh. Our briefing had omitted that detail, so I had to assume it was not important or, worse, thought to be none of our goddamn business. Our leaders were conspicuous by their absence, so I wondered on. Interpreter Chin had the Vietnamese pilot clear up the puzzle as soon as the two Vietnamese Air Force officers arrived on the scene. The head man said, "We will fly to Thailand and return, Trung Si [sergeant]. The green light should go on exactly at 0200. No sweat, GI." The briefing ended.

Delong and I took one last look at the darkened, misty sky

that hung over the China Sea before we enplaned at 0050 hours Wednesday morning. A boring forty-five minutes later I stood 'em up using hand and arm signals only and went through the jumper's litany: (1) stand up, (2) hook up, (3) check static lines, (4) check your equipment, (5) sound off for equipment check, (6) stand in the door. The last command was for myself only, and I obeyed the order. I didn't have long to wait on the last command while I watched the red light on the left door panel. I saw flashlights on the ground just as the light turned green. (7) *Go!* I was out of there at six hundred feet or so. My chute opened and brought me up just as I heard a scream above me. A static line around the neck often gets that type of response. I had no time to diagnose the noise and wished with all my heart that the Viet Cong hadn't either. On the ground, I stood up just like you're not supposed to and took off my chute, bundled it up in a figure-eight roll and tied it to the backpack. I traveled only a few yards to the two Americans who were manning the ground lights. They checked off my name before I spoke.

"You heard the scream, Paul?" I asked.

"Yeah," SFC Paul Tracy replied. "Ho hum. Just another static-line-'round-the-neck job. They were warned and forewarned. Hope he ain't dead. I have Cowboy on the way, or at least he's awake. Torres here"—he pointed to the stocky Puerto Rican NCO—"can attend to him until he's in the hospital. Here they come now. You okay, Bill?"

"Yeah, Paul," I replied. "Shit, I never had it so good."

Delong and four Yards were carrying a groaning mountain man who was bleeding from the neck. They turned him over to Sergeant Estevan Torres, and without further fanfare we were on a 95-degree heading looking for cover, darkness, and quiet. Delong walked slack man (second) and I stayed in the center with Chin and the radio operator.

By the time Cowboy and the H-34 choppers arrived for their hospital victim and the parachutes, we were in total darkness, outta sight and outta mind. Then came the rains. We halted in trees growing in the sand dunes and waited for the dawn to come and the rains to go. Well, daybreak came and we got the dawn, but the rains continued. We were all soaked but we managed to eat cold rations and move out. This set the pattern for the entire reconnaissance trip. Noise discipline was excellent, as was movement—until I began coughing on the third night. The rains halted only briefly in the afternoon hours and we never completely dried out. By the fourth afternoon, I was coughing so bad that the Viet Cong in I Corps should have been worried about it. By then I was running a fever as well. I stopped the patrol and talked to my young, able assistant.

"It's over for me, Chuck. I can't go on. We'll have that Viet Cong platoon on our ass with all the noise I'm making. Call that air relay on the PRC-25 and tell 'em we want out at darkness, and give 'em our location in the clear. Hell, everyone around here knows where we're at by now anyway. I don't want any shit outta our headquarters, either. All we want is Cowboy and those whirlybirds."

We placed our listening posts alongside a prominent trail and waited until dark. My coughing was making everyone nervous, but I couldn't stop it.

The sun was sinking outta sight when Cowboy and one other H-34 appeared. Our position was in low second growth, void of trees, and we threw smoke. When Cowboy saw our red signal, he showed off a tad, coming straight down, loading our five bods and going straight up. Good training, I guess, not that he needed it. The second aircraft removed Delong, Chin, and the three remaining Yards. We were in Nha Trang in only minutes, never getting higher than treetop level. I kept a handkerchief over my face the entire time in order not to inconvenience anyone or pass on whatever I had.

Having showered later, and lying naked with two GI blankets over me, I awaited SFC Torres, my favorite medical 91B5S. My head was on fire and my cough becoming worse so I was glad when he arrived with Delong by his side.

Torres spoke while shoving a thermometer into my mouth,

"You look like shit, Bill. Roll over and I'll give you a penicillin shot!" I complied after damn near coughing up the idiot stick under my tongue.

When I rolled back, Torres took the thermometer. "It's 105 degrees, Bill! You've got to go to the 8th Field Army Hospital, old soldier."

I coughed and lighted up a coffin nail.

"Goddamn, Bill," Delong said. "you don't need cigarettes just now. Give yourself a break for God's sake."

Torres continued shaking his head while I resumed the coughing and smoking. "Torres, you don't know how much I hate those damn horse mills. I don't wanna go! Hell, you're a brain surgeon—you can cure a cold, can't you?" I asked.

"It's gone past that 'cold' stage, Bill. Do you have any pain in your back below the shoulder blades as yet?"

"Yeah, Doc! How in the hell did you know that?"

"You have lobar pneumonia, and that's serious business, William. You need to go to the 8th Field Hospital, I just don't have the equipment or drugs for the long haul. Delong will get a jeep, and we'll take a ride, pal."

Between coughs I said, "Fuck a bunch of lobars, I ain't going nowhere, Doc. I like the local facilities."

Finally, Torres said, "Tell you what, Bill, it's ten P.M. now, and I'll wait until around six in the morning, but if that temperature hasn't gone down by then, it's off to the 8th Field Hospital we go. Deal?"

"It's a deal, Doc. I'll be okay by mañana!"

Torres and Delong left the tent after leaving me some aspirins and two canteens of water. I smoked another cigarette and dozed only after the noise subsided. I woke up several times during the night and sipped water and APCs before dozing off again, and frankly, I felt like death warmed over. I was even glad when 0600 and SFC Torres arrived in a dead heat. He repeated the thermometer bit and the shot in the ass trick before he began his morning lecture.

"Get some clothes on, Sergeant Craig, your fever is 107

degrees and the congestion in your chest is worse. Time for the 8th Field. You agreed, remember?"

I protested, but not too strongly this time. My dislike of hospitals was heard once more but it fell on deaf ears. "Sure would like a cup of coffee," I begged.

"I'll get you a cup while I'm rounding up a jeep and reporting the situation to NCO-in-charge Duarte. Get some clothes on, ol' pardner!"

Torres departed amid my complaining and attempts to wiggle out of the dreaded assignment. When I bent over to blouse my boots, my lungs almost burst from some form of pressure. I finished the chore and felt the same response when I straightened up.

The 8th Field was a one-story, cross-shaped complex of wooden buildings connected by corridors. Truthfully, it looked a lot like the Army medical facilities of the thirties and forties. I should have felt right at home, having been born in one of the damn things.

Torres drove the jeep slowly on the macadam road to the hospital, only a mile from our tent city facade. He parked the jeep and we walked the few steps into the emergency room. I hadn't finished my cigarette yet but I was working on finishing it, gagging and coughing, and Torres was turning in my medical records and attending to other administrative chores. I seated myself in the lobby. I was told to extinguish the coffin nail when a pretty young nurse began taking my blood pressure and temperature. She looked at the thermometer in alarm and scooted out of the room as I coughed, sighed, and lit another cigarette.

This was the scene when the nurse returned with a doctor in tow. He eyed me and literally shouted, "He's got 108-degree temperature and he's puffing on a cigarette? *Put that out, soldier!* Get him in hospital garb, Nurse, and assign him a bed! We'll be along with the portable X-ray machine shortly." Dr. Panic walked off mumbling obscenities under his breath.

I was in an Army blue hospital gown when the doctor and

the portable machine came into the ward. Propped up in the GI hospital bed, I felt like a heat lamp with a cold. Again the officer in charge begin to berate the help. "Ice wraps in towels under both armpits and his crotch, plus a water bag with ice for his head! We must get that fever down." They rolled me over and pumped the miracle drug into the biggest muscle in my body.

After the doc left with the chest X rays, ice packs were the order of the day. I still managed to doze off, but how, I'll never know. When I awoke, the doctor and two nurses were examining me and my hospital chart as well. As usual, the doc did all the talking.

"We have your fever down to 100 degrees, so you should feel a little better, Sergeant. Your lungs are now classified as disaster areas. One is half full of fluid, and the other is three-quarters full. That fluid has to come out, and the drugs should do the rest. How do you feel now, by the way?"

"I feel much better, Doc, but my lungs hurt if I bend over. At least now I know why. Do I have to stay in bed all the time, sir?"

"Yes, at least until we remove the fluid and your fever is back to normal. You can go to the latrine on your own, however. Any more questions, soldier?"

"Yeah, Doc! How you gonna take out the fluid?"

The Army doctor grinned in fiendish delight. "With a suction needle. You may not enjoy it, but it's a necessity if you are to recover anytime soon."

Three days later my fever was zilch and, except for my lungs, I was a ready teddy. The day the doctor ordered me into the operating room to remove the fluid was not one of my good days, but I went along with it for a while. The room contained a portable bed with clean sheets and a few instruments of torture that I was not yet familiar with.

"Remove your pajama top and place your upper body on the bed from the standing position. These two male medics will assist and steady you during the procedure." Or did he say "ordeal"?

Then the doctor showed me the largest needle I had ever seen, precipitating a near-revolt. The instrument was a foot or so long and was attached to a tube with a movable handle.

"You can't stick that grease gun into a human being, sir!"

"It won't hurt much, Sergeant. You guys are supposed to be tough. Bend over!"

"We are tough, sir. Smart, too. I ain't going for it."

Doc Panic nodded at the two medics, and one of them went for reinforcements. When five large men dressed in whites entered the operating room, I was forced to make a choice—fight or submit to torture. Not much of a choice, considering my condition. I bent over while Panic stuck the sword in one lung, through my rib cage, and emptied the tube's contents before moving to the other. At the conclusion of the removal, I was released and stood up before admitting that the pain had been endurable.

I was escorted back to my bed and lay down on a very sore back, mumbling to myself.

Four or five days elapsed before I got a shot at the bureaucracy. Major Shepard, the OIC nurse of the 8th Field, came around early one morning and went to each bed. "General Westmoreland will be here around 1100 hours," she said. "I want all beds made, and the patients who can stand to be at attention by their racks." She gave me a smirk and waited for an affirmative answer.

"No can do, ma'am. I ain't allowed outta the bed except for latrine duty. I'll talk to him from the prone, if you don't mind."

Displaying no surprise at my refusal, Shepard countered smartly. "I'm giving you permission to be outta bed, so just do as you're told, Sergeant!"

"You ain't my doctor, ma'am. If I can do all that, release me back to my unit! Hell, I'm ready."

"I can't release you, or believe me I would," Shepard said. "Just be at attention when he comes around, soldier." The battle was joined but she couldn't win, and I knew it. My time at the Fort Sill, Oklahoma, Station Hospital had taught me that much.

General Westmoreland came around at the appointed time with Major Shepard and a few other opportunists at his side. My bunk was in the front row near the entrance. Besides me, the only other patient abed was a lieutenant who had a punji stake infection of the leg. Everyone else braced. "Here comes Westy, Bill."

I watched him approach. Major Shepard appeared to be in the final stages of shock, and Westmoreland was smiling in a knowing manner, but his aides were looking rather stern. As for me, I wondered if the general would remember me; he was famous for that feat. He often forgot officers' names, but never NCOs. He glanced at my chart secured to the bunkstead before he spoke.

"I heard you had a hard time of it, Sergeant Craig. How do you feel now?"

I smiled before replying. "I'm fine, sir. Hope I'm outta here soon and back to the Delta Project ASAP, sir." I coulda sworn that Shepard nodded along with the general.

He began to walk away but looked back and said, "I was over there this morning, Sarge. What is that commander's name again?"

"Captain Richardson, sir."

"Yeah, that's right. Get well, Bill. See ya around."

So much for Major Shepard. But the war wasn't over just yet. The battle of wits would last the entire thirty days of my confinement. Frankly, Shepard just didn't have the experience or know-how to be very competitive. At the very least, she would learn that the NCO Corps was alive and well.

My companions from Delta Project came to see me when they could, and Clarence Counts and Paul Tracy kept me posted on the haps. The project had the trained reconnaissance teams assembled and was ready to operate. It would be the forerunner of all recon units in the Republic of Vietnam—

units such as the 75th Rangers, Command & Control, and even Recondo School itself. Unknown to us, many people would be counting on us. But with the talented NCOs we had heading up the project, I never believed we could go anywhere but up.

Doctor Panic released me after thirty days, and Master Sergeant Duarte came by and told me that the project was moving downtown. All the NCOs would be on operation, he said, so please take care of the move. Panic had not only released me, he placed me on thirty days of no-field-duty, so I wasn't gonna bust my hump.

The 5th SF Group donated the hired hands from their Vietnamese labor pool, and in one day we were no longer living in tents. The two-story homey structure we'd moved into was elegant living for us poor folks. Whose idea it was, I never found out, nor really cared, but it had CIA written all over it. The roomy abode was almost in downtown Nha Trang, a city that had beaches, clubhouses, and even a lighthouse that was manned by our own U.S. Coast Guard.

The troops of Delta were back in garrison and enjoying the good life in only a few days. I was glad to welcome them back and meet the new guys who had joined since my stay in the hospital. It's hell when you call men with ten to fifteen years "new guys," but that was the nature of the beast in the early sixties. Paul Tracy, my new roommate, took the place of Charles Delong, who had departed for the Rock. It didn't go unnoticed that the permanent change of station (PCS) people from the 5th were replacing the 180-day TDY personnel from the 1st SFG on Okinawa.

Some of the handshaking came from Jack Smythe, Lloyd Fisher, Frank Webber, John Miller, Ronald Terry, Donald Duncan, and Bill Freyser. Except for a few like Duncan, experience abounded with the new guys. We all got acquainted at the beach bars at night. SFC Donald Duncan was a well-constructed five-foot-ten-inch, 185-pound California prune picker, originally from Canada. But after only a night or so of listening to this highly opinionated individual, the entire group began to shun him.

Why? If you've read his book, *The Legions,* you already know. The book was banned at Fort Bragg for a spell when it first came out. Special Forces people were—and still are—clannish, and share many other characteristics. Politically, they tend to be right-wingers. By that I mean they believe it's their country, right or wrong.

I sipped Ba Muoi Ba as Duncan said, "In other words, I'm saying we should not interfere in an international conflict that's been going on forever!"

"We should not stem the flow of communism?" I interrupted between sips.

"Bullshit, why not let the Reds have it? They couldn't be any more corrupt than the government. It's wrong, Bill, and you know it."

"The economics of South Vietnam's government," I said, "and the corruption, for that matter, will not get much better until the war is over, Don. It's been that way in every war that has ever lasted over a week. For instance: go to a bar or a whorehouse, and you will find women selling their ass. Most of these women would not be in that business if it wasn't for the war. When the North Vietnamese and Viet Cong quit selling their ideology with the gun, things will change."

"Tell me what's so wrong with the government of the North, Bill?" Duncan asked.

"Communism rules with an elite few," I said slowly. "They have a way of screwing up everything they control. Why? Hell, I don't know. Name one commie country whose standard of living will even touch the U.S., Japan, or South Vietnam's, for that matter. Don't try, 'cause it doesn't exist. They can screw up a wet dream."

"A military government is not all bad, especially during wartime," SFC Frank Webber chimed in. Webber's face was becoming red with anger at Duncan's opinions.

"I don't buy it," Duncan said. "I think we're helping the wrong people."

The table full of SF personnel exploded, and I took the opportunity to escape the near riot. Regardless of the verbal debate, apparently no one changed SFC Donald Duncan's mind or opinions. After that hitch, he gave up ten years or more of service and wrote *The Legions*.

Some of the arguments I have mentioned here were recorded in the book, but from the author's point of view. After his discharge, Duncan began to write for the pinkie *Ramparts* magazine and to associate with people who believed we were the bad guys.

But events in III and IV Corps of South Vietnam postponed, for a spell, the communism versus democracy debates that were alienating SFC Duncan from his peers.

CHAPTER 3

Delta Project was organized to (1) collect intelligence, (2) conduct long-range reconnaissance patrols, (3) direct air strikes on inaccessible targets, (4) execute hunter-killer teams, and (5) recover allied prisoners. Because of an unmitigated disaster in III and IV Corps of South Vietnam—a South Vietnamese division was practically destroyed along the corps boundaries—we were called upon to execute parts one and two.

The North Vietnamese finally proved to the doubting U.S. and ARVN commands that they were in-country. This was a good example of one aspect of the war that afflicted the commanders throughout our twelve-year involvement: ignoring or disbelieving intelligence that was bought and paid for by our tax dollars. They didn't get away with their disbelief that time, and a bunch of poor-slob Viets paid the ultimate price. Our job was to find the NVA and fix 'em for our reserve units to finish. In this case, we would have the best reserve forces the South Vietnamese government had to offer.

The Vietnamese Airborne Brigade was one unit that would be on standby as a reaction force. Its strength at the time was approximately three thousand gung-ho paratroopers with equally gung-ho U.S. advisers. My informant, SFC Al Combs, a former Special Forces NCO, had been with them for a long period of time, and he swore by them. That Al Combs knew what he was talking about, I harbored no doubts. Our other reaction force, the Vietnamese Marine Corps, had a reputation almost as good as the Airborne Brigade.

Delta Project moved to a tent city on the outskirts of the resort city of Vung Tau. The Vung Tau airbase was the scene of the most serious climate I'd ever witnessed since my assignment to the project. The beer drinking and partying were held to the bare minimum. Each and every team was to be committed, and I drew S.Sgt. Ronald Terry and a Vietnamese team that I knew nothing about. I had nothing to say about the insertion. From Master Sergeant Duarte, I gathered Terry had just survived some close calls and would bear watching. He was a young, hard-core SF soldier and I wasn't too worried about it at the time. Our job was to find 'em, not eliminate 'em. Terry and I were issued .25 caliber pistols for hideaway guns by the CIA before we departed. I left it under the pillow on my GI cot.

Cowboy and his H-34 helicopters were to insert us on the boundary line between III and IV Corps, and I marked the point of insertion on my map the afternoon of the briefing. We were to be inserted that very night around 0200. The area was flat, and I liked that, but small trees and second growth were the only concealment available. The Vietnamese lieutenant team leader was busy taking notes. The patrol would last from three to five days or until we were sighted, compromised, or made contact. At least I was assured in my own mind that Cowboy would take us out, whatever the situation.

Terry and I left the briefing and went to our tent cubicle to pack rucksacks, and yes, we packed them very lightly. Terry seemed very nervous, so I tried my best to be reassuring by stressing the positive aspects of the operation, and there were many, I thought.

"These eight Vietnamese have the experience," I told him, "and we have good backing. You know damn well Cowboy and his crews will come get us, come hell or high water. Just relax, it'll be okay, Ron." Terry calmed a tad, much to my relief.

We loaded our ten bodies at one o'clock in the morning, as planned. We flew at ground or treetop level and touched down twice, the third time being the real insertion. We exited quickly and the point man followed his given azimuth for thirty minutes before halting. I moved up with Terry and looked at the dark growth of vines and shrubs scattered among teak trees. I nodded at the patrol leader and we moved into the brush and set out a perimeter and listening posts to sustain us during the dark and humid evening. Unassing the rucksack, I breathed deeply in contemplation of a few hours sleep. Terry, on the other hand, thought it was a signal to begin a whispering campaign.

"Aren't you gonna stay awake, Bill?" he asked.

"No, Ron," I said. "You couldn't get a mouse in this growth without us hearing it. Sack out and be ready for mañana! Okay? The listening posts are fifty percent on and fifty percent off. So don't sweat it!"

I was happy at daybreak to gag down my indigenous ration, rice and beef jerky. A long pull on a canteen of water and I was ready to move. I talked to my rested partner before we moved.

"In this flat terrain with no landmarks, it's tough to tell exactly where we are on this damn map. If you write down the azimuths and the time we spend on them, at the end of the day—or anytime—we can say with some certainty where we're located."

Terry mumbled okay before we saddled up and began our trek. The Vietnamese patrol leader acted very confident and was watching his map intently, and that eased my mind somewhat. In only minutes, after I reported in over the PRC-25, we were off. I did as I preached, and recorded my azimuths and times in my notebook.

The land was flat, thank goodness, and we had to work at remaining in the trees and shrubs for concealment. At 1400 or so we stopped at a stream to replenish our water supply, remaining in place for over an hour. After emptying my water supply and quickly refilling it, I checked our location on the map. The calculation with the azimuths and times spent on each took only minutes. I marked our location and turned to Terry.

"Do you know where we're at on the map, Ron?"

He reluctantly took the map from his camouflage fatigue pocket. "I think we're here." He pointed.

I breathed deeply in disgust and marked our location. "Please keep closer track of where we're at, Terry!"

For three days and three dark, lonely nights we continued checking out the terrain without any success. The fourth day, we heard voices coming south on a trail we had just staked out. We watched as uniformed soldiers with strange garb laughed and meandered down the trail. The soldiers appeared to be well-fed, well-clothed, and clean. They had their AK-47s at sling arms, probably feeling secure because of their recent victory. Their conceit hacked me off for some damn reason. Nevertheless, I motioned that there would be no firing. We had accomplished our mission, which did not include greasing four dummies from north of the DMZ and bringing a million troops down on our ass. I marked their location on my map, and suddenly the laughing and chatter ceased. The four halted, looked around and moved quickly on down the well-worn path.

I looked at Terry before whispering to the Vietnamese team leader, "Find a landing zone, *now!*"

He nodded, and we backed away from the trail for about twenty minutes before finding a suitable place for a pair of helicopters to land. I called the RTO (radio operator) to my side just about the time Terry was heard from.

"They went for help and are coming after our ass, Bill," he told me.

I only glanced at him and nodded before repeating the call signs for Cowboy and our trip back to base camp. "I'm doing all I can do to get us outta here, Ronald!"

I had no sooner got it out of my mouth when we began receiving small arms fire on the west side. The fire was high and inaccurate. Our NVA counterparts were guessing and wanted us to confirm what they didn't know ... like our whereabouts. I just wasn't going for it. I shook my head at the native sons and watched Terry hug the ground and stare straight ahead. He was taking it okay, and I breathed a sigh of relief when the metallic sound of the PRC-25 brought me back to the LZ.

"Go, Cowboy!" I said.

"On the way, GI. Give me coordinates, ASAP! Over!"

"Wait one. Over!" I checked with the team leader, but that proved as futile as trying to verify anything with my American partner. It dawned on me that I was now the only person involved who knew our map coordinates. "We're at LZ245668 and we're now receiving sporadic gunfire from west of our location. Read back the coordinates while I get out the red smoke. Over!"

"I read you GI One. LZ245668. On the way, sir. *Out!*"

As a team, we had rehearsed our evacuation under fire over and over, so I saw no problem. I'd seen Cowboy in action, so I had no doubt that he would land, fire or no fire.

We heard the choppers before we could see them. Shortly, the gold-dust twins were overhead. We laid down a base of small arms fire by emptying one magazine clip from M-16s and carbines before I threw the red smoke. We received no return fire until we were safely on the helicopters. The team leader returned fire from the doorway of the H-34, and we were on our way home to the Vung Tau airbase. I wiped the sweat from my brow in relief, and Terry seemed to lighten up a little as well. As far as I was concerned, the mission had been accomplished.

After being unloaded at Vung Tau and making our report, we joined our teammates in Tent City. We were surprised to find that every team inserted had sighted NVA troops, and Duarte and Duncan had the worst encounter of us all. They finally holed up in a Buddhist pagoda and waited until gunships extracted them under fire. Once the powers that be had finished placing pins marking our contacts on their wall maps, it was obvious where the enemy units were holed up. The Airborne Brigade and Marines were inserted, and our part of the operation was over. I wrote out my after-action report shortly after landing in Vung Tau.

That night the Delta drunks had a few beers in the Vung Tau AFB NCO Club and discussed everything from insertions to desertions. We let off the steam that builds up during this type of mission. We were finished in that part of the war zone and moved out smartly for Nha Trang. Shortly after the Vung Tau insertion, my 180 days were over.

I was on the Nha Trang airstrip with my original B-detachment, but its members chose to stay aloof from me, the Delta Project deserter, and I really couldn't blame them. In some ways, I guess I had let them down. I'm human and not always right, you know. But I had graciously helped load the C-130 cargo aircraft despite not being a member of the B-team. I would even help 'em unload it in Kadena AFB if they behaved properly. Besides, I didn't need any companionship from them; my Delta pals had come out to see me off. I helped 'em accomplish their mission by starting a conversation that would continue until the aircraft departed for Okinawa, the "Rock," situated between Japan and the Philippines, which by then had become my home. Though I tended to forget it at times, I was married and the father of a young son, then ten months old.

Johnnie "Slip" Miller, an old pal from Fort Bragg and at that time a newbie in Delta, was grinning as usual. "You TDY assholes have it made, Bill!"

"Slip, I hate to agree with you," I said, "but you're right. About the time things are gonna get chickenshit in Delta, we leave you hanging for a year. Sorry about that!"

My ex-roomie, Paul Tracy, leaped right into the fray. "How's Delta about to get chickenshit, Bill?"

"Well, Paul," I answered, "Charlie Beckwith is taking over from Captain Richardson and there'll be some changes, won't there, Johnnie?"

"I have never had any trouble with the guy, Bill, but admittedly he's a little gung ho; what with just coming off a year with the Special Air Service in merry ol' England." That was a long speech for Slip Miller, and I let it lie.

Unconvinced, Paul Tracy muttered, "I hope you're wrong, but then I only have a short time left. TDY, ya know."

The men of the B-detachment loaded their bods on the cargo aircraft and we were told we would land in Kadena AFB sometime that night. I was headed home to my young family. To my way of thinking, thanks to the pneumonia, the 180 days were a disaster. I waved at my Delta pals as we broke ground, Okinawa bound.

Delta Project aftermath: In September 1965 Delta detachments were composed of teams of eight Vietnamese Special Forces (LLDB) and two U.S. Special Forces personnel. By January 1966 in the An Lao Valley, the 1st Cavalry requested Delta to find the local NVA. The project was committed but the detachment composition had been altered by some ambitious individual. By then the detachments were composed of six U.S. Special Forces troopers and had taken on the appearance of the Special Air Service, Vietnamization be damned. Three Americans, as good friends as I have ever had, footed the bill.

Staff Sergeants George Hoagland, Ronald Terry, and Huston Badaloti checked out of the net. My old pal from Okinawa, Garry Stamm, and others were wounded and scattered, but were eventually evacuated to the 8th Field Army Hospital, or to safety.

Delta did recover and resumed its mission as was originally intended. A tribute to a helluva fine group of dedicated men.

CHAPTER 4

The C-130 landed on Okinawa that night and we wasted little time unloading the aircraft. It was good to be home. We were escorted to a room in the terminal, and we brown baggers (married personnel) were greeted by our wives and children, if any. It was my first experience at this sort of thing, and much to my surprise, I enjoyed it.

Hatsuko looked fine, and Jimmy, at just ten months, was bright and lively. Except for the fact that he didn't know who in the hell I was, everything went fine. When we arrived at Kadena Circle, a small village outside the airbase, things did not improve much. In fact, to tell the absolute, Jimmy had to be moved from the bed back to the baby crib and he cried most of the night.

Those of us who'd returned from the TDY were given the next five days off to attend to administrative matters. The last day of the absence another incident taught me some things about living away from the barracks that I'd been unaware of.

In February 1965 our Okinawan estate was located on a side street, a block from "Highway One." I call it Highway One for many reasons, the foremost being that it was the only one that existed on the island. It meandered from Naha, the capital city, to the northernmost part of the large coral reef.

The wooden structure, behind a board fence, was composed of a large living room, a small but comfortable bedroom, and a kitchen with none of the modern facilities except running water and electricity. The outdoor privy had running water also, but not much else. It consisted of a floor-level wax basin hole in the floor. Now you know why most Orientals can squat for hours at a time without discomfort. I couldn't, and really didn't want to pick up the habit.

That particular night, like good married brown baggers, we retired at ten o'clock. When we awoke around daylight, we were greeted by several surprises. Most important, my billfold, under my pillow when I fell asleep, was gone. Dressed in shorts only, I rushed through the house and followed a trail of my personal items. I found my empty billfold outside. My wife was up and at 'em as well, and we quickly dressed and made a list of our losses before breakfast. Okinawa's "stealie boys" had convinced one Oklahoma boy that they were the best in their illicit business. Our losses were numerous, but why didn't we awake while the robbery was going on?

Another hairy part? Hatsuko saved silver dollars and had them inside the headboard stand of our bed. To reach them, the stealie boys—we knew there were two—had to reach over Jimmy's baby bed and just above my head as well. Thank God no one woke up during the heist. We lost our TV set and about three hundred dollars, a heap of loot in 1965. How did we know there were two? After we listed our losses and cleaned up the mess, Hatsuko directed me to the comfortable backyard.

She pointed out two piles of human excrement where our ungracious intruders had relieved themselves after relieving us. Only then did she enlighten me on her police work.

"They do it every time, Daddy. Call it stress, strain, or tension, stealie boys relieve themselves after each job. Everyone who has been through this knows that, and the police know it best of all. They always dump the evidence or anything that they don't want, your billfold in this case, in a pail of water when available."

Admittedly, I'd learned all I really didn't want to know about the stealie boys of Okinawa. I was ready to place my counterattack on the front burner.

We bundled up Jimmy and, after the noon meal, departed for the hooch shared by Frank Fowler and his wife, Shizue (Suzie), only a city block away. After the usual greetings and watching Jimmy attempt to scarf the large German shepherd dog's bone, we got with the program.

"Yeah, it doesn't happen to us, and you're watching why it doesn't, right now," Fowler said.

Much to Jim's delight, the police dog growled when my son attempted to move the bone away from the dog's water container. I was not worried that the well-disciplined animal would injure the young soldier.

"I was convinced of that before I arrived, Frank," I said. "The reason I'm here is that I know you can find us one. The stealie boys have convinced me that everyone living off-post needs one. I'll pay the going rate. Can you help?"

Frank Fowler looked down at the two playmates before answering. "Yeah, Bill, I'll look around. It'll take me a few days but I'll find you one. How's that?"

In three days we had a large German shepherd roaming our fenced-in yard. I had a doghouse for him, but we had one small disagreement. Apparently, he didn't approve of smoking and would run up behind me and knock the cigarette out of my hand whenever he caught me indulging. How to counter that idiocy? Simple, I quit smoking when "Butch" was around. Hell, you can't win 'em all.

February and March of 1965 rolled on by while C Company toiled away from Camp Kue and nearby Buckner Bay. The Armed Forces hospital was near the company team rooms and headquarters. The Quonset huts were WWII-era arcs of galvanized tin, not the modern facilities other units enjoyed. But they got the job done. Special Forces still was not the apple of the High Commissioner of Okinawa's eye, and never would be, at least not in my lifetime. If it was of any interest to the general, we were not exactly impressed with him either.

The assignments continued to pile up on the 1st SF Group, and we just didn't have the personnel to accomplish all of them adequately. We were involved with assistance to the SF detachment in Taiwan, to include permanent change of station replacements and temporary duty detachments to Vietnam, Laos, and Thailand, in addition to recruiting our replacements and training them as best we could, in view of the Special Forces' very high requirements.

These replacements came, in the main, from the 503rd Airborne Battalion, then expanding to become the 173rd Airborne Brigade. Recruiting in this manner, we did not have to put them through MOS training, at least. The NCOs were proficient in such specialties as light and heavy weapons, but their demolition was still only passable, although they were strong in other engineering subjects. Operations and intelligence people needed on-the-job training, as did the medics we were fortunate to have. All of them had one deficiency that the non–Special Forces Army had never explored in that day and age: cross-training. In other words, we were receiving one-dimensional soldiers of the first water. Certainly, this was not the fault of the GIs, as the extra skills were not needed in the conventional units they came from. It would be years before the garrison-based units would defer to experience and place some emphasis on cross-training, but then what else was new?

Our most exacting job with our new people was giving them the opportunity to learn the six basic SF skills: intelligence, operations, demolitions, light and heavy weapons, medical subjects, and map reading and methods of instruction. Some were even sent to short language courses to bone up on that often neglected necessity.

These endeavors took up our on-island time in 1964 and 1965. Admittedly, because of our off-island commitments, many had to qualify for their S prefix under combat conditions, but no one ever told them it was gonna be easy. This was the scene when the word of the contest went out to A, B, and C companies, 1st Special Forces Group (Airborne), in April 1965.

CHAPTER 5

Sergeant Major Wally Klink announced the revelation to the undermanned company of 145 people on a Monday morning during the third week in April 1965. The 0730 formation was not alert to such pronouncements, but it hindered Klink not an iota.

"The contest will take one week to complete and begins next Monday, so you have a week to get your business in order. The results will be graded. For you newbies who may have gone into shock, I will go over the rules and regulations one more time. If you have any questions, see your team sergeant after this formation. Each military occupational specialty will be tested in the following manner, no exceptions. First, everyone must swim two hundred meters using whatever stroke or strokes they desire!

"Second, everyone will give a presentation on any subject in his field. For instance, an 11B [light weapons leader] could give a one-hour class on the care and cleaning of the M-2 carbine, or a medic could give an hour presentation on the treatment of shock, etcetera.

"Third, and in conclusion, you will give a presentation on a cross-trained subject of your choice. Again, you will be judged and scored and winners will be announced before the middle of May. Good luck to all of you!"

After being dismissed, my detachment discussed the latest twist by the Group and I came away not too concerned, but not so the younger people. They felt threatened; I did not. Why should I?

Contest or no contest, my military occupational specialty (MOS) read 12C.5S, in other words, I was SF qualified. The 1st SF Group was hurting for personnel, so I if flunked, would I get kicked out of the group? Get serious, that's not the way to solve your shortages. Something was going on we didn't understand, or it was just a new training vehicle. Regardless, I got my program laid out and was ready for the contest on the appointed date.

Matsuda Range, known as the Northern Training Area, is located halfway between Oku in the north and Naha in the south, near Kushi on the east coast and Kyoda on the west side of the lovely island of Okinawa. (Okinawa, by the way, is located halfway between Japan and Taiwan or the Philippine Islands; 1,000 miles from Tokyo, 6,000 miles west of San Francisco, and 1,750 miles from beautiful Saigon.) The judges found the place and graded my presentation only after I swam my two hundred meters off the shore of White Beach located close to nearby Matsuda Range.

I was very busy in preparation and execution so I cannot report on anyone else's activities during the so-called competition. I presented a two-hour class on basic explosives, and the platform time I'd accumulated at Bragg's demolition school eased me into the performance rather nicely. I heard no adverse remarks from the graders.

On to my cross-training exhibition, which is what it was, so to speak.

On GI folding tables, I laid out all the submachine guns that were available in the group weapons pool. The center table contained the granddaddy of 'em all: I presented the nomenclature, assembly, and disassembly of the .45 caliber Thompson submachine gun. During the presentation, each student was told the similarities of each submachine gun to the Thompson. I then escorted them to each table and answered any questions concerning the Swedish K, MAS .36, AK-47, Uzi, and other foreign weapons. I had long since grasped the often stressed teaching point that the instructor should always have the widest grasp of his material.

The next week, the winners were announced, and unfortunately I was among 'em. The winners, military occupational specialties, and units were as follows:

113.7S: Operations & Intelligence, SFC William R. Card, Company B. Willie was an old friend of mine from the 7th SF Group, in 1959 and 1960. An all-around soldier, including being scuba qualified, he could do a little of anything in the SF field. Card was a veteran of the 187th Regimental Combat Team during the Korean War. Thirty-six or so years old, Willie had a different outlook on the contest than I did, simply because he couldn't stand to lose at anything.

12B.5S: Engineer, Me, 'nuff said, Company C, thirty-eight years old.

05B5S: Radio Operator, S.Sgt. Gilbert L. Hamilton, Company B. The winner must be able to send and receive twenty-five words a minute in Morse code. Hamilton had the reputation of being the gutsiest and fastest learner in the entire group. An example: Gil was volunteered to attend scuba school despite not having been able to swim at all before he volunteered for SF. When told by the recruiter that he had to be able to swim two hundred meters, he asked for two weeks to learn. In two weeks he completed the swim, and a few years later he graduated from scuba school.

11C.5S: Heavy Weapons leader, Donald Snowhite, Company A. Only a passing acquaintance of mine at the time, but we hit it off great and he was quickly listed among my best friends. Tall and with a thin build, his dry sense of humor kept you on your toes. He was knowledgeable in the heavy weapons field, including field artillery.

91B.6S: Medical Specialist, Wilbur Donaldson, Company C. A tall, light-haired southern boy, Wilbur had the trait common to all SF medics that I was acquainted with and admired: he knew what he was doing.

Two days after the circus, we MOS champions were told to be at headquarters at Bishagawa at 1400 hours. We were ushered in by Group Command Sergeant Major (CSM) George Dunaway. After being seated, we were greeted by the ol' man, Colonel Kelly, who proceeded to tell us "that we had been selected" for a classified mission in South Vietnam, and that if we didn't care for such an assignment, we could leave.

The ruse of the contest had finally been exposed. Every time I thought I had the U.S. Army figured out, they came up with something new and different.

The colonel said, "I will give you a smoke break at this time, and if you return, I must conclude that you have volunteered for the assignment. Take ten!"

Five silent individuals shuffled out into the humidity and tropical sunshine of Okinawa. Four of us did as ordered; being a nonsmoker, Willie Card disobeyed.

"Been wanting to get off-island for a spell," Hamilton ventured. I could only grin.

"We're all gonna go, hell, we're wasting time out here!" Willie Card said.

"Maybe, Willie," I told him, "maybe not. I just got back, you know. I think I'll just stay out here while you heroes listen to the fox-fuck you're gonna be involved in."

That rang Card's bell. "Yeah, I'll bet. Around Group they'll be calling you an asshole for years to come if you stay out here."

Somehow, I knew he was gonna say that. But before I could reply, Dunaway came out the screen door. "Those of you who are of a mind to, return to the office."

Willie Card had finally won an augument. I put out my cigarette and headed back to the briefing room, as did everyone else involved.

Colonel Kelly went to work and I finally became curious. Among the lowly enlisted men, Kelly had not earned any respect with his water-jumping tactics. But in my case, he had. I'm not saying that I admired those who, incessantly, avoided the hard earth as a parachute-landing locale; I thought everyone should earn jump pay in an equitable manner. However, in my quest for a college degree, I'd taken a college course—the subject escapes me—from Kelly and had been won over by him; he was easily the best informed professor I ever had the privilege of making a C under. He motivated me to continue the quest for a bachelor of arts degree that I should have had even before I came into the Army.

"This is the twenty-first day of May. You will leave, bag and baggage, on the first of June 1965, from Kadena Air Force Base at 1000 hours. You will be allowed no farewell visitors and will be transported from this location. . . ." Kelly paused.

"You will report to the Joint Chiefs of Staff and will be given your assignments at that time. It is a hush-hush mission, and it would serve no purpose to reveal it at this time. These entire proceedings are secret, and the less you say or know, the better.

"Your orders will read, 'Temporary duty to Saigon to the JCS for 180 days.' The rest of the administrative details I will leave to Sergeant Major Dunaway. But before I leave, good luck to you. Do us proud. You're the best we have to offer." Kelly shook each man's hand before departing.

Dunaway took little time to wrap up his part of the "contest." Come Monday morning we were gone. Willie Card was again in hog heaven, but I was not.

After a visit to the S-1 Personnel shop, we headed for our homes. Willie was still wallowing in it, while we both looked forward to our first beer of the day. He's wound up like a Swiss-made watch, I thought. We entered the American Legion Club at 1630. Unlike Willie Card, I was in a pissed-off state of mind as we selected a booth against the wall where we could talk. Willie was having a tough time containing himself while waiting for the waitress.

"Why are you unhappy, Bill?"

He didn't give me a chance to answer, so I could do nothing but bide my time.

"Here you are, selected as the best SF man in your specialty on Okinawa; selected to work for the bosses of Vietnam; selected to draw per diem from Saigon at twenty-one dollars a day for six months, and you're unhappy! Everyone in Special Forces wants to be in our shoes; excepting you, of course. Are you nuts?" At last he paused long enough to down half of his bottle of Bud. Whew!

"Willie," and I did start slowly, "I don't want to go for more than one reason, dammit. Number one, my kid will be one year old on Friday and I'm leaving a few days later for a place I just came back from a month or so ago, and that's just a starter."

"Hell, I'm a brown bagger, but you don't hear me bitching. If the Army hadda wanted us to have wives and kids, they'd have issued them to us. What else?"

"I didn't like the way they selected us. That was kid shit, and you know it. A contest . . ."

"I thought the way they selected us was unique, and kinda smart, too. If a colonel sends duds from his unit to work for general-grade officers, what does that make him? Probably a colonel for the rest of his life. You'd have done the same thing if you'd been Kelly. Admit it!"

"I wouldn't! You're saying that a colonel can't make general without good NCOs, so what else is new? The sonsofbitches couldn't make captain without us. Screw the officer corps. I ain't in here because of them assholes. You're beginning to sound like one, come to think of it. There are 12C.5Ses in this unit that can do anything I can do and maybe better. Someone musta tipped 'em off. They're smarter than I am."

I had him fuming by now. He knew that I knew he was a Reserve officer, so I enjoyed my beer while he tried to get his blood pressure down. "There are good officers and bad officers, just like there are good sergeant majors and bad sergeant majors. Your hang-up over the caste system is blurring your thinking. You can't beat 'em, so why don't you join 'em, Bill?"

"That's an easy one. Because I think they're promoted off of the blood, sweat, tears, and *brains* of the NCOs, that's why! I'll pull my own weight, thank you."

I had won a point that Willie Card refused to concede, so he changed the subject matter a tad.

"If you're so wrought up about this assignment, why did you go back in for the briefing? Go home to the baby boy and Mommy. Don't go back in for the briefing!"

"I went back in, Willie, because if I hadn't, you would have been jackin' your jaws about it from now till doomsday, and you would've had plenty of help, and listeners, for that matter. No one would mention that I just came back from a wasted tour in the Delta Project; no one would've mentioned that it was my second trip in 1965. Oh, *no*! Bill's got shit in his neck! Now you know why all five of us went back in. See ya at Kadena Air Force Base come Monday morning!"

CHAPTER 6

The Friday before departure was James J. Craig's first birthday. We had the party at our mansion in Kadena Circle, and people showed up from the fighting 1st Special Forces Group. Before the blast, I had told my wife of my departure come Monday morning. She paid little heed to it; by that time she was immune to that sort of thing. Everyone had a blast, including the recipient, Jimmy. I never knew about everyone else, but I had a very large head the next morning.

Monday morning, rucksack, duffel bag, and the ditty, I was suddenly proud to be boarding a C-130 cargo aircraft with, according to the test scores, the best that the 1st SF Group (Abn) could muster. This did not mean that SFC Willie Card—the NCO in charge, by the way—had won the argument. What it did signify to me was a lesson learned: when things don't go your way or you think you've been had, sit down and talk it over with someone with a different viewpoint. You will learn many things, just as the person you're arguing . . . er, discussing, the subject with will. A few days after your chest is clear and your wounds salved, you'll have a better outlook on the problem and your emotions.

We landed at Saigon's Tan Son Nhut busy, busy airport in the afternoon and were met by a Master Sergeant White, an SF soldier I knew vaguely at Bragg. He herded us to a waiting H-34 helicopter which flew us to Vung Tau. We were quartered in the lighthouse outside the city. Our GI cots had been set up by some Lac Luong Dac Biet (LLDB; Vietnamese Special Forces soldiers). We were told by White that we would be briefed by a lieutenant the next morning, then he departed for Sin City. Being old soldiers, we unpacked what we needed and stored the rest. The LLDB left a guard on the place, so we departed in our two jeeps for chow in Vung Tau proper. White's orientation was not much help, so we decided to help ourselves to the resort city.

The resort town could be seen from our lighthouse perch. I let Willie Card drive, and the other three winners followed in the second jeep. We wound down the hillside road and were on the beach in good time. Willie pulled off the road and parked at the first food and beer establishment he spied. We were all famished, and Willie was thirsty as well.

The Dynasty Club and Grill had booths on both sides and down the middle, all leading to the bar in the rear of the establishment. Some Army aviators in gray coveralls were making noise as we passed their booth. I had just cleared the controlled disturbance when an older flyboy sounded off and stood up in the booth.

"Bill! Bill Craig, it's me, dammit!" Due to the dim lights and my having come out of the sun, I could not distinguish the individual from his companions.

"Bill, it's me, S. A. Lund." Only then did I recognize my old Lawton, Oklahoma, buddy from the 179th Infantry Regiment in Frozen Chosin days, during the Korean War.

S. A. Lund, a few years older than I, was a Lawton boy like me. In Korea he was a first lieutenant and the communications chief of the 2nd Battalion, 179th Infantry, back in '51, '52. He was skinny at 150 pounds, and five feet nine inches. I embraced the Okie and released him, while Willie and the boys seated themselves in a booth a few feet away and watched us; a hug's not really the proper military way to greet a lieutenant colonel. Lund invited me to sit in an unoccupied booth and promised introductions later. A petite Vietnamese lady brought us each a beer. Our rendezvous wouldn't take up much time but we both felt it was important. Out of respect for his rank, I allowed Lund to lead off.

"I went to fixed-wing and helicopter schools after we came back from Korea, and I've been flying ever since. I'm now the commander of the Army Air Wing here at Vung Tau Air Force Base. There are two of my pilots that you know very well."

"Bullshit, who are they?"

"Billy Boucher is a young chopper pilot," Lund said. "Remember him? He's much younger than either of us."

"Yeah, vaguely. He pitched baseball for LHS a few years back. Right? He's more Joe Bob—my younger brother's—age. I'll be damned! Who else does thou speak of, Lieutenant Colonel?" Lund blushed when I called attention to his rank, but being a loyal Lawton High School grad, he continued.

"Walter Dunegan, now Major Walter Dunegan to you, flies a Mohawk reconnaissance aircraft for the Army. He's in Hawaii right now but he'll be back in about a week. He'll shit when he sees you, of all people."

"I ran around with Walter when I first got out of Korea," I said. "He moved to Lawton from Altus, but I didn't know that he went back in the Army."

"I didn't either, Bill. He'll fill you in when he gets back. Now tell me about yourself. I heard you came back into the Army and were in Special Forces, but I've never met anyone who had run into you. Fill me in!"

I completed the saga in good time, then said, "Let me introduce my pals to you. We can't tell you why we're here, but we may be able to later on. It's not too important anyhow," I added, downplaying the assignment I knew nothing about as yet.

I took Lund to Donaldson, Card, Hamilton, and Snowhite and did the honors. The SF people knew I had scored heavily, missionwise, with my knowing an Air Wing commander. The reasons were obvious: Special Forces assignments had normally been funded by the CIA, and they furnished plenty of loot, but were dreadfully short of equipment and know-how.

Now we could scrounge aircraft off of S. A. Lund, the commander, and screw the CIA ineptitude.

The pilots, Lund in charge, came over and spoke with us for a few minutes before they were on their way. A few beers, a light meal, and we followed suit. I drove back on the winding road and let Willie rave on.

The next morning we ate C-rations for breakfast and the coffee was delicious for a change. Snowhite drove to the Vung Tau airstrip to pick up Master Sergeant White. Snowhite outdid himself by not only bringing back White, but Black as well. A black first lieutenant was introduced to us in a makeshift classroom next to our quarters. Lieutenant Black was a leg—that is, nonairborne—light-skinned Negro who seemed very amicable.

"Your mission is to train infiltrators who can penetrate North Vietnam by land, sea, or air to disrupt the NVA resupply efforts as well as place some pressure on their internal forces," Black told us.

For myself, I was just happy that it wasn't going to be us doing the infiltrating.

"As far as I know, you will not be on the ground with them. You will be moved into quarters in downtown Vung Tau, while your troops will live here at the lighthouse. The Vietnamese Special Forces, or LLDB, will be responsible for their behavior, so discipline will not be your problem, only the training. The trainees? They will or should arrive in approximately two weeks, because they are still being recruited. They are being recruited, and I use the word loosely, off the streets, jails, and skid rows of Saigon City."

The bombs continued to fall.

"You weren't supposed to know that, but I thought you should have an idea of what you're in for. Your job is to train these infiltrators in weapons, demolitions, medical subjects, tactics, and the use of communications equipment, in addition to being able to infiltrate by land, sea, and air.

"I'll now take your questions as best I can," Lieutenant

Black concluded. "Master Sergeant White will help when I get baffled."

SFC Willie Card spoke up smartly. "What is their state of training, sir? We can't make out any training schedules unless we know for sure."

"When they arrive here," Black said, "they will be airborne qualified and will have had at least basic combat training. Some may be better trained than others, but use that as a guide when you write your schedules. What next?"

"How long will the training last and will it be by teams, sir?" I asked.

"The training will be by teams, just like Delta Project, but unlike Delta Project, they may be dropped as individuals or by teams. The time available for training has not yet been determined, but you should know soon. Perhaps they are waiting for your training schedule before they commit themselves."

The situation was becoming confusing, at least to me.

"It sounds to me that they need field exercises and some specialized training, sir," Hamilton said.

"Very good, Sergeant, I think you're on to it. You people make out your schedule based on what you've been told, and the Joint Chiefs of Staff will add or delete. The troops won't arrive for a few weeks at best. If there're no more questions, I'm gone."

We spent the next few days moving into luxurious quarters in downtown Vung Tau. It was a week, at best, before we started on the training schedule.

Snowhite and I roomed together, and everyone else had a nice room as well. The house had a large living room with a bar in the back section. We needed a bar like we needed an extra nose, but we didn't complain about it. At least we now had a place to eat three meals a day that we could afford.

While we unemployed contest winners were making up our training schedules, I was called, through channels, to give demolition classes to a hush-hush organization that was also just getting off the ground.

The Phoenix Program was training down the beach from us, behind a barbed-wire enclosure. The classes came off without a hitch, and I used my old arguing partner, Willie Card, as my assistant instructor, and in the process found that Willie didn't know a helluva lot about demolition. Willie was a fast learner, though, and by the end of the week was quite proficient. It would help when we began our own instruction. I was impressed with the success of the Phoenix Program. Before the Tet Offensive was over, the infrastructure of the overrated Viet Cong was all but destroyed, and the Phoenix Program played no small part in the process. Regardless of our detractors, we sometimes did some things right.

In several weeks our own trainees were tucked away in the bottom floor of the Vung Tau lighthouse and awaited our guidance. We wasted no time on the preliminaries, but Sergeant Donaldson, our medic, had to check them out before we began the instruction. The findings were a disaster.

Of the forty or so trainees, about eighty percent had syphilis. Why weren't they cured during their initial training? Why bother to ask? Donaldson cured the problems with a fresh case of penicillin. This unexpected turn of events opened our eyes to many facets hereto unthought of. First of all, I never in my many trips to Vietnam heard of any U.S. personnel catching syphilis; gonorrhea, "the clap," yes, but never the dreaded. Maybe the JCS was going to try some biological warfare, dropping the infected soldiers into North Vietnam to infect the entire populace. The JCS may have been a lot sharper than we had given them credit for.

Finally, I realized why we had such a good medic: in addition to our own needs, he had other chores to perform. The JCS ruined his day near the end of the training by allowing the by-then cured individuals to go home on leave. When they returned, all but a few were infected again, and he had to start the whole process over.

Our training started out with Card's water infiltration tactics, and in the afternoon I pitched in with immediate action drills and/or demolition classes. As a team, we were finally busy, busy. To our surprise, most trainees could swim, and many of them very well. Card did teach the use of scuba gear, so the water time wasn't just a physical conditioner. We all pitched in for the air-infiltration training. We started out using the most obvious and least desirable method: the T-10 or MC-1 parachute. The advent of the helicopter had made this type of infiltration almost obsolete except for HALO, or free fall from high altitude to a low opening. We began the training with a night training jump on the back beach of Vung Tau. Not really a perfect choice for a clandestine drop zone, but good training, regardless. The maneuver, despite its drawbacks, came off perfectly. It was the first night drop for our Saigon cowboys.

On our next air infiltration I had a team inserted by helicopter into an area infested by Viet Cong not far from the R&R center. My after-action report said it all: "They performed very well, as did the LLDB cadre who was my assistant." One drawback bothered me on the excursion, but I did not report it; I discussed it with Willie Card on one of our excursions to the Vung Tau AFB watering hole a few nights after we returned.

Card was sucking up the beer that made Milwaukee famous, while I got off the cognac and Coke kick, a combination I'd treasured since I first began drinking the hard stuff during my second hitch.

"So you didn't feel good," Card said. "What's the big deal? Patrolling is tiresome and drains you anyway. What's there to worry about?"

"I really wish I knew, Willie. I really do. I've just never felt that way before. Sometimes I would only move two or three hundred yards and have to stop. It never happened to me before. I'll stick with the beer from now on."

The very next day, I cleaned and repacked my field gear before going to the Army Air Wing Headquarters to see Lieutenant Colonel Lund, my old Korean pal. I seated myself in his office in my camouflage fatigues and got his attention in an instant.

"Bill, your old Lawton buddy just got back from R and R in Hawaii yesterday. He's supposed to take his refresher flight today in his favorite Mohawk aircraft," Lund said.

"No shit? You're talking about Walt Dunegan, ain't you, S.A.?"

"Yeah, he'll be here in about thirty minutes; they're checking out his ship right now. You ever been up in that new Army recon aircraft, Bill?"

"Hell no, boss. I'd never even seen one up close till I came to your outfit. Tell me something about the damn thing." That was a mistake!

"The Mohawk is made by the Grumman Aircraft Engineering Corporation," he said. "It's a reconnaissance ship made in 1959. It has two Lycoming T-53 L-3 turboprops that generate a thousand horsepower each. At five thousand feet you can hit the top speed of 317 miles with a two-man crew."

"You sure it won't go 318 miles per hour at four thousand feet?" I asked. I got a grin out of him. "Seriously, Mr. Facts, how do you get outta the damn thing?"

"Yes, William. All you have to do is hit the eject button and you'll go up and out the cockpit. Wear your helmet so you won't hurt youself going through the Plexiglas."

"Hell, I'm a ready, Teddy."

Thirty minutes later Dunegan briefed me again, but his was a little more practical. I was very proud of Walter Dunegan. From a Tanker NCO during the Korean Police Action to a major and a Mohawk pilot ten years later. Not bad for an Okie.

Dunegan and I had a ball on the test flight but I hadn't changed any in relation to aircraft; I disliked landing in the damn things. Dunegan showed me where the U Minh Forest had suffered a B-52 strike a few days prior. The results were startling, even to an old warrior. The bombs had cut a swath through those teak trees that would have even shocked the

Environmental Protection Agency. Jane Fonda wouldn't have defected if she'd seen those gaping holes.

And I think Dunegan reached the top speed of 317 or 318, whatever, before he rolled the Mohawk over once, for my benefit. I enjoyed the ride no end. Like everything else in the Army, the recon vehicles were becoming more sophisticated. Dunegan and I had a long talk after the ride and I promised to stay in touch, at least while I was in Vung Tau.

A week later found me taking a team to the field again. My physical condition was again acting up. I became exhausted after only a few hundred yards of snoop and poop in the tangled wait-a-minute vines and vegetation. When we returned without contact, I stayed in Saigon Hospital one night while they took a biopsy of my liver, among other tests. The doctors sent me and the results back to the dispensary at Vung Tau Airbase the very next day. My new physician minced no words with me at all.

"First of all, you have the beginning of cirrhosis of the liver. We caught it in time so there's still hope for you. What do you drink and how often? Lastly, do you eat regular meals or skip supper from time to time?"

My naive answer told him all he needed to know. "How did you know that? Yes, I skip meals quite a bit. I drink cognac and Coke whenever I can."

"That's the liver-problem pattern, old soldier. It has not progressed too far, but I want you to eat three meals a day and knock off *any* alcoholic drink. Report back here in three weeks for another exam. Got it, Sergeant Craig?"

Because I couldn't go to the field for a while, I assisted with classes in base camp. I did get to fly in an 82nd Division helicopter once during my restriction, when a Donald Snowhite patrol snatched a Viet Cong prisoner and called for extraction. I boarded the chopper at the strip and noted a major was the pilot; very strange circumstances considering the times. Warrant officers were being commissioned every day at Fort Rucker, Alabama, warrant officers who did not care to do anything but fly and maintain helicopters. Very strange. The major kept glancing back at me and the Viets, like he didn't trust us. The enlisted crew chief was busy looking out the door but he paused long enough to keep us informed. "We're going in, the pilot's kinda nervous."

"I noticed," was about all I could say. I spotted the people as we touched down. Snowhite, an LLDB, and a young Viet Cong in black pajamas with his hands tied behind his back were waiting. My helpers and I jumped off the aircraft and literally threw the little bastard on the ship. I waved at Donald Snowhite before I boarded.

The major turned and watched us strap the enemy in with a seat belt. Personally, I saw no threat from the Viet Cong, but the major apparently was on a different frequency. During the flight, he kept turning and telling the chief to have me watch the Viet Cong closely.

Finally I had to speak up. "Inform your boss that we have done this two thousand times without incident." We finally landed safely at Vung Tau. The Vietnamese SF turned the bad ninety-pounder over to the proper authorities and I headed for the house, thinking how fortunate we were to have warrant officers flying practically all of the rotary wing aircraft.

I stayed with my solid diet and was very bored some nights staying in our boardinghouse alone. I even began jogging down by the beach on days I had no assignments. Much to my surprise, I began to feel great. Could it be that the doctor knew something I should have known? Three weeks passed swiftly, and at the second examination my blood tests and X rays were quickly done. The doctor finally called me in for the prognosis.

The captain was smiling, at least when he started off. "You have the heart and lungs of an eighteen-year-old, Sergeant Craig. Stay away from the booze and you may live to be a hundred or so, if the VC don't get you first."

"Okay, sir. I can do that and I'll stay with the diet and

regular hours when I can." Unknown to either of us, three weeks earlier I had drunk my last hard liquor.

Things were going smoothly at the lighthouse training center until JCS pulled a funny: the trainees, apparently ready to leap into the North, were given a ten-day leave!

Sergeant Donaldson, our all-knowing medic, bitched endlessly about that.

When the trainees straggled back, Donaldson waited not one day before checking them for venereal disease. Over sixty percent were once again infected with syphilis. Another case of penicillin was sacrificed. We all wondered if North Vietnam was ready for an invasion of sex-crazed syphilitic commandos. But unforeseen events on the Rock would prevent my being around to see our trainees off to war.

CHAPTER 7

I finished my two-mile run on the back beach and was walking back to the hooch. The buildup of U.S. troops was well under way, so there were a lot of GI vehicles around, whose occupants waved or hooted at me. It bothered me not; let them learn the importance of physical fitness the way I had. The heavy U.S. military traffic triggered recollection of a scene and conversation that had taken place in a team house in a CIDG camp in 1964.

Detachment A-132 had finished supper when Staff Sergeants Sherron, Green, Pronier, and I, and Captain Victor Hugo hung around, much to the disgust of Cookie, the Rhade (Montagnard) mess honcho. Hugo had just asked why I thought General Westmoreland was another mistake made by the U.S.

"Because he's a conventional warrior attempting to fight an unconventional war," I told him.

"Big deal," Hugo said. "It's not the first time. Probably not the last time. What's wrong with that, gentlemen?"

"There will be a big buildup of U.S. combat troops, sir," Bob Pronier answered.

"Hell, the 173rd Airborne Brigade could kick the shit out of the NVA," Don Green, our 05B radio operator, declared.

"Bullshit," Sherron said. "Not so, Don. The NVA will not fight them toe-to-toe. They'll fade away and come back another day."

"Let's get back to the basic argument, men," Hugo pleaded. "Why is Westmoreland's appointment a mistake?"

"The buildup of U.S. troops will include draftees, sir," I said. "The first time a draftee hits Vietnam soil, we have lost the southern part of Vietnam. Right, Hugh?"

"When that happens," Hugh Sherron said, "the mothers and apple pie will start raising hell about our having no business over here. Our country will throw in the towel, sir."

Now, in September 1965, I continued my walk back to the boardinghouse as the draftees and the southern half of Vietnam went down the road. General Westmoreland had made prophets, or seers, out of the enlisted men of Detachment A-132. In my heart I knew we had blown it, but I just didn't want to believe it. At my quarters something else awaited me that I didn't want to believe as well.

Master Sergeant John White had a solemn face and a message from the Red Cross on Okinawa. I had no inkling what was taking place. I was still in my PT shorts and T-shirt when he asked me to be seated in my own living room. I was exhausted anyway, and obliged.

"We have a message to you through channels from the American Red Cross in Camp Kue, Okinawa, Bill," he said, and read: " 'Your wife, Hatsuko, gave birth to a premature three-pound, six-ounce baby. The baby has succumbed at Camp Kue Hospital, and your presence at your home base is desired ASAP.' "

I was stunned.

"I'm sorry, Bill. We've made travel arrangements for you on the first available out of Tan Son Nhut Airbase in Saigon. My helicopter is waiting for us at the Vung Tau facility. You did know your wife was pregnant, I assume?" he concluded.

"Yes," I replied softly, "I knew she was pregnant, but she had about a month and a half or so to go. I'm stunned, really."

"Again," White said, "I'm sorry as hell!"

"Yes, I knew Hatsuko was pregnant, hell, we even named

the baby before I left. We have a son, and we named this one Katherine Ann. Hell, I guess you'll never miss what you never had. I'll be ready in a second, Top," I said sadly.

I had brought no Class A dress uniform, greens or khaki, so I boarded the waiting helicopter in the Special Forces camouflage fatigues and bloused jungle boots that were being tested then, so my attire would pinpoint me during the entire ordeal. At the time, I did not think it a pressing problem. I did check my pockets for the military passport that we all carried and my immunization record.

Despite the Saigon air terminal's being a beehive of activity, White guided me to a counter where a clerk checked my passport, relieved me of my duffel bag, issued me a flight number and a ticket. I didn't even glance at the flight schedule on the board, nor the ticket in my hand for that matter. I was in deep thought about the loss of someone whom we had both wanted so badly, someone I had named after my mother. This was my mental state when I strolled to the gate with my ditty in my hand.

My uniform received some stares from the civilian flight attendants and the GIs in Class A uniforms as well, as I continued to my seat on the luxurious aircraft. Okinawa must really rate, went through my numbed skull. The civilian pilot got my attention with his first announcement.

"Welcome aboard 707 Flight 123 for the good ol' continental USA, with stops at Clark Air Force Base in the Philippines, and in Hawaii."

I was going to have to change aircraft in the Philippines before getting to the Rock. Sonofabitch!

In a few short hours I was in the terminal at Clark AFB, fuming at the check-in counter.

The attractive Filipino lady behind the counter was gracious about it. "We already have you booked on the first flight to Okinawa, Sergeant Craig. Have your passport and shot record confirmed at the next counter, so we can confirm the flight and your reserved seat number."

The U.S. Air Force NCO glanced at my passport and returned it, but the shot record was another matter altogether. "You need a cholera shot, Sergeant," he said.

"The dispensary is behind the counter and two offices down. When you're finished, come back here for your ticket."

"Go screw yourself, junior. I ain't taking no goddamn shots. I didn't want to come here to begin with. 'Nuff said." When I reached for the shot record, he summoned two short, dark Filipino Military Police who were standing a few yards away.

Knowing damn well they spoke English, I still spoke slowly, so the riot wouldn't evolve any faster than it already had. "I'm taking no goddamn shots, and two Flip MPs are not going to get the job done. You had better get a few more so we can all have a good time." I was ready to defend myself and to take my frustrations out on anyone who wasn't on my side.

The American nodded at one MP, who moved to the telephone area where a group of GIs was gathered. Clearly reinforcements would soon be on the scene.

I was attracting attention among the Air Force and Army bystanders, which I could have done without. An Oriental individual put down the phone and the MP took up the slack. Dressed in U.S. Army fatigues with no rank or insignia except a U.S. Army nameplate, the Oriental approached, stopping when I cautioned him about his proximity to danger. Still, I could not help but think that I had seen this person somewhere before.

"I'm Al Chiang, a photographer with *Stars and Stripes*," he said. "If you'll permit me to say so, you are starting something you cannot win."

I nodded. "These assholes are not giving me any shots," I told him. "I didn't want to be here to begin with. I'm Bill Craig, Al."

Al Chiang stared at me a bit before he spoke up. "You're making a mistake, and you don't really care? Why don't you tell me what the real problem is, Bill."

We remained standing close to the counter as I recited the episode to the photographer.

"You're feeling sorry for yourself," he said, "and I can't blame you, but have you thought about how your wife feels? A riot at Clark Air Force Base is not the answer. I have a compromise solution if you will permit?" Chiang said.

"Say what's on your mind, Al," I replied.

He smiled. "I'll call Okinawa and Camp Kue Hospital. You talk to your wife, and maybe it'll help everyone concerned. Whatcha say, Bill?"

Al Chiang begin his duel with the overseas telephone system, and in only minutes he offered me the phone. Still, I was very suspicious. Finally I reached for the receiver.

Hatsuko Ago Craig came through loud and clear. "Hi, Papa-san," she said. "Where are you and when are you coming home?"

The words spoken then will be etched in my memory forever. "Hi, baby doll. How are you feeling?" I asked.

"I'm fine and feel much better than yesterday. You okay?"

"Yes, I'm fine. What was the baby, honey, a boy or a girl?"

"She's a girl. Can you come home?"

I thought I'd missed something in the translation, so I reacted rather loudly. *"You mean she's still alive?"*

"Of course. At least she was two minutes ago, when I last looked."

My grin affected the observers, causing a chain reaction led by my ol' pal, Al Chiang. "I was told she . . . was dead," I said. She quickly filled me in on the details of the delivery, and we finished with my saying, "I'll be home sometime tomorrow. Take care of yourself and the baby. 'Bye now."

Free of the telephone, I grabbed Al Chiang and repeatedly shook his hand. "It's a girl and she's in an incubator. Are you ready for that?"

Al returned my handshake but not my hand as we walked a few yards to the dispensary. He smiled broadly at the nurse attendant and said, "One cholera shot, there, young lady."

The Philippine MP force that had now grown to ten also smiled when I pulled up my sleeve. I handed my yellow shot record to the nurse and held the piece of cotton over the mark she'd left on my arm. I was not making sense, but everyone within hearing distance was on my side for a change. "She's still alive, she never was dead. She's still alive," I babbled. The nurse handed me the shot record and pointed to the check-in counter where the commotion had all begun. Even the Air Force sergeant was smiling as he checked my shot record.

"You're home free, Sergeant Craig. Your aircraft will leave at 1100 hours in the morning. Check-in time is 1030. Here's your boarding pass. The guest house is across the street from the terminal," he said, pointing. "Good luck and congratulations, Dad."

I was still smiling as I walked into the bar and ordered a beer. I made sure I thanked Chiang one more time before he departed. Those ten MPs ought to have thanked him, too. How can a simple phone call change such a desperate situation? "My life will end someday, but until that time, certainly the learning process never will," I said quietly to myself.

After only a few sips of my beer, the inevitable question came to me: Who screwed up the message to the Red Cross, or did the Red Cross blow it . . . ?

I left Clark AFB forever, I hoped, the next morning promptly at 1100 hours in an Air Force C-82 aircraft. Not luxury, but a safe, quick ride to my home. I wished against wish that everything was going okay for my mother's namesake, Katherine Ann Craig. Knowing Okinawans as I do, I knew that Jimmy was in good hands.

I claimed my duffel bag and marched from the Kadena air terminal to a cabstand only a few yards from the station. At Group Headquarters I signed in under the watchful eyes of Command Sergeant Major George Dunaway and gave him the good news from 'Nam. "Everything is apparently going as planned, Sergeant Major."

I was not going to reveal what I knew about the screw-up concerning my young daughter; he didn't mention the subject, so I responded in kind. He hustled me to a waiting jeep that took me to C Company. No big deal for the most powerful CSM in the U.S. Army.

I dropped off my baggage at the house in Kadena Circle, then the driver and I moved out smartly for Chibana and Charging Charlie Company, where Sgt. Major Wally Klink supervised my signing in.

"How's the wife and kids, Bill?" he asked.

"Soon as you get my autograph, I'm off to find out, Top."

"Good luck, William. Check back in about a week and we'll put you to work. Can do?"

"No problem, Sergeant Major. I'm gone!"

At Camp Kue Army Hospital, I was directed to the fourth floor, where the incubator babies were located. "Don't you want to see your wife, first?" the reception clerk asked sweetly.

"I'm sorry," I said. "Would you call and have someone tell her I'm here?"

When the clerk hung up, she said, "She's fine. She'll meet you in the incubator ward."

The incubator ward was waist-high stucco then glass to the ceiling. Hatsuko and I greeted each other, then she pointed out the incubator that held Kathy, all two pounds eleven ounces of her. I had a hard time believing what I was seeing. She was so small, yet seemed fully developed. At last I now knew what the word miracle meant.

After a few minutes, a nurse interrupted us and I had to present my ID again before she would answer our questions.

"No one is allowed in here for whatever the reason, except the parents, period. Your daughter is normal in all aspects except for her weight. Do not get your hopes up too high; it's going to be touch and go for a while."

"When can we take her home?" I asked.

"She will not be released until she weighs five pounds or

more. You will be afforded the opportunity to take her home only when she has reached that stage of development."

As we strolled back to her room, Hatsuko said that she would be home in a day or so. "Jimmy should probably stay with Frank and Shizue Fowler until I'm released, Daddy, but it's up to you."

I agreed. I'd had a ton of experience, but very little of it concerned monitoring a sixteen-month-old boy.

Leaving Camp Kue, I visited Frank, his wife, and my son. Jimmy didn't appear to be too happy with the intrusion, because he didn't really know who I was. I couldn't fault him for that. I was, thanks to the situation, only a part-time papa-san. I left while Jimmy continued to play with the dog.

In only a few days Jim and his mother were home in Kadena Circle and Kathy had regained the weight she lost after birth, diaper or not. Visiting now became a ritual that would not go away for three months. A few things transpired during this period besides the periodic visits to the fourth floor of the efficient Camp Kue Army Hospital.

When I reported in for work, I was informed that I would not go anywhere until the baby girl was out of there and doing okay. I was also informed that my new assignment required a Top Secret clearance, not just the Secret clearance I then had. I filled out the paperwork and was assured that it was only a for-mality, that the upgrading was only a matter of time.

I began refresher training with Company C, 1st SF Group (Abn), and Hatsuko and I decided that our run-down living quarters were not commensurate with my rank and pay grade of E7. We moved to Ojana, located nearer Hatsuko's mother in Naha but farther from Camp Kue and Kathy's incubator. I even coughed up the money to refurbish the modern two-bedroom stucco building, which featured a fenced-in yard. My Top Secret clearance arrived about the same time, and I drove my '56 Ford to my new assignment the very next day.

Site Yara was a small coral hill just off Highway One, near Kadena Airbase. It was a small fenced-in compound with just one gate. Once inside, the gate locked behind you for security reasons. A lone cement-block building greeted my Top Secret eyes. SFC Ed Clough, my new boss, showed me the new working quarters, but because I'd been a demolition man, I was not impressed with the hush-hush environment. I had jumped an atomic demolition device (ADM) for my graduation exercise before becoming SF qualified at Ford Bragg.

The classroom was not large, perhaps twenty-five by forty feet, with a platform, podium, and Army steel chairs. A door behind the platform led to a smaller room. When you came in the front entrance, the office containing three desks and four file cabinets was to the left. I noted that the file cabinets were bolted and locked. I was informed they all contained Secret Restricted Data documents that were not allowed off the premises.

The tour ended abruptly, and Clough, all seven feet of him, told me to return at 1400 for my briefing and to meet my fellow instructors and the officer in charge. I exited the golden gate and heard it slam and lock before I reached my car.

Captain Peters, a slender Negro about my height, rose from his chair at 1400, mounted the platform and began the briefing. After fifteen minutes he was relieved by SFC Clough, who kept his remarks to twelve minutes. To summarize the combined twenty-seven minutes: using simulators, we were to teach Special Atomic Demolition to two-man teams selected by the 1st SF Group. Butch Fernandez, the Portuguese-Hawaiian SFC sitting next to me, and I would be trained first by Clough and Peters before we were allowed to pass our wisdom on to the Group's selectees.

"The weapon" is a man-size load for one man to jump. So why two-man teams? Because the awesome destructive power of atomic munitions demanded that one person not be given so much responsibility. One man could go off his rocker and do something foolish; the two-man rule simply decreases the chances of "something foolish" occurring.

The simulated nuke device taught at Bragg would be used

as a familiarization expedient. The simulators were stored at the Kadena ammunition supply depot located a few miles down the paved highway from Site Yara. I concluded that this would be a good assignment: the job would keep me on-island for a spell and further my education in that particular field, and I'd have the time to attend the University of Maryland extension courses at night and get back on track for the B.A. I had let slip by in 1950.

The last months of 1965 found me and my family settled in for a while without facing the threat of TDY for a change. The neighborhood in Ojana consisted of modern housing occupied by Air Force and Army personnel. Approved family housing was still at a premium off-post, and I had no desire to move on-post for numerous reasons that dated back to my childhood as an enlisted-man's son at Fort Sill, Oklahoma.

Much to the relief of everyone involved, the daily trip to Camp Kue Army Hospital ended December 19, 1965. After eighty-two days and nights in an incubator and a week in the real world, Kathy weighed five pounds, two ounces. Hatsuko held her daughter for the very first time the day we exited the confinement area and headed for our new home in Ojana.

The hospital bill for the delivery and nearly three months' care came to just over ninety dollars, and we gladly surrendered the money, thanking God she was born in an Army facility. The daily trips to Kue in the 1956 Ford convertible were also over. In addition to the bumper-to-bumper traffic on Highway One, the 30 mph speed limit on the Rock was enough to make one consider giving up driving altogether.

The year of 1966 would be our first as a family of four making the usual daily adjustments, not only to our environment, but to one another. The year passed quickly.

At the very beginning of 1967, I decided to make some changes in our living conditions. In the main, I wanted to eliminate the long, torturous drive to Site Yara and to the post exchange and commissary; not including my drive to the University of Maryland classes every other night. A new housing development near Kadena Circle attracted my attention just before "the incident."

I had just taken my annual flu shot, but after only a few days, I was experiencing difficulty opening and closing my eyes, and then I experienced another troubling phenomenon: I began to have speech problems, and even found myself opening and closing my mouth manually.

I immediately called on my friend since Fort Bragg days, my favorite 91B medical specialist, SFC Hugh Hubbard. "You appear to have some form of paralysis, Bill," he told me, "but damn if I can figure out what's causing it. May I advise the Camp Kue emergency room? Like right now, Bill!" After some argument from me, we left.

About 1900 we arrived at the emergency room, and it was in an uproar. A young woman had threatened to commit suicide and had locked herself in the women's latrine. Hubbard got involved, and I sat through the entire farce in the reception room with my head in my hands. I was still seated in this position after the fiasco quieted and Hubbard went to the counter on my behalf.

A medical doctor was summoned. He took only one look at me and ordered me admitted. The medics took blood samples and the doctor administered the spinal tap. Then no one told me a damn thing for a spell. It was near 2400 before the doctor gave me a minibriefing in Room 301.

"You have a form of creeping paralysis that has started from your head and is working itself down. It's about here now," he said, pointing to my throat. "If it gets down to your chest, we will need that resuscitator next to your bed. A neurologist will be here tomorrow from Japan. He's a specialist in this sort of thing, and you are fortunate that he's on his way. Sleep should be no problem for you, so hang on. See you tomorrow."

I did sleep very well, but didn't dream about how fortunate I was because Major Speck was on his way.

Dr. Speck, a very businesslike individual of medium height

and weight, was looking down at me when I awoke. He asked me some questions and I manually opened my mouth to answer, but only after opening my eyes in the same manner. He had apparently seen enough to diagnose the problem. "He has Guillain-Barré syndrome, a disease of the nervous system. It's very rare, and few people have survived it that I know of. One, to be exact. Treatment to activate the nervous system must begin at once. A quarter gram of steroids every four hours, beginning now!"

The four tagalongs were scribbling furiously on small pads but it didn't slow down Speck at all. "Make eyedrops available immediately for him to use until he can open and shut them without help. He must stay in bed for a while. No visitors. He's critical, so get busy. I'll be back in ten days to see if he's still with us. I must run as I have a plane to catch."

I wish he hadn't said that, I thought. I'd already died so many times that I just brushed off the remark. I was rudely interrupted in my deliberations by a lovely young nurse.

"Open wide," she directed.

Using both hands, I did as directed. The steroids were followed by a glass of water. My arms were soon draped with intravenous tubes, one for feeding and one for fluids. Frankly, I was in one helluva shape, and felt like it.

I was bedridden for three very long days before I noticed some improvement; I had to strain myself, but I could open my eyes without help of any sort. Closing 'em was a different matter. The eyedrops had also helped the dryness that resulted from my eyes being open over a prolonged period.

After a week I was allowed to get out of bed anytime I wanted. In ten days Dr. Speck came back to the Rock and smiled at the second survivor of Guillain-Barré syndrome he had encountered. He brought a battery of doctors who wanted to interview me. "All you have to do, Sergeant, is to answer their questions. It will help them, perhaps, to recognize the symptoms and perhaps save some lives."

"Sir, I owe you my life," I told him, "whatever that's worth, so it'll be a pleasure to return the favor."

The questions began after the noon meal, which, because I was no longer tethered to the IVs, I had no trouble devouring.

After lunch I sat in a chair at the open end of a semicircle of eight doctors in white smocks. I fielded the questions with no problem, but the person who I had seen at the Sukiran dispensary was embarrassed when I pointed out that the dispensary on Saturday mornings appeared to want cut-and-dried cases of venereal disease or colds. That when the personnel on duty couldn't diagnose my illness, I was told that if my condition didn't improve by Monday, to come back. I thought that cop-out could have cost me, and I said as much in my usual tactful manner.

Dr. Speck nodded in agreement; Dr. Guilty blushed. Before I left the room, Dr. Guilty apologized for his indiscretion.

The session had been an eye-opener for me as well as the doctors. I certainly never knew that "French polio," as it is sometimes called, was such a mystery to the medical profession.

Guillain-Barré syndrome usually starts at the feet and works its way upward. My infection started from the head and was working its way down. Why? What causes it? No one even ventured a guess, so I did, and it caused an uproar in some military circles. That godforsaken flu shot I took a few days before got my vote. No one could confirm or deny my WAG (wild-ass guess), but I still believe it, to the extent that I have never taken another flu shot. I'd rather chance the flu virus than anything the French have to offer.

Three days later Major Speck departed for his home station in Japan, but not before leaving word to take me off the steroids. Major Cline did just that the next morning.

At bedtime I couldn't sleep and felt restless. About two in the morning I gave it up, rose from the hospital bed and turned on the lights in my room. I felt hyper and had to move around; my legs ached and I felt depressed. I rang for the nurse and looked out my fourth-floor window. I had the urge to jump, and it was more than just a passing fancy.

The nurse entered and quickly told me I wasn't supposed to be up with lights on. While she was berating me, instead of doing her job, I realized what was wrong with me.

I hushed her menial worries about hospital regulations with a quick violence-tinged outburst of my own: "Lady, I feel like I'm having spasms all over, and I feel like jumping out that damn window, and you're worried about the light bill. I want something to make me sleep, and I mean right now. I mean *now*, Lieutenant."

She looked at my chart and moved from the room at quick time. I resumed my pacing, gritting my teeth, but made sure that I stayed away from the window. I also continued to run up the light bill. In less than thirty minutes Dr. Cline was in my room, dressed like he'd just gotten out of bed. I opened my big mouth but he held up his hand for the floor.

"I goofed, Sergeant Craig," he said. "I forgot about the aftereffects of long-term steroid use, because you're the first patient who's been on steroids since I've been here. You're going through withdrawal because I took you off cold turkey. The nurse will be here shortly with a lesser dose of the drug. It'll take a few days to ease you off of them, and this won't happen again, I assure you. Sorry 'bout that."

It only took a few more days of lessened doses to ease me off of the drug. Shortly thereafter I was free of any medication except the tranquilizer Valium. I had never heard of the drug, but I enjoyed its calming effect. I began to receive visitors, and felt great. In a week or so Major Cline brought the good news that after some tests that day, I could leave! The only restriction was that I was not to jump from a perfectly good airplane for thirty days.

My longtime friend and teammate James L. Lewis brought my ten-year-old '56 Ford, with wife and kids attached, to pick me up. Jimmy was still trying to figure out what part I played in his life, but his sister Kathy at least pretended she knew me.

We all laughed and joked on the way to our castle in Ojana. Hatsuko had taken excellent care of the home and the joint was shipshape. I was more than happy to be home, but as usual, duty called.

I reported to my unit the next day and was well-received by my new sergeant major, Maddox. He duly informed me that because of my thirty-day medical restriction, I wouldn't be going near Site Yara for some time. Instead, for the time being I was assigned as an assistant operations sergeant. I needed more experience in administrative chores, especially in light of my ambition to be a Special Forces A-detachment team sergeant. I was given three days to get myself together before I was to report back to duty. I thanked the sergeant major and departed for home to be with the wife and kids for a while.

Traveling from Sukiran along Highway One continued to be a chore. Bumper-to-bumper traffic through the carbon monoxide and fumes that shrouded the two-lane thoroughfare made the thirty-five-minute drive between duty station and home a test of mental and physical endurance. Site Yara had been farther away but quicker to get to.

The next day we inspected the newly constructed homes at Kadena Circle. They were of cement-block construction and fenced in. There were tile floors inside, small living room, kitchen, two bedrooms, but only one indoor latrine. "Four thousand will pay the way and it can be financed," the realtor said. We passed up half of the good deal and paid in cash.

We now owned our first home, bought by money paid me when I was in places where I was unable to spend either my paycheck or the per diem, and supplemented when we Special Forces types were dispatched on temporary duty. We did not own the land on which our new home rested, however. In those days the Okinawans and the Japanese would lease land to foreigners but not sell it to them, which only proved what I already suspected—in many ways they are smarter than we are. A ninety-nine year lease was included in the price.

I went back to work, and things settled down after our move, with the tranquilizers keeping my beer drinking down to zilch for a spell. I wanted to continue drawing fifty-five dollars a month jump pay, and my three months without a jump—after which jump pay would be withheld—was fast approaching. Finally, my thirty-day restriction was over and I was placed on a jump manifest for the first time in ninety days.

A few miles north of Kadena Circle lies the Japanese WWII airstrip named Yomitan. It is surrounded by coral rock covered with a few inches of soil. On the west side is Suicide Cliff, also of WWII fame. If you miss the drop zone, you're in a hurt or in the Pacific Ocean, whichever comes first. I would jump-master a U.S. Marine helicopter and eleven other jumpers. A jumpmaster can lead the stick of parachutists out or push the stick and jump last; it's up to him in most cases. Jumping a rotary wing aircraft with an MC-1 parachute is stealing money from your employer. No prop blast greets your exit, there's not much opening shock, and if you miss that formidable airstrip, there's a fairly soft landing.

I rigger-checked my jumpers in good time and we lay around waiting for one of the three rotary-wing aircraft involved. Hatsuko, who had never seen a parachute jump, had come out with the kids and Shizue Fowler, and they were observing from the end of the runway.

The first unusual occurrence of the day happened to an SF jumper who failed to make a vigorous exit, his open parachute hanging up on the rear landing gear. We watched as the Marine pilot flew the luckless trooper out over the Pacific Ocean, where the jumper released himself from his chute and fell into the sea. Our own ship, appropriately named the *Green Beret*, picked him up. He was a little nervous but otherwise in good shape.

The second incident was a little more serious. The MC-1 parachute is like a T-10 canopy with a gore cut out. The open gore makes the chute much more steerable than the T-10, but it must be turned into the wind when landing in order to minimize the landing speed. The open gore, turned into the wind, supposedly takes eight knots from the lateral speed upon descent. This old soldier came in with the gore out of the wind, adding speed to his landing. He broke both femurs, or thigh bones, and was carted away to the hospital. He died a year later of his injuries.

By this time, my eleven-man stick was becoming apprehensive. I just continued to march, relying upon the Valium to keep me loose. I was so loose that the two near tragedies never even ruffled my feathers, and I was still grinning when I stood 'em up in the CH-46 helicopter and began the jump commands. Despite not having jumped in three months, I was near laughter when I exited the noisy, two-engine aircraft. My gore was facing the right direction as I approached a landing spot away from the concrete airstrip near the turn-in point. I fell upon landing, but only because SOP said we were not to stand up. I had to wait on my stick, being the jumpmaster, before turning in our chutes as a complete unit.

It may have been my first jump in three months but, thanks to the Valium, I enjoyed it. My wife told me afterward that she never wanted to see another parachute jump as long as she lived.

Finally, the question of Valium being addictive? I've heard that as well, but I do not believe it because I quit cold turkey before my six-month stint was over.

CHAPTER 8

By the summer of 1967 the haircut policy in the U.S. Army had not changed or been altered in my seventeen years of service. Unlike our civilian counterparts who had lost control of their children, we still conformed to a no-slack policy.

A few incidents about this controversial situation might be enlightening about a period that would set the hair trends for decades to come. One youngster of sixteen or so was shipped to the Rock with his Army sponsor, his father, who just happened to be an officer. The young man's hair confused the GIs about his gender. Most of us in Special Forces had not been to the Hugh Hess Hay in so long that "undisciplined" hair was a source of amazement and, generally, good-natured humor.

Not so the military that ruled the Ryukyu Islands, of which Okinawa was the capital. The youth was refused a space on the school bus and his long walk to school was accompanied by lewd whistles and unsought attention. The High Commissioner ordered the sponsor to see that his dependent's hair conformed to the military's hair policy or to leave the island.

Failure to heed the directive would have finished the sponsor's military career. What the man did, I never learned, nor was I interested enough to investigate. However, the youth was thereafter conspicuous by his absence in the enclave.

In the main, I went along with military policy concerning head and facial hair. I became concerned about it only in extreme cases. I was involved in a confrontation, for instance, in the early 1960s, in the 1st SF Group on Okinawa, when

CSM George Dunaway issued a blanket order directing *all* enlisted members to shave mustaches they had grown (despite Army regulations that permitted them). By their silence, I concluded that the commanders were on his side and approved of his unlawful action.

It bothered me because I was born with a harelip and had been teased since childhood about the scar that remained after corrective surgery. I wore a mustache for cosmetic reasons.

To come to a workable solution and not throw sixteen years down the tube, I had to think through my path of action. At the time, I wished I was single again and could tell Dunaway, the second-most-powerful NCO in the U.S. Army (who would go on to become the *most* powerful Sergeant Major of the Army) to jail me.

I went to work on it before the confrontation that would inevitably occur; Dunaway undoubtedly knew of my boast, for God only knew I had repeated it in every NCO Club on the wee island of Okinawa: "It'll be a cold day in hell when I shave my mustache. Screw Dunaway."

One Monday I fell out for sick call and picked up my medical records. At the 1st Group Dispensary at Hizagawa, I handed them to a 91B medic doubling as a clerk, saying that I had "a technical problem" and that I would like to see the group medical officer.

The enlisted medic returned without my records in a New York minute. "Step into his office, Top," he said. "Major Sky is ready for you."

Sky got up from his desk, smiled and extended his hand when I entered. His dark, graying hair and large shoulders made him look like one of the Vikings I had read about in high school.

"Sir, Command Sergeant Major Dunaway has passed the word that there will be no mustaches in the First Special Forces Group," I said.

"So I've heard," Sky said.

"I am harelipped, as you know, and wear a mustache to cover the scar. I just won't go for it, Major. Jail me!" I insisted.

"You don't have to shave your mustache, Sergeant, and you know that. It looks good on you. Your speech is excellent, by the way. You've obviously worked hard at overcoming your cleft palate."

"Thank you, sir, but I haven't convinced the Group command sergeant major, or his flunkies at company level, of the necessity for my mustache, so what do I do now?"

"The solution to that problem is at my very fingertips, William. I am going to notate the fact in your records that will follow you the rest of your Army career." I smiled.

"In addition, due to the circumstances and the characters we're dealing with, I will give you proof to carry on your person!" Dr. Sky handed me a small document with his signature attached. I could not help but grin at law's triumph over illegality.

Driving back to Camp Kue, I was still smiling. I had shaved my mustache twice in my career since my second-hitch enlistment in 1954, once for jump school and once for Captain Cull at Fort Campbell. Never again! When I arrived at Kue, I showed Sgt. Major Wally Klink the document from Major Sky. He shook his head and said, "Good luck, Bill." But the issue was soon over, resolved, as Klink left the unit and Dunaway departed Okinawa to take over the 5th SF Group. The 5th had never been my favorite unit to begin with. But an incident was brewing on the front burner that would erase my peace of mind over my recent victory. Fate, for some ungodly reason, has a way of evening the score.

During the few years I soldiered in the continental U.S., I had my hair cut once every two weeks, mainly due to the expense. In Okinawa, however, the service was so cheap and the lady barbers so good-looking, I got the chore done once every week.

A Sunday evening around 1600, or four P.M., in July 1967, I took a Valium and drove off to Camp Kue. The young lady trimmed my locks in good time and I moved out for Sukiran's Coral Hill NCO Club, where the beer flowed while I easily passed my capacity, despite knowing damn well that I was on Valium and wasn't supposed to be drinking at all. Around nine P.M. I was hardly in any shape to drive home, or anywhere else for that matter. Have you ever tried to tell a drunk that he shouldn't do something? It's a lost cause, I assure you.

I stopped the Ford at the stop sign upon leaving Sukiran, then turned right, toward Kadena, but felt a little sleepy from all the effort and bowed my head and drove into a four-foot drainage ditch.

I was sore from the encounter but climbed laughingly out of the wreck, up the incline, and stood by the highway, but not for long. The Armed Forces Police on Okinawa were composed of soldiers, sailors, Air Force, and Marine Corps personnel. What particular service detained me that night, I couldn't say. I did note, however, that they weren't enjoying themselves as much as I was. I soon found myself in a cell.

When the cell door clanged, I smiled and remembered why I was in a cell, while the other drunks were afforded the luxury of waiting outside on cushioned benches.

In the early sixties some Ryukyu Armed Forces Police came to Company A, at Sukiran, and went to the orderly room. When they insisted on looking upstairs, the charge of quarters, a tough staff sergeant named Gene Bell told 'em the unit special operating procedures: "No one can go upstairs except the personnel who live here, officer. I will have to call the commander for permission to deviate from those procedures."

"You need no one's permission," was the reply. "We'll handle it without all that." A confrontation ensued, to say the least.

By the time Gene Bell had gone through the two MPs and was working on their backups, the commander had arrived. In addition to denying them access to the billets, the lieutenant colonel chewed ass and took the names of the intruders. From that day on, Special Forces had a special place in the hearts and souls of the Ryukyu Armed Forces Police.

The appearance of Sergeant Major Maddox interrupted my remembrances. I followed Maddox to the desk, where he signed for me before we moved to his privately owned vehicle.

"Bill, you're in a heap of trouble," Maddox commented.

"Why, Sergeant Major? You don't really think I'm drunk, do you?"

He didn't go for it. "Get serious, Bill! Yes, you're drunk. Let's work on another line. Like the truth, for a starter."

I described the evening's entertainment to Maddox, and he pulled up to my abode before he spoke again.

"Colonel Munger will see you at 0800 in the morning. Get some sleep and I'll help you as best I can, but expect the worst."

Hatsuko listened to my tale and she was just as frightened as I was. She did have the presence of mind to call Frank Fowler and relay that I would need a ride to work the next morning.

I was dressed in OD jungle fatigues bloused into Corcoran jump boots, and was wearing a beret, when Staff Sergeant Fowler honked the next morning. A cup of coffee would have to hold me. I had a hangover and felt horrible. On the way to work, Fowler didn't improve my state of mind by relating his encounter with this DUI business at Fort Bragg.

Sergeant Major Maddox was not grinning when I knocked and entered. He motioned for me to be seated. "Lieutenant Colonel Munger will see you very shortly," he said.

"Sergeant Major," I began, "I screwed up this morning and I know it. Thanks for the ride home last night. I owe you one. I know a DUI is not to be sneezed at, but I have some other thoughts on it that I would like for you to be aware of."

The boss jumped right in. "Before you continue, Bill, I want you to know that we're both on your side. Your experiences and conduct in the past will be considered."

I wasn't too sure what that meant, but it slowed me not. "At Bragg, they bust 'em one stripe, Sergeant Major. I think it's wrong as two left feet; I've never seen an officer busted for DUI. It's bullshit, and I fail to see how it reflects on my duty performance. That's it, Top. The Valium and the beer let me down. That's my only excuse."

"I need to see your medical slip authorizing the Valium, Bill. I'm on your side, but don't come on too strong with Munger. I think he'll be with us on this, too. Okay?"

I reported to Munger at 0900. He returned my salute and requested Maddox and me to be seated. My hangover was noted by the alert commander, and it didn't surprise me. The short, heavyset officer probably already had his twenty years in and certainly wasn't a rookie. He appeared to be gritting his teeth when he spoke, causing his jowls to appear flabby.

"You've never been in this kind of trouble before, Sergeant Craig! What's the problem?"

"I only have one excuse, sir. I was taking Valium and wasn't supposed to be drinking. I was duly warned by the doctor not to do it. No excuse, sir!"

Maddox handed the medical slip to Munger, who accepted it and continued, "Yes, I heard you had a close shave, and I don't really know what to say except that I am required to render justice." He looked at me and back at the medical slip. He stood up and began to pace. "I'll look into it, Sergeant, and you'll hear from me and the sergeant major when we're finished. You are dismissed!"

I rose, took one step back, saluted and quietly left. The worst part was over, as best as I could tell. For some reason, I felt relieved, and went back to work in the Operations section. That I had left my driver's license on the Military Police desk—and it would remain there for a *year*—was punishment enough as far as I was concerned. Two days later I was given an official reprimand by Munger, closing the last chapter of the novel. I sincerely thanked Sergeant Major Maddox for his assistance.

After only a week of catching rides, hitchhiking, and riding suicidal skoshi cabs, I realized that the solution wasn't as good a deal as I had figured. But Sgt. Major John T. Lockhart of Company B, who was visiting our Operations shack one day and heard me sounding off on the subject, had an interesting solution.

"How long before your hitch is up, William?" he asked.

"Almost a year, Sergeant Major. Why?"

"It's not commonly known, but if a GI reenlists, all forms of nonjudicial punishment must be erased from his records. There's your solution to the driving problem, old soldier."

"I'm not sure I understand, Top."

"Listen up! It's on your record that your license was suspended for one year. Right?"

I nodded.

"If you are accepted for reenlistment, and you will be, they must wipe the slate clean and return the document. I have said all I'm going to say except good luck. And I wouldn't want word of this procedure getting spread around."

I was stunned but skeptical. I went back in the Quonset hut and pretended to shuffle papers while I rolled it around in my head. It was June 1967 and I only had two more months on Okinawa, because of the regulation that a person could only be assigned in one overseas command—in this case the Pacific Command, or CINCPAC—for six consecutive years. I still needed three years to complete my twenty years. What did I have to lose? It was too good to be true, so I'd go for it!

The Group Recruiting Office found me at parade rest come Monday morning. While waiting for the E7 to open the joint, my conscience began to bother me. I finally decided to pacify both parties in my skull and enlisted for six years.

Tuesday, I was sworn in and received my discharge with a promise that my recorded DD 214 record of service would follow. By Thursday the big deal was completed, and come Friday, instead of being sworn in, I would be sworn at. I came out on orders as having reenlisted for six years. I asked and received permission to visit Military Police Headquarters that very afternoon. I was in good humor by the time I entered. The desk sergeant referred me to the sergeant major himself. I told the sergeant major that I wanted my driver's license and handed him a copy of my reenlistment orders.

He read the orders before he even had the courtesy to pull my file. "You still have eleven months to go before your license can be returned, Sergeant."

"I realize that, but I reenlisted, Sergeant Major, and that suspension is a form of nonjudicial punishment, so it must be erased from my records." I was very polite.

He studied the enlistment orders then tried to bribe me; a common law violator, he was. "I'll do it, if you'll tell me who told you how to do this."

I was shocked. "Top, I learned about it through my own studies. No one had to tell me. May I have my license, please?"

By that time I'd had a year in Laos and a year and a half in Vietnam. All I had to look forward to was a permanent change of station move to Fort Bragg come September 1967. Ms. Alexander, the Special Forces records-and-assignment chief in the Pentagon, was famous for taking care of her boys. Here's one old soldier she certainly took good care of—my orders came down in August, and the Pentagon had a strange way of spelling Fort Bragg, North Carolina—Republic of Vietnam. I was to report to Nha Trang on or about September 15, 1967.

I wasn't too thrilled about the turn of events, because I'd wanted to take my wife and kids to their new country, but it wasn't to be, at least for a while. I had too many things to do to lose any sleep over Ms. A.'s solution to my reenlistment.

My wife and I had a lot of planning to do before my reporting date. My mother, in Oklahoma, had been complaining about not having seen me in four years and never having seen the wife and kids. Due to the shortage of time, Hatsuko and I decided that she and the kids would stay on Okinawa during my tour. Before leaving for Vietnam, I would go home on space-available aircraft, see my mother, return to Okinawa, stay a week or so there, then report to the 5th Special Forces Group on the beaches of Nha Trang. I knew my mother was going to be disappointed at not seeing Hatsuko and the kids, but that arrangement was the best I could do on such short notice.

Before leaving for the States, I went to the company headquarters and they assigned a sponsor to look after Hatsuko and the family. As she was a native of Okinawa, I didn't believe she would need one, provided nothing out of the ordinary happened to me in Vietnam. Very quickly I was aboard an aircraft to the States, a place that was by then only my home away from home. Although I had been gone only six years, I no longer felt any kinship with my native country. A nice place to visit, I guess. That feeling would take a long time to erase.

At San Francisco I purchased a round-trip ticket to Oklahoma City, and was home two days after departure. As I'd thought, my mother was very sad at not getting to see her daughter-in-law and two beautiful grandchildren. I explained why that just hadn't been possible and solemnly swore that they would be home after my year in Vietnam, which consoled her to a degree. I spent three weeks looking up my friends and Korean War buddies. Despite not really wanting to be there, I had a refreshing time and arrived back in Okinawa with two weeks to spare.

On the thirteenth of September, after two pleasant weeks with my family, I arrived in Nha Trang. It was gonna be a long year. Thirteen not being my lucky number, I should have waited till the fifteenth.

Signing in, I was billeted in the transients' quarters of the headquarters complex near the Nha Trang air depot. The personnel sergeant told me to report to the top enlisted soldier the very next day. I knew in my heart that Dunaway would be thrilled no end. I cursed Ms. Alexander for a few minutes before dropping off to sleep.

Eating in the very well-supplied headquarters mess hall

confused me no end. The food was out of this world (eggs were cooked to order!). Was I really in Vietnam and drawing sixty-five dollars combat pay every month for it? Special Forces was no different than any other Army unit in some ways: the headquarters personnel had it tough, receiving sixty-five dollars a month also.

I reported to Command Sergeant Major Dunaway's office after being told that he wanted to see me in person. Now I was worried. When I walked in, my fatigues, beret, and jungle boots were spotless. He offered me a seat and I complied, warily. "This is kinda confusing, Sergeant Craig, but bear with me," Dunaway said. "Your name went out a week ago, so all corps areas knew of your pending arrival." Damn, I'm in some kinda trouble, I thought.

"The reason I haven't any assignment for you at this time is because a sergeant major asked me to hold it up. He apparently has some plans for you that I'm not privy to. So report back in each morning and I'll keep you posted until it's time to move out. Any questions?"

"Yeah, Sergeant Major. What sergeant major and what corps area are we speaking about?"

"That's privileged information, Bill. See you tomorrow morning. Enjoy our facilities while you can," he said curtly.

I would, but soon even the excellent food during the day and visiting the NCO Club at night began to drag. I can't tell a lie, though, I did enjoy visiting with the troops who were in from the A-detachment sites, Delta Project, and other units I'd been connected with. If nothing else, it brought me up to snuff on the buildup of U.S. troops and the many missions Special Forces had inherited since my departure in September 1965.

My picnic ended Friday morning when Dunaway gave me my assignment. "Yes, William, you're off to Company C, in Da Nang. You do know Sergeant Major Harmon Hodge, I presume?"

"Yes, Top, I knew him at Fort Bragg," I replied.

"Well, he's waiting for you. He was the one who requested

you to begin with. So, providing we can get you an aircraft out of here, you're gone."

The C-130 flight was uneventful, as was the jeep ride through Da Nang and across the bay to the Company C compound. I did note the boom and hustle of Da Nang. Many new buildings and overpopulation were a result of the U.S. troop buildup. The only thing that really surprised me was the abundance of U.S. Marines now in the I Corps (northernmost provinces of South Vietnam) area. The United States Marine Corps had other surprises in store for me before the tour was over.

In-processing was well-organized, and completed by 1300. The facilities at the company level were not as luxurious as the accommodations in Nha Trang. But when I walked into the mess hall, my old pal Mess Sergeant Norman "Pork Chop" Racibor made me feel like I was back in Okinawa again. He was just as surprised to see me as I was to see him. The reunion was short, but I told him to meet me in the small Enlisted Club after supper. It was old home week over a few beers, and I ran into Billy Boggs before the lights went out. Boggs was an old roommate in the One-Oh-Worst at Fort Campbell, Kentucky. The homecoming did not prepare me for my interview the next day, but I enjoyed it regardless.

An L-shaped wooden structure contained the headquarters of C Company, which governed up to ten A-detachments, several B-detachments, and classified units in I Corps. What little administrative in-processing I had remaining was dispensed with and I was ushered into the neat, square office of the sergeant major.

Harmon Hodge was six feet two inches, 195 sturdy pounds, and no man to argue with except with a smile on your face. A few Marines would find that out the hard way before Hodge finished his permanent change of station in Da Nang. An altercation with this gentleman usually meant hospital recovery time. Just to be on the safe side, I smiled when I entered.

"Have a seat, Bill. I want Lieutenant Colonel Schungel to meet you before I mash this great assignment on you."

While Hodge exited, I studied his well-kept desk and thought briefly about what I knew about my new enlisted boss. Hodge was apparently a very religious man and didn't tolerate drinking on the job. How could you fault that? He didn't really care for it at all, but I never heard him come down on anyone unless the pastime became a problem involving job performance. The "Preacher" was his moniker throughout Special Forces. I never used the term because I didn't think it applied, nor did I have enough guts to call him that to his face.

His brown hair and brown eyes sparkled as he returned with his boss. Schungel was about the same height but thinner, and his brown hair was rapidly turning gray. His "At case, Sergeant Craig" put me at rest. He motioned for me to be seated but remained standing, as did Hodge.

"Bill, tell the colonel what type experience and tours you've had in Southeast Asia."

I did just that, as briefly and as modestly as my conscience would allow. Despite my having had no one-year PCS tours, Schungel was impressed with my six TDY tours, three years of on-the-job training. When I completed my brief history, Hodge asked if I'd been in Korea.

"I was there from November of 1951 until I rotated in June 1952, Top. I spent eight months in the Pioneer & Ammunition Platoon, 2nd Battalion, 179th Regimental Combat Team. I also served a month or so in a battalion reconnaissance platoon."

The colonel had heard enough, and I stood up as he offered me his hand again. "You'll do fine where you're going tomorrow. I'll ride up with you, if I can find the time. Good luck, and welcome aboard."

I stood at attention as he exited, as much in the dark as to my destination as ever. Hodge snapped me out of it and motioned me to be seated while he did likewise.

"Bill, we desperately need a team sergeant on the A-detachment at Lang Vei, near Khe Sanh, so I had Dunaway put you on hold when you arrived. Hope you didn't mind the wait, but I was all but snowed under."

My morale soared. At last, a team sergeant in Special Forces—my ambition for eight years of study and toil had been fulfilled. Still, I couldn't believe it had finally arrived. A team sergeant called for the rank of Master Sergeant E8 and I was now only an E7.

"It's gonna be a tough assignment Bill," Hodge said, "but if I didn't think you could handle it, I wouldn't have recommended you. In addition to an A-detachment, you'll have SeaBees and Vietnamese Special Forces. If I told you they have not jelled, I would be making an understatement. When you need help, give me a call. Khe Sanh has changed a lot since you were there in 1962, but Master Sergeant Godaysik will give you a briefing at 1400 this afternoon. Good luck, Team Sergeant!"

Dressed in jungle fatigues, and jungle boots made for walking, I floated to Racibor's slop shop still on cloud nine at high noon. The sultry summer was ending and the rainy season was about to begin, but I couldn't have answered what year it was if someone had asked. Pork Chop came into the dining area from the kitchen and sat with me while I babbled in a daze. Before he departed, he brought me back to Da Nang, September 22, 1967. "Good luck, Bill, you're gonna need it! You've got a tiger by the tail!"

Except for two desks in the center, the Operations room looked like a Rand McNally workshop. Maps of all sizes depicting South Vietnam and I Corps covered the walls. I sat at one desk and turned my chair around in order to face Master Sergeant Godaysik, my 1400 briefer. Having roamed I Corps in 1962–63 while scouting for new A camp locations, I knew much of the information about to be presented. Nevertheless, I was very attentive.

Master Sergeant Godaysik was a burly, muscular troop. He

retrieved a pointer. Beneath light, cropped hair his bronzed face was dominated by expressive eyes. He flashed a broad smile as he began. "Company C, Fifth Special Forces Group, now controls A camps located in Ba To, Con Thien, Gia Vuc, Ha Thanh, Mang Buk, Minh Long, Huynh, Thuong Duc, Tien Phuoc, Tra Bong, and Lang Vei.

"The Lang Vei A-detachment is now located in the north-westernmost corner of South Vietnam, eight kilometers west of the Marine base at Khe Sanh. You've been to Khe Sanh Combat Base, haven't you, Bill?"

"Yes, Operations Sergeant, but just carry on. I need any refresher on the area that's available."

"You follow Highway One from our present location in Da Nang until you reach Dong Ha." He pointed. "Take a left at Dong Ha and you're on Highway Nine, heading for Khe Sanh village, the Combat Base, and the new campsite of Lang Vei."

In order to be more explicit, he moved to the Quang Tri Province map before continuing. "Just before you hit Khe Sanh ville, you take a right and a few miles down the road and you're in the Khe Sanh Combat Base. We'll come back to this Marine hangout in a few minutes. Stay on Highway Nine, and minutes later you'll be in Khe Sanh ville. Five miles down the road sits what is now the new Lang Vei camp and your detachment, A-101. The old campsite is not on Highway Nine, it's just off to your left, but your new camp straddles the damn interstate." Godaysik paused and lit up when I asked my first question.

"I remember Sergeant Steptoe, who had A-101 at the old camp. Tell me what happened in that cluster-fuck."

"It happened four months ago, but the U.S. Air Force set the stage in March of sixty-seven by mistakenly making a bombing run on the Bru [Montagnard] village of Lang Vei. The F-4 Phantom jets killed about 125 civilians in that fox-fuck."

"Yeah, that's a good recruiting ploy for the CIDG!"

"I know," Godaysik agreed. "Steptoe and A-101 had no one

else to turn to, and that's the scene in May 1967. Some infiltrators in the CIDG cut the wire on the south side of the camp for the NVA. By 0330 it was all over. The rescue platoon found three survivors, including Steptoe, who is still in a helluva shape. We lost seventeen CIDG and had a bunch of wounded. Now you know why they wanted A-101 in another location. The Bru are easily spooked, and in this case they may be right. Your camp is on *this* dogbone-shaped hilltop, eight hundred meters west of the old one. It overlooks the border with Laos and has better fields of fire. Any other questions, Team Sergeant?"

"The Viet Cong infiltrating the CIDG will be a problem forever, Top. We just have to live with it. How far along is the construction of the new camp?"

"I've never been there, but I have Operations people who have been, recently. The Navy SeaBees are working their asses off but still have a ways to go. They have one large timber-and-reinforced-concrete bunker in place, and A-101 sleeps there at night. The SeaBees and Viet Special Forces sleep in the smaller completed bunkers. You have at least six weeks' to two months' work to go before completion, Bill. What else?"

"How do those factions get along, Top?"

"Problem number one, Bill!" he replied.

"I'll leave it alone. I'll find out soon enough. How about Khe Sanh Combat Base?"

"Problem number two. Not much cooperation at all."

"Who's in charge of who?"

"Problem number three. The 26th Marines are under the 3rd Marine Division, and you take orders from the Company C detachment located here."

I'd gotten more from the briefing than I expected to. "Some of those problems go a little higher than an A-detachment team sergeant's pay grade, but I'll do what I can." Actually I gave very little thought to the problems; worrying about them would be a waste of time until I could see them for myself.

At the club that night, Norman Racibor brought over a friend and prodded him into giving me some insight on what my assignment's real problems were. Again, I had heard all I needed to know; problems cannot be solved with bullshit and theory. I listened to the individual, but I was more interested in the San Miguel beer than in faraway Detachment A-101.

"You've got four rifle companies, 101, 102, 103, and 104," Racibor's informant said. "They're at about half strength. How ya gonna recruit the Bru after you've bombed their villages?"

"I really can't do anything about it just now. Let's talk about women or beer, or something we can do something about," I responded. "How's Harmon D. on the troops from the field, Pork Chop?" I asked, hoping to steer away from Lang Vei for the rest of the evening.

"Hodge don't change, Bill, and you know that. When you or your people come in from the boonies, clean up, shave, and get a haircut. Once that's accomplished, you can party. He runs a tight ship, but the people that catch hell are those who violate those basic requirements. He brings more smoke on his own headquarters people than he does the field soldiers. Hell, I don't have any trouble with him." Pork Chop's conclusions would be my doctrine in the months to come for people fortunate enough to earn R&R in Da Nang from isolated A-101.

I was mildly surprised the next day when my helicopter companion on the long trip to Lang Vei turned out to be Lt. Col. Daniel F. Schungel. He greeted me warmly before we were jeeped to the Da Nang air field. Our ride to Khe Sanh to refuel and on to Lang Vei was otherwise devoid of significant conversation. But for some reason, I felt better having him aboard.

We landed parallel to Highway Nine in the heart of the construction of A camp, by the wooden outhouse. We were met by my new team leader, Captain Frank C. Willoughby, who shook my hand and greeted me warmly after Schungel's introduction. He, in turn, introduced me to the man I was replacing,

SFC Richard Chamra, who hustled me away from the chopper pad and into our quarters. Except for Willoughby and the executive officer, 1st Lt. Miles Wilkins, the entire detachment was quartered in a huge bunker on the western perimeter overlooking the Sepone River and Laos. The two team officers were living in what would eventually be our tactical operations center (TOC). I dropped everything on the GI cot but retained my M-16 and webbing for the tour.

The walk-through was to last until suppertime. Like the Yards, the thin Chamra was sheathed in camouflage fatigues, while I stomped along behind him in the jungle fatigues worn in garrison by SF only. I knew this stamped me as a newbie. Through an interpreter, we met some of the officers and men of the Civilian Irregular Defense Group (CIDG) Companies 101, 102, 103, and 104. Judging by appearances, they were the most ragtag, undernourished, deprived Montagnards I had ever set eyes upon. I told Chamra that very thing while we toured the perimeter.

"History has not had a kind spot in its heart for the Bru," he said. "They've been shit on by the Viet Cong, the NVA, the Marine Corps, and the U.S. Air Force. If I left out anyone—oh yes, the South Vietnamese!—it was only a temporary oversight. I would hate to be playing out their hand. The poor bastards!"

"I know about 'em from Khe Sanh back in 1962, so I know you're right," I said. "But the fact remains, we have to recruit some more of the poor bastards to fill up those half-strength CIDG companies, Dick."

Inside the as-yet-unfinished TOC, I met the two SF radio operators, S.Sgt. Emanuel Phillips and Spec. Four William McMurray. They both gave me the impression that they knew what they were doing, and they welcomed me aboard before we moved on to the SeaBees' spare bunkers. The Navy engineers were all on the job, building what would soon become the best fortified A camp in South Vietnam. I would meet them at the supper meal, along with the remainder of the detachment.

I had met the Vietnamese Special Forces (LLDB) team leader, Lieutenant Quy, at the helicopter pad and looked forward to meeting the team sergeant, Lu Minh. I was not disappointed. We came upon him on the small hillside, supervising the supervisors of a work detail excavating for a bunker. The Bru NCOs had been lying down when Lu Minh came upon the scene, and they were braced at attention, receiving their just desserts.

The LLDB team sergeant was, without a doubt, of Chinese extraction mixed with Montagnard ancestry. At first glance he seemed roly-poly, but that impression faded after watching him move around. He had a clear, loud voice to go with his almost six-foot frame. When he finished his one-man critique of the labor and its supervisors, the dirt begin to fly. The interpreter was introducing us as Minh came toward us through the second growth on the hillside. His face lit up and he damn near broke my hand when he shook it. I was very happy when I finally retrieved the mangled implement. Team Sergeant Minh's command of English was unique: mixed with slang and profanity, he sounded almost the way I did when I lost my temper.

It was time to move on before I finally got in a sentence. "We'll straighten it all out, ol' Team Sergeant, just you wait and see," I said. He slapped me on the back as we walked away toward the Sepone River and the Kingdom of Laos. We stopped considerably short of the kingdom however, at a spot where two SeaBees on bulldozers were repairing the road and the lines of sight. We spoke to the 'dozer operators and I received the same complaints from each driver, who were both dressed in Navy dungarees. Pistols hung from their hips.

"The job security is lax and not supervised, and we're discriminated against in the chow hall."

I told them that both situations would be corrected ASAP. When the tour was concluded, Chamra and I headed for the aboveground dining facility. Just because I could live on a can of C-rations a day did not mean that I thought food wasn't an important morale factor, as was discrimination. I stood inside the facility and observed. Only when everyone was fed did I venture through the line and feast on the remains. The last hour had opened my eyes very wide about friction at Lang Vei.

CHAPTER 9

The officers had already eaten, so I seated myself on one of the long benches next to the Navy chief (E7), who had gone through the line after his people. From that alone, I knew he knew something about leadership. Our conversation only reinforced what I had suspected from my observations. It was clear that there was no trust or respect between the twelve to fifteen SeaBees and the ten SF people. I believed that after a long talk with our captain and some unkind hints to the noncommissioned officers of A-101, only two or three major problems would remain.

First and most important was finishing the construction of the camp. Second was to fill up the line companies with native sons, and third was to obtain some cooperation from the Marines at Khe Sanh. But the talk with Captain Willoughby had to come before all other considerations.

The site of the conference was his makeshift quarters in what the blueprints made out to be the fabulous tactical operation center (TOC). We were both drinking Vietnamese 33, Ba Muoi Ba, beer he had borrowed from someone. I started off the session that would be a learning experience for both of us. I certainly didn't want to start the thing off like a battle of wits, so I smiled as best I could before I began. The dialogue is reasonably easy to recall, perhaps because the topics touched upon policies that I would insist on regardless of the situation or location for the rest of my military career. "I'll run the detachment and you'll command it, sir!"

"That's what Colonel Schungel said before he departed," Willoughby answered in a resigned tone. "So I'll live with it, Sergeant Craig."

"We have minor problems that even an outsider can see, sir. I saw that today in my tour. Let's start on solving them before we get down to the major drawbacks that will take everyone's help to solve," I said sincerely.

"Carry on, Team Sergeant!"

"Chow will be on a first come, first served basis, but officers, I, and the Navy chief will eat last. We need the SeaBees very badly. The better our relationship, the faster we won't need them at all, sir."

Willoughby nodded, so I continued to march. "Guard details for the SeaBees working down by the Sepone River will include an American or two, for insurance. They feel like they are in danger down there. I talked to the Vietnamese SF team sergeant, and he'll furnish some ass-kickers as well!"

"Sounds good to me," Willoughby said. "It would help immensely if you and he get along, Top."

"Sergeant Major Hodge has promised to bring us up to the twelve-man level ASAP, and I trust him to do just that. He also said to abide by the regulation that stipulates that we must have an operation out in our area at all times." I paused and looked at my team leader.

"We have little field experience at this point," Willoughby replied, "nor do we have the indigenous personnel. How do you propose to satisfy the head shed in that requirement, Top?"

"The exact size of the operations was not specified, so we'll satisfy it with small operations of twenty to twenty-five people and two of us. I hope our people and the indigenous will get the experience as we go along. I'll run a duty roster of U.S. personnel so we can all gain the experience. I'll juggle the roster to be sure you and I are never out at the same time, or Lieutenant Wilkins, for that matter. The Bru companies furnishing the personnel will be rotated as well."

Because I now believed the team leader to be on my side, I moved on. "What, if any, high-angle fire support do we have . . . from Khe Sanh, for instance?"

Willoughby chuckled. "We have none from Khe Sanh, but we do have two 81mm mortars here for our own support. Our heavy-weapons man is trying to instruct our people on the M-1 sight just now, and that's it, Top."

I was not surprised, and my head-shaking confirmed that. "Well, I can fire the damn things, but we need to improve the fire support. I'll send a message to Hodge. If the conventional forces commander in Da Nang tells Khe Sanh to 105 artillery support us, they will. I'll work on it, with your permission of course." I didn't give the commander time to answer and rushed on. "Where will the 4.2-inch mortar go when it's air-dropped, sir?"

"How did you know that, Top?" Willoughby seemed astonished.

"I picked it up in Da Nang. We'll place it in the center of our perimeter, I guess. I'll need some instruction on cutting charges for that damn thing. Tiroch had better know his business!"

Lastly, I said, "There will be no women or alcoholic beverages in camp!"

"You mean no beer, Top?"

"No, sir! No hard liquor. Three beers a night is the limit on beer. That won't hurt anyone. No drinking beer during duty hours, either. That's an Army regulation, so I don't give a shit what people think of that one, or the women part, either."

"We have one Bru movie star who picks up and cleans our clothes in the daytime, Top."

"Great, sir, as long as she's gone by sundown, no problem. No screwing the girls in camp, sir, is what I'm saying!

"What I've seen of the Bru women and their betel-nut-stained teeth, I don't think we'll have a problem there. After I make my rounds in the morning and talk to the Vietnamese team sergeant, I'll have our patrol unit designated for the five-day move, and their U.S. accomplices as well. Unless you have something, I'm gone. I'm on watch from 1200 till 0400 so I need some sleep."

I moved north and west a few yards from the TOC before reaching the troop bunker. Although eight people were sleeping on cots in the thirty-by-fifty-foot reinforced steel and concrete bunker, room was adequate. I unpacked my winter sleeping bag and laid it out on the bed as a cushion before I flopped for three hours of rest.

The next morning, after putting on jungle boots and clean socks, I climbed the very steep stairs. Two suspended water bags and a wooden table with holes for steel helmets awaited my arrival. I brushed my teeth and washed my ugly face. Then I moved out for the aboveground mess hall.

I waited outside the four-by-four lumber construction that featured screening waist high to a ceiling that was covered with galvanized tin. The Navy chief joined me, and after five or six SeaBees and SF people exited, we went in to nourish up. The two Army officers were not far behind, so we all sat at one of the wooden tables and chatted. Even my team leader noted the difference in the happy bantering that went on at the breakfast meal. I literally devoured the meat, toast, and eggs our cook had secured from somewhere. One thing you learn at an early period in Special Forces is never to look a gift horse in the mouth: who gives a damn who stole it or from whom? I drank one more cup of java, told Willoughby and the chief my schedule, and departed.

I was already gloating; the war with the friendlies was in its last stages. Only one more step to go.

My first stop was the half-completed tactical operations center, and I looked it over before descending the steps. It was gonna be a beaut! The small two-room commo shack was operating and keeping the two CW operators busy. Between receiving and deciphering the Morse code, they had no time for idle conversation. In thirty minutes the traffic quieted and I read each message before I began my short dissertation. Both operators were obviously proficient, but to satisfy my curiosity, they gave me a rundown on their Army background.

Staff Sergeant Emanuel E. Phillips told me that he had arrived about a month before I did. He'd been in Group (SF) a few years and had never been anything but a CW operator since basic and advanced training. He was married but had no children. It was his first tour in Vietnam.

Specialist Four William G. McMurray said, "I've been at Lang Vei seven months and only in the Army a few years. I got married just before I left the States, and like Sergeant Phillips, also have always been a radio operator."

After reciting my experience in SF and my family life, or lack of, I began with a few policies that they may or may not have been familiar with, and I didn't bother to ask. "Every message that goes out of here will be read by me and/or the old man if I'm not here. Every incoming message will be read by me before distribution and filing."

Neither showed any surprise. In fact, McMurray grinned knowingly.

"When we get this bunker completed, and I'm going to get some priority on that project, you, the executive officer, and the ol' man, will live here. Any objections?"

McMurray surprised me with this retort: "I speak for myself, Top, but I'd rather not live where I work, if you don't mind."

I considered his request before saying anything. "How do you feel about that, Sergeant Phillips?"

"I kinda agree with him, Top, but someone has to be around here twenty-four hours a day, so it's up to you, I guess."

"We'll have a guard here once our perimeter is completed, Phil, so just continue to march until then. I'll go along with living quarters on the perimeter at that time."

Everyone seemed satisfied, so I asked a question they both knew was coming. "You monitor the PRC-25s when operations are out. Right?"

McMurray grinned before he answered. "Yeah, Top. But there hasn't been one out lately."

"That will change come Monday morning. Believe it! My last question, and I've got to be running along. What kind of contact do you have with Khe Sanh Combat Base?"

They both looked stunned, but McMurray came through again. "The same as we've always had, Top: *none*!"

"Son of a bitch," I murmured. "Things have got to change. They need us as bad as we need them. For the time being, Hodge and the C-detachment are trying to lay on 105 artillery support. Hope it comes through! At least then we'll have commo with the artillery, and that would be a start. I'm not going over there until next week, but I'll keep you informed. I'm heading for the Viet team sergeant's hooch to lay on a patrol for next week. My operations order will let you know when, where, and who. You guys are doing a good job and things will get better. 'Bye!"

CIDG Company 101 was on the south end of the camp perimeter, about seventy-five meters from the TOC, separated by a single concertina barbed-wire fence. I went through the wire gate and heard Viet SF Lu Minh's ass-chewing before I started my descent to the military crest. When Minh saw me, his expression changed from a scowl to a wide grin, and he shook my hand as well as that of Tung, my interpreter, who had tagged along when I left the TOC.

Minh squatted, and the interpreter followed suit. We were all dressed alike in cammies, jungle boots, soft caps, and pistol belts with harnesses and weapons. I sat on the hard earth, not my haunches. We formed a small circle.

Because of Minh's interest in English as a second language, I used the translator sparingly, but I laid on an operation from the 101st Company in short order. Minh assured me they would have twenty men from the understrength seventy-four-man company rarin' to go at 0630 Monday morning. When he asked what U.S. would participate, I said that I had no roster as yet and was unable to answer the inquiry. I promised him an answer the next day, and we put the operation aside.

"We need your men to begin placing barbed-wire fences around the outer perimeter, Minh."

He nodded in agreement.

"Can you have each company draw enough wire to build three fences sometime today? If you can, I'll have an engineer supervisor beginning tomorrow."

"I'll see my team leader, Lieutenant Quy, and we'll arrange it, Trung Si. Where you go now?"

"Tung and I are headed for the SeaBees detail down by the Sepone. Want to come along?"

"Yeah, Trung Si, we go!"

The three of us headed for the work party that was just short of the Laotian boundary. There, a bulldozer was hauling sand that was being screened before being moved by truck to the TOC and other U.S. bunkers for the concrete overhead cover. I was mildly surprised to find the chief in Navy blues, harness, and weapon. At least he had requisitioned a pair of jungle boots to go with his odd attire. Of course, he stood out like a sore thumb. I wasn't too happy when I found out the rest of the crew of seagoing engineers were dressed the same. I called his attention to the fact that they should be dressed in cammies like us. He agreed but said, "Your detachment said the cammies were not available. We each got a pair of jungle boots, but that's about it."

The U.S. specialist five came out of the brush and approached. I was very glad to see him and his interpreter. He had issued me four sets of cammies the night before, so I knew that they were indeed available. He came up to us with a greeting and a smile. The six-foot blond was named Johnson, and he seemed to know his business. I asked him the story on the Navy SeaBees' uniforms, and he said that he had been told by the captain that they were not to be made available to the SeaBees.

"Okay, I'll buy that. Tonight after supper, set up a time with the chief here and make 'em available!"

Johnson and the chief both grinned widely. "Can do, Top," Johnson replied.

"When you get through, Chief, come over to the mess hall," I said, "and have a beer on me."

"Can do, Bill. See you at chow!"

Minh appeared to know the subject and grinned as well, saving me an explanation. "Let's go check security, Team Sergeant Lu Minh!"

"Can do," Minh said.

Johnson and the interpreters led the way to the makeshift SeaBee security. Probably due to the location, the squad on the Sepone River, just above the bank, appeared to take their duty very seriously. They hardly turned around when they heard our rather noisy approach. Minh moved up with Johnson and made sure the prone figures were up to snuff and wide-awake.

We moved to the sides of the perimeter and were not quite as pleased with what we found. Some of the troops there were slumbering in the humid sunshine, but my biggest concern was their proximity to the people and equipment they were supposedly guarding. I asked Johnson if he was completely satisfied with their displacement. He shrugged before he replied.

"I'm supposed to advise, not kick ass and take names."

Specialist Five Johnson was fortunate that day, for he was going to learn some lessons the easy way, and I told him so. I conferred with Minh through the interpreter before I admonished Johnson. Minh shook his head in agreement before giving Johnson a lesson in advising.

Lu Minh walked over to a trooper who was still slumbering, and his size-nine boot interrupted the fellow's nap by creasing the largest muscle in his body. When the Bru snapped to attention, the ass-chewing in Vietnamese ended with an order: "Get your platoon sergeant over here, *now*!" The trooper quickly had the Bru Montagnard honcho in front of us, then he eased back into his guard position.

Another ass-chewing fouled I Corps' clean air. The platoon sergeant moved the soldiers out a distance and reported back to Minh and me when he had finished. I took over from Minh and made it short. "If I catch them asleep on guard duty again, I will hold you responsible. You could be drawing a private's pay, ya know.

"Specialist Johnson, we pay these people and no one else. You're in charge and you will be obeyed or else, and if anyone else has told you differently, disregard it. Your perimeter was too close to what you're guarding. If you ever have any problems or anyone gives you any shit, see me. Carry on, soldier boy!"

"Okay, Top." This session taught me as much about Lang Vei and A-101 as it did Johnson about being an adviser.

"Adviser, my aching ass," I said, moving back on the road to base camp.

That's how I spent my few first weeks in my new assignment. I learned as much about my detachment as the men learned about me. Getting it ironed out would take time, and I only hoped we had some time left to spare. As I look back on this period before the Tet Offensive of 1968, I realize that the NVA and North Vietnam were in a state of transition also.

October 1967 was highlighted by a chow run to Khe Sanh Combat Base. It was time for me to visit a site I had not seen in depth since 1962. While the convoy readied, I asked McMurray if he'd spent much time at the base. His reply set the tone for the trip.

"No, Top, I've been there about three times. If they had their way, we wouldn't be allowed to set foot on the place."

CHAPTER 10

The 9th Marine Expeditionary Brigade came dramatically ashore at Da Nang on March 8, 1965, to great worldwide media fanfare.

In May 1965 the 9th Marines were succeeded by the III Marine Amphibious Force (III MAF, pronounced "three maff"), consisting of the 3rd Marine Division, the 1st Aircraft Wing, and 1st Marine Division. The commanding general of III MAF was given responsibility for U.S. operations in the I Corps Tactical Zone, which incorporated the five northern provinces of South Vietnam. In June 1965, Major General Lewis W. Walt assumed that role.

In grudging cooperation with the Army of the Republic of Vietnam (ARVN) and Special Forces troops who had been in place since 1962 or earlier, the government wrested control of the populace in I Corps and helped reassert the authority of the central government. By 1966 the allied military and civic-action operations were slowly eroding the enemy's elaborate infrastructure and his dominance over the people.

To overwhelm a combined force of such a great size was not within the North Vietnamese Army's capabilities, regardless of what the liberal news media might have thought. The Communists believed the answer lay along the 17th Parallel. Gradually, they massed large troop concentrations within the Demilitarized Zone (DMZ) in Laos and in the southern panhandle of North Vietnam. But the Marines made their forays across the DMZ very costly. By March 1967 the NVA had lost 3,492 confirmed killed in action (KIA), the Marines 541.

The Khe Sanh Plateau, in western Quang Tri Province, provided the NVA with an excellent alternative. Khe Sanh is located at the heart of the rugged Annamite Range; studded with piedmont-type hills, the plateau provides a natural infiltration route. Most of the mountain trails are hidden by tree canopies up to sixty feet high, cleared elephant grass, and bamboo thickets. North and south dominate the two main avenues of approach. One of these, the western access, runs along Route 9 from the Laotian border through the village of Lang Vei to Khe Sanh. The only stumbling block to the NVA along this route in 1967 was the 26th Marine Regiment (-), a Popular Force (PF) company comprising Bru and Vietnamese soldiers with U.S. and ARVN advisers, and several groups of Marines that constituted a combined action platoon. And Special Forces Detachment A-101's four undermanned CIDG companies, of course!

On August 12, 1967, Colonel David Lownds relieved Colonel Padley as the commanding officer of the 26th Marine Regiment (-).

While our small convoy consisting of a jeep, deuce-and-a-half, and a three-quarter-ton truck was slowly edging the long five miles to the Combat Base, the Khe Sanh airstrip was shut down for reinforcing. Army helicopters and the C-7 Caribou fixed-wing aircraft were tasked to resupply the area.

McMurray and I were in the jeep and leading the tiny convoy into the city of Khe Sanh, just three miles from Lang Vei on Highway 9. Popular Force troops and civilians alike waved as we crawled through the small ville. It was obvious that no one knew we were coming, so I just had to open my big mouth. "How come we have no commo with the rough puffs, Mac?" I was referring to the Popular Forces.

"Top, I've been here seven months and can't answer the

question. You're right to ask. This area is about as coordinated as a Chinese gang bang!"

"Too many factions not working together and too many field-grade officers trying to build empires, Mac," I said. "We're going to try to change it, but it won't be easy. Mac, you've been here seven months. Have you ever thought it was SF or A-101 against the world?"

McMurray continued our slow exit of Khe Sanh ville while he pondered before committing himself. "Many times, Top, but I don't want to believe it. Conventional units will help us, but J.C. himself would have to order 'em to do so. I think they believe we shouldn't be here; in other words, screw the civilian population that Special Forces is helping to help themselves. Sometimes, I think they're right, but down inside I know they're wrong. Thank God we have Special Forces Mike Force units that will ride to the rescue. Hopefully, there'll be no more Ashau Valleys."

"Very good, Mac," I came back. "I've got three years in Southeast Asia and I know you're right. The only thing I can add is that the conventional assholes in uniform are learning, but how many of us are going to pay for their education remains to be seen. Where's the turnoff to the Combat Base?"

"We're only about a mile from the turnoff, Top. It's tricky and easy to miss if you're not paying attention."

About a mile and a half out of Khe Sanh village, we turned left off Highway Nine onto the trail that led to the Combat Base. The overhanging tree limbs and second growth made it difficult to see the road, much less into the brush and tree-covered terrain on the flanks. With our having no commo with the friendlies, I didn't like the tactical situation, and said so. Things had to get better.

Our open trucks with troops facing the sides stopped when we did, at the command of the Marine gate guard who stood beside a very small guard shack. I left my weapon in the jeep and approached the apprehensive young man who was armed with an M-16. He greeted me cautiously. I told him who we

were and what our mission was and that we didn't work for
Ho Chi Minh. He was still apprehensive but notified his partner in the guard shack. The PRC-25 radio cackled and popped
before the radio operator nodded his approval. I reclaimed my
weapon from the jeep and hitched a ride with the deuce-and-a-
half-ton rough rider. We turned left at the runway and went to
the supply hut that lay fifty yards from the strip. Behind the
hut were mounds of food and equipment marked for their
recipients, proving to me that they did know Special Forces
A-101 was in the area.

An Air Force sergeant showed us our weekly food supple-
ments. I left Mac and the Bru to get it loaded while I headed
for the French command bunker. Built in the center of the
Combat Base, the underground headquarters had been a land-
mark even in 1962. I needed some contacts and knew no other
way to go about it. "I'll be back as soon as I'm able, Mac," I
shouted.

Parking the jeep beside the underground regimental command post, I glanced down the runway to where vehicles and
men were clustered around an area that was being resurfaced.
I walked down a spacious stairway and into the waiting room
of the tactical operation center in seconds. A Marine staff
sergeant rose from behind his field desk and came to the
counter to greet me. "What can I do for you?" he asked. He
sounded less than happy.

"I would like to speak to your Operations sergeant if he's
around. I'm from Lang Vei Special Forces Detachment A-101
and need some information."

Before he could ask where in the hell Lang Vei was, a
broad-shouldered, dark-haired gunnery sergeant came out of
the entrance of the S-3 Operations complex. He spoke before I
could close my still-open mouth.

"You the new team sergeant over at Lang Vei, Top?" Meanwhile, the confused staff sergeant went on about his business.

"Yeah, Gunny, and you're the S-3 NCO, I hope," I replied.

"You got it. What are you doggies doing this far from home?"

"I guess I wanted to see if you'd brief me a little on your situation."

He turned toward his two-room mansion and said, "Come on in, and we'll trade off."

I smiled, checked my weapon once again to make sure it was unloaded and locked, then followed the huge Marine. I was not curious about the maps that adorned the room's concrete walls. His domain was separated from the other offices by a small wooden gate and plywood fence. He seated his 230 pounds of muscle behind his desk and motioned me to be seated.

"You want me to start off, Team Sergeant?" he asked.

"Sure, Gunny, rank has its privileges."

The 26th Regiment was scattered, and only a battalion or so was then at Khe Sanh Combat Base, and those personnel were busy maintaining the occupancy of Hills 881 and 861. The mess halls, constructed of wood and squad tents, served hot meals for the jarheads when they came out of the field. "That's it," he concluded, "unless you have some questions I can answer that are not classified."

"I haven't been to Khe Sanh since 1962, when this airstrip was being constructed. The place has really changed."

He sat up straight, like I wanted him to, before I continued.

"With the NVA activity around here and in Laos at this time, you'll need more than a damn infantry battalion and a 105 artillery battery very shortly."

"I only work here, Top, but I think it's gonna change. What else?" he asked.

"Why are there no communications with Lang Vei? Why do we have no artillery support for our area of operations from your artillery?"

"Good questions, and I've asked them myself. Here's the answers I got. We here at the 26th Marine Regiment cannot coordinate with Lang Vei or the rough puffs at Khe Sanh city because permission must come from the top in Da Nang."

"You mean the 3rd Marine Amphibious Force that controls the U.S. effort in I Corps?"

"Correct, Team Sergeant. You've got to go to your control detachment in Da Nang, who must ask permission from the 3rd Marine Amphibious Force. If the coordination is approved at that level it trickles down!"

"That's the only way to arrange radio contact as well, I assume?" I asked.

"I know of no other way. I would like to do it here, but no can do."

"Before I go, I'm going to tell you some things I don't tell every swinging Richard, Gunny. Like every A-detachment, mine has an intel sergeant whose main function is to establish an intelligence net. The agents he recruits and trains are mostly civilians who have knowledge of enemy units and movements in the AO. We pay them from allotted intelligence funds. We send our information to the C-detachment in Da Nang and on to Nha Trang, home of the 5th Special Forces. For the most part those headquarters don't really need that kind of poop."

"Get to the point, Top," the gunny said.

"Why not bring the information to Khe Sanh Combat Base and send an information copy to our headquarters?"

"It's not authorized by 3rd MAF, and we would be required to disregard it completely."

We shook hands and I left.

McMurray anxiously awaited my arrival at the air depot, and we mounted up our indigenous warriors and headed home. I briefed the radio operator as we cruised slowly on Vietnam's answer to the Alcan Highway. "The intelligence system is a crying shame in our armed forces. A few men with personal ambitions are allowing their egos to kill, or cause to be killed, our very own people."

Like all personnel E9 and below, McMurray could only shrug. "I don't understand how we ever won the big one—or any other war. Certainly wasn't through our intelligence effort or distribution of the product," he concluded.

All in all, the trip was an eye-opener. Detachment A-101 had no way to go but up. Qualified personnel, camp defenses, reconnaissance patrols, recruiting of indigenous personnel, Khe Sanh Combat Base's lack of cooperation—all those would keep us swamped for a while.

Sleeping a few weeks with practically the entire detachment in one bunker, we all began to exert ourselves with camp defenses. Our first patrol was out and twenty Company 101 people with S.Sgt. Peter Tiroch and First Lieutenant Wilkins returned from their first operations with no contact or sightings. At least that part of the plan was going smoothly. The patrol experience gained by the people involved would prove to be invaluable.

The SeaBees were busting their humps trying to complete the bunkers on top of the small hill. Once that was completed, the inner perimeter would be fenced, separating the U.S. personnel from the outer defenses to ensure that after sunset, no indigenous would have physical access to the U.S. quarters or the tactical operations center. The only ex-engineer on A-101, I supervised the fence-building, double apron and triple concertina fences around the U.S. perimeter and the entire outlay. Each day for a week to ten days, I finished my administrative chores in the radio shack then journeyed with an interpreter and an indigenous radio operator to the outer perimeter for my daily physical training. Nine times out of ten my ol' pal, LLDB Team Sergeant Minh, would show up and help supervise as well. One day I told him that I had a secret desire to send a recon team across the Sepone River and check out Laos along that river line. He told me that our area of operations ended at the waterline. He surprised me by saying he'd thought about it as well. My interpreter then informed us that we were both living in a dream world; that the Bru would no more cross that dividing line than they would take up residence in Saigon city. We were taken aback.

Team Sergeant Minh and I polled many of our CIDG troops about reconning Laos, but their answers were unvaryingly negative: "Never hoppen, Trung Si! Beaucoup VC. We all die!"

The NVA and their agents had certainly impressed the Bru Montagnards around Lang Vei. There was just no way they would invade Laos, we thought.

The SeaBees Navy Chief assured me one morning, in the mess hall over a cup of coffee, that their labor at Lang Vei was near an end. I knew that the job was progressing, but not to that extent.

"We have one more very large airdrop of materials and we'll wind it up shortly after that, Top!"

"Yes," I replied, "I have the date and time of the drop, Chief. It's the day after tomorrow; the message implies that it will be by C-130 aircraft and will be a large one. How long after that will you be hatting up?"

"A week to ten days, and your bunkers will be ready for anything they can throw at you, Top. We're gone!"

"That's great, Chief. You're lucky to be gone from this place. We'll miss you."

"We'll miss you guys, too, Top. What all is on that cargo plane's packing list for the drop?"

"Glad you asked," I said, removing the list from my fatigue pocket. "We'll have a Bru company of about eighty souls on recovery, besides three SF and a couple of Viet SF people. Here goes: large timbers, concrete, steel rods, and indigenous food supplies. Those timbers and concrete are heavy, so we'll mark the drop zone and move back to the apex and wait till they're finished. Facing the Sepone River and Laos, we'll have one unit on security on the cleared area that we're using as a drop zone. Okay?"

"Okay, Top, we'll be ready."

The morning of the largest airdrop I'd seen since my 326th Engineers days in 1959, we laid out a large T of International Orange panels to mark the center of the DZ. The C-130 cargo aircraft, with load limits of eight thousand pounds, came in first at about twelve hundred feet. Many of the loads were slowed by three or four cargo parachutes. The Bru seemed to be pleased with the technology, but knowing the work that would follow the drop, the Americans were unimpressed. The C-130s unloaded ASAP, then two smaller, two-engine C-123s followed with the ration drops.

A wooden crate containing Vietnamese pigs exited the second C-123, but the chute barely opened, slowing the load very little. Upon impact, the crate spilled open and the cargo chose their path to freedom. Unfortunately, the Viet pigs seemed to feel that the road to freedom lay on the opposite bank of the Sepone River, in Laos. The drop zone detail wasn't going for it. With a simple follow-me wave by a Bru platoon leader, an unscheduled invasion of Laos was on. Was Phoumi Nosavan ready for us?

We moved the rest of the detail down to the supplies and began removing the chutes. An hour went by before the aggressors returned from the forbidden land of the VC, each one carrying at least one squealing pig.

Sergeant Lu Minh and I had learned there were factors that would motivate the Bru to cross the Sepone.

True to his word, the SeaBee chief and his naval engineers completed their construction at Lang Vei in a little more than the seven-day week and were gone. The SF detachment had mixed emotions about their departure, but the majority had a good opinion of the hardworking sailors.

I moved into a concrete, timber, reinforced-steel bunker facing the Laotian side of the inner perimeter. I slept well at night when not on watch.

Meanwhile, our Da Nang headquarters was trying to solve the detachment's personnel problems. Willoughby and I were speechless over the caliber of people unloading at the campsite of Detachment A-101.

CHAPTER 11

The detachment communications were in good hands with Emanuel Phillips and McMurray; I'd never seen operators with more dedication or savvy.

SFC James Holt had come on board right before I arrived in September, and thanks to the SeaBees, his bunker-type dispensary was in operation. I cannot recall his prior experience in SF, but his performance at sick call for the natives was impressive. Holt was a very mature, likable Arkansas lad, a blessing to his humble detachment and profession. He would soon be joined by a comparable youngster who would need his guidance and had all the qualities and ambition to put it to use. Buck Sergeant, three stripe E5, Nickolas Fragos, was a team sergeant's dream, a young medical specialist with all the Army schooling in the 91B medical field. All he needed was cross-training and leadership. Upon his arrival, a new strain of malaria believed to have been delivered from north of the DMZ by Hanoi Jane's minutemen began to gain ground in I Corps. The health services of the U.S. Army was soon issuing dapsone tablets to combat the deadly peril. Each team member was issued a week's supply, and the detachment stressed that the result of not taking them could be sudden death.

An Australian attached to the detachment apparently didn't believe the threat and refused to take the preventative. He came down with the new strain of malaria on a Tuesday and was evacuated that day to the Naval Hospital in Da Nang. He died on Friday.

We immediately instituted a new policy to counter the falciparum malaria potential. Holt was on operation, so implementation fell to the young 91B, who was still in his early twenties. Like many briefings at busy, busy Lang Vei, that one came over one of the three authorized Budweisers in the team house/mess hall a few hours after supper.

"Here's what I want, Nick. Each Monday morning after breakfast, all U.S. will line up in formation. At that time you will see that they take their dapsone tablets. The Ol' Man has given a direct order, but it's up to you to see that it's carried out."

Nick nodded. "Don't you trust people, Team Sergeant?"

"That was a dumb question, young man, but I'm gonna answer it anyway. We just had a man die because he knew every goddamn thing and failed to see the importance of the tablets. Now, would you like for me to write his folks, or wife, and tell them I trusted him? Bullshit! Tomorrow you'll see that they take 'em. And besides, as busy as we are, everyone's apt to get a case of CRS from time to time." The last statement got his undivided attention.

"What's CRS, Top?" Fragos asked.

"Can't Remember Shit!"

Next morning, after breakfast, the detachment fell out in a single line, Captain Willoughby not excluded. I had watched Phillips take his dapsone, so he was on the line with the CW commo system while we dawdled.

I spoke a few words then motioned for Nick Fragos to enforce the medical directive. He did as ordered and I fell back in line with my dapsone in hand, waiting for the order before drawing the canteen that dangled from my pistol belt.

"Everyone take your dapsone tablet now!" the medic ordered. It brought compliance, but not from me. I just wasn't going for it. I retained my pill and watched the goings-on before I took a swig of H_2O and countered Ho Chi Minh's form of medical genocide. The line broke as the detachment went about their varied chores, except for Fragos and me. We both stood fast, but not for long. He came striding to the end of the line with a grin on his face as big as Texas. "Well, Top, I did good. Huh?"

"You still don't get it, do you, Sergeant Fragos? Here's the way it's gonna be come next Monday morning, whether it be Holt or yourself. You or Holt will step in front of each member and witness the individual as he swallows the dapsone. Only then will you move to your next victim. You got it, soldier?" I didn't wait for a reply, but moved out to the TOC.

The implementation may have seemed extreme to the trusting young sergeant, but that mattered not one iota to me or to the U.S. Army. What did matter was that we suffered not one case of malaria of any type once the procedure was in place.

When Fragos finally left Lang Vei, he was right up there with the best of the best and aiming to be a doctor. But the good Lord had other plans for the soldier boy.

SFC (E7) Ronald Knight, a young intel specialist, came to A-101 via the 101st Airborne Division, Panama, and training group at Fort Bragg, North Carolina. He was in his twenties and an eager SFC of the best kind. A Kentucky lad, he, too, was at the right place to receive the experience he needed. A southern-born, southern-bred lad, he would learn something all of us white boys—and blacks—learned before we were through. The detachment would not forget the lesson Knight was taught, either, and that's for sure.

Whether on operation or camp defenses, he worked day and night with the Bru. While he was keeping late hours at his profession, he found time to have a brew in the team house after dark from time to time. He had a few weeks' on-the-job training and an operation under his pistol belt when an "infantry leader, weapons," came on the scene from Da Nang via training group and the 82nd all-American unit at Fort Bragg.

SFC Kenneth Hanna was a good-looking black soldier, experienced in every facet of his job except getting shot at. Like many of us, he could not have selected a better place to get baptized in that particular field.

One of a team sergeant's minor tasks was designating the living quarters for incoming replacements. Having only one vacant bunk made the decision very simple, I thought. The Kentucky white boy would have a new bunkmate when he returned from his operation. I made sure Hanna was situated at once. When Knight returned, he turned in his operation report and was told of his new bunker mate.

That very night after supper, and after my third and last beer, Knight braced me. "Top, why me? You know my raising. I'd rather he had another place to stay if you don't mind."

I was not angry or surprised. "I know much more than you're giving me credit for, Ron. You'll get over it and be a better person for it. The discussion about this particular subject is closed. Anything else you'd like to discuss?"

In about ten days Kenneth Hanna was formally initiated into the Vietnam GI's club. It was claimed by our doctors that the dysentery, headaches, and the "I wanta be somewhere else" disease was due to the effects of treated water and untreated food in the humid climate. I guess they're right because I'd only been there six times, and I'd only had it six times. Fortunately, the discomfort only lasts two or three very long days and very long nights. SFC Holt gave Hanna a day of bed rest, and the establishment at Lang Vei was smarter than to go against the doctor's wishes, even though we knew that doses of Kaopectate and antibiotics would have had him up in no time at all.

That night at the team room, team members not gainfully employed sat and had their usual one to three beers from Saigon. SFC Ronald Knight drank only one and did that very quickly. When he rose from the wooden-bench table, he wore a serious look on his face. Nick Fragos, the young medic, asked him what the rush might be. Knight hurriedly answered, "My teammate's not feeling up to snuff and I'm gonna keep him company. See y'all mañana!"

The speed of his transition surprised every team member

aware of Knight's earlier feelings. I, for one, was pleased to no end.

The next week, after Hanna was feeling much better, I accompanied him on another initiation of sorts. We took twenty-five Bru warriors from the 104th CIDG unit on his first combat operation. The patrol lasted the full five days, and we covered the area near the Ashau Valley just as my operation order directed. It was baptism without fire for both of us. The first combat operation for me in two years, and the first ever for Kenneth Hanna, taught us points about our Bru partners, points that we needed to know to survive and to prevent premature cardiac failure.

The first night location, we were perched on a small ridge with the headquarters element, the radio operator (RTO), platoon leader, and the medic. The moonless evening limited visibility to yards if not feet. Yet once the listening posts and security were in place, campfires were lit! It rattled Kenneth Hanna to no end. I pointed out that "if they're cooking over the fires, and telling everyone where we're at, it's for a good reason, Kenneth. They want them to know. Regardless of what you may have read or heard, they value their lives just as much as we do ours. They may know, in advance, that there's no Viet Cong or NVA in the area. I've seen the Rhade do it in Darlac Province, so I no longer worry about it. Learn from the indigenous, Kenneth. I have over here, and in Korea as well."

Nevertheless, one American and one Bru from the small headquarters were awake at all times during the uneventful night. This was not illogical or contradictory, it was just a commonsense standing operating procedure (SOP) on any and all operations, like our SOP requiring two, never just one, U.S. on all operations.

Moving west, nearer the Ashau Valley, the Bru became cautious and nighttime fires were no longer lit. Hanna and I followed suit. Hanna and I survived the excursion in good shape. I knew in my mind that I had a reliable old soldier, now a combat veteran, who could, and would, cut the proverbial mustard.

These people were the heart and soul of Detachment A-101. They carried the cause during camp construction and did it in a superb manner. If a team sergeant in Special Forces had his pick of personnel for an assignment, he couldn't have made a mistake by selecting any of these people.

CHAPTER 12

November 1967 was eventful and vital to A-101 for reasons pertaining to survival. Not surprisingly, the events also pertained to the Marine Corps base at Khe Sanh.

From Captain Willoughby on down to Spec. Four McMurray, the men of A-101 knew that Khe Sanh's so-called higher command treated us like dirt. In an area where Americans were a minute minority, we were treated like orphans by our own people. Admittedly, because of the distance that separated us, Da Nang's C-detachment also often made us feel neglected, but at least we knew they were trying. We also knew that eight kilometers away, as far as the Marines were concerned we did not exist.

Our situation did change during this period. We could go no way but up, and we appeared to be doing just that.

Leaving Lang Vei on Highway Nine, you passed Khe Sanh ville and came to the secluded intersection that led to the Combat Base. Known as the French Fort, this location was also used by the first A-detachment at Khe Sanh, led by Captain Korcheck in 1962. Special Operations Group (SOG) also abandoned the post and moved its operations to a compound on the southwest corner of the Khe Sanh perimeter, calling it Forward Operations Base Three (FOB-3). How did an Army unit manage that? Simple enough, if you work for the right people in high places.

SOG was composed of SF people and Viet SF, and it worked for Military Assistance Command Vietnam (MACV), that is,

General Westmoreland. The unity of command, a universally accepted principle of war, did not exist on the Khe Sanh plateau, but it did several hundred miles away in Saigon—neither Khe Sanh nor the Marine Amphibious Force in Da Nang had any say in FOB-3's move except for the exact perimeter location.

The first available chance, I made a social call on FOB-3. I was again on escort duty for supplies at the Combat Base air depot. Once again I left my running partner, McMurray, and with the jeep driver in tow, we made our social calls, such as they were. The French Fort was our first stop. The Marines had nothing for me so I departed. Once outside, I saluted the commander, Colonel David Lownds, of the 26th Marine Regiment, who asked me if I was from Lang Vei before he moved into the complex. Then the Bru driver, the Viet and SF escort and I approached the SOG compound on the secluded southwest corner of the base. We immediately knew we weren't in the Marine perimeter—no squad tents were blocking our view, for one thing. Construction almost identical to our recently finished perimeter at Lang Vei greeted us, and like Lang Vei only a month earlier, the construction was not yet complete, except for the wire fences to the front. Communication trenches connected the soon-to-be-completed bunkers, overhead cover, and so on. An American in one trench hollered my name and got my complete attention.

Sergeant First Class Billy Waugh climbed out of the commo trenches, said a few words to his Viet counterparts, and came over to shake hands. We chatted about the old days in Okinawa before anything of any importance came up.

"Bill, I want you to meet Sergeant Major Pegram," Waugh said to me. "I think you know him from Bragg. We all know A-101's standing with the jarheads, so you need all the friends you can get."

I agreed but added, "Yeah, Billy, and considering our location, we might be of some assistance to you as well." SOG's border-crossing missions were known to everyone in SF. He nodded as I followed him to the command bunker. I waited outside while Billy Waugh went to fetch Pegram. Why didn't I go in with Waugh? For the kind of work they were doing, your clearance, whatever its level, didn't amount to much unless you had a need to know. I didn't. It would just be more information I couldn't reveal if I was captured.

"Bill, you ol' bastard," said a large individual in camouflage fatigues. I greeted my old Fort Bragg buddy and we told a few lies before Waugh went back to digging. Only then did we get down to business, business that in the next several months would help A-101 and SOG no end. I waited to see if my pal would volunteer the open door policy so it wouldn't appear as though I was begging. He finally did.

"I know, or think I know, you're not getting cooperation or communications from the Marines here at Khe Sanh," Pegram said. "What I can do is very limited, but try me out and I'll help when I can."

"I've thought about it ever since I heard you people were taking over part of the perimeter over here, Top," I replied. "Just a radio frequency with someone over here would be a starter."

"You've got it, Bill. As soon as we're through getting organized, I'll give you our call sign, a frequency, and time to call. What clse?"

"We nccd artillery support from the Marines, like bad, Top. Sergcant Major Hodge assures me that the C-team is working on it, but any pressure SOG could exert with MACV would be appreciated."

"I'll see what I can do, Bill. Nothing is free, so I know we can count on Lang Vei if we need assistance down by the creek. Right?"

"That will be no problem," I replied. "Anytime we can help, just let us know. After all, we are in the same unit."

"I'll hold you to that, Bill. Come see us when you have time. There's a temporary duty detachment from Okinawa joining us in about a week, so you'll know everyone over here, shortly. See you around."

After thanking Billy Waugh for his assistance, I rejoined my driver and scooted back to the airstrip. Before we took off for our home port, I enlightened Specialist Four McMurray.

"I know you hate to have to wait on anyone, Mac, but believe me, you're going to agree it was worth it!" I told him about getting our foot in the door, and he was smiling in no time.

The command party jeep was the leading vehicle in our small convoy. Our supply deuce-and-a-half truck was second in line, and what little security we had was bringing up the rear—the three-quarter-ton truck carried twelve well-armed Bru. The side curtains were rolled up and all the Bru were facing outward, hands on weapons pointing in the same direction. In guerrilla warfare, we were the most lucrative target that came down the pike. If the Viet Cong hit us and disappeared into the forest, we had just two options: (1) run the ambush at full steam ahead, or (2) stop and charge the ambush, the method the immediate action drills advocated. For me, time spent in convoy was the most terrifying time during the tours I spent in South Vietnam and Laos. I had little faith that we would live through the initiating fire, so I avoided convoys whenever I could. Everyone has hang-ups, I reckon.

We passed through Khe Sanh ville and waved at the adoring locals and cleared the city limits before we ran head-on into someone who did not share my views on motor vehicle traffic in relation to guerrilla warfare.

McMurray slowed the jeep in amazement. As for me, my mouth fell open as I held up my hand to stop the two trucks that trailed us. I found it hard to believe what I was seeing— a solo Marine Corps jeep, a driver, and the full-bull colonel who commanded Khe Sanh Combat Base. We were all halted approximately a mile and a half from Lang Vei, straddling Highway Nine. I recovered faster than McMurray, but not by a helluva lot. The colonel had a slight grin on his face, but his driver seemed to take the situation a little bit more seriously than his boss.

"Sir," I said rather loudly. "Do you know where you're at?"

"Yes, Sergeant Craig," Colonel Lownds replied. He held up a folded area map to emphasize his point. I wasn't convinced of his knowledge about guerrilla warfare. Judging by what I'd seen at Khe Sanh—tents with no overhead cover, ammunition in craters with no overhead cover—it seemed to me that the commander of Khe Sanh in 1967 did not believe any of the intelligence passed to him; that is, he did not believe there was a war going on. The grunts he commanded on the hills around Khe Sanh were well aware of it, but here beside me in a jeep was a man who just wasn't convinced. Even as an E7 in the U.S. Army, I couldn't pull rank; I could only advise.

"Sir," I said, "you shouldn't be out here with less than a company. This road is not secure."

"Don't worry about it, Sarge, us Marines are tough, so there's little danger."

Despite the rage I felt deep inside, I surprised myself at my calmness. "Sir, I'll loan you the security team in the open truck. They'll see that you get back safely, if possible."

Lownds seemed unimpressed by our kindness, but he accepted the offer. McMurray and the Bru security force would see him back to the village of Khe Sanh. His small Marine and rough puff (Regional Force Popular Force) units could take it from there. Our reduced convoy was home and unloaded before a pissed-off McMurray was back with the security troops. I was awaiting his arrival in the safety of the mess hall. When Mac opened the door and found his team sergeant drinking Colombian Kool-Aid, we both burst out laughing.

Our discussion revealed nothing startling but the fact that perhaps guerrilla warfare just wasn't the Marine Corps' cup of coffee. I hoped that if the commander decided to repeat his mistake, someone would step in and prevent it. By then, the Viet Cong probably had the word about his excursion. Another mistake like that would cost the allies a loss of face, and give the Viet Cong and NVA reason to carry on.

We continued to field one operation at all times, but none were making sightings, or contact, despite intelligence that said the better part of two divisions was being diverted to the Khe Sanh plateau. We were too busy to lose any sleep over it. November was still in its prime and progress was being made on completion of the camp. Construction had finished, and that included three outer fences in addition to the concertina that shielded the inner perimeter from the native sons. The hilltop site included the team house (mess hall), U.S. living quarters, dispensary, fuel dump, supply bunkers, and, most important, the tactical operations center.

The last days of November brought some incidents of the good news, bad news variety.

First, the good news. The message from our C-detachment was on a positive note for a change. "The paranoids," as we were becoming known, were finally getting a break: Khe Sanh Combat Base had been directed by the 3rd Marine Amphibious Force Headquarters (III MAF) to lay in, and have on call, artillery support for the area of operations assigned to Lang Vei. Captain Willoughby and I talked about it that night after a hot meal.

"Well, Team Sergeant, what do we do now?" Willoughby asked. "Do we wait for them to contact us or or what?"

I was in deep thought about the same subject but hadn't come to any conclusions. "Sir, if we wait on them," I said, "it'll be a Christmas present, so let's don't. What'cha say?"

"Hell, I'm willing to contact Khe Sanh, but haven't a clue as to how to go about it. I'm for any solution, conventional or unconventional. Any ideas as yet?"

"SOG, SOG, SOG, has been going through my mind for ten minutes, dammit! Why not? Let's use that route. It's the way I can think of," I said.

Willoughby and I moved the few feet to the radio shack and

bugged Phillips with our solution. He dug out the frequency and looked at me before speaking.

"What do you want me to say to 'em, Top?"

"Tell 'em that Spunky Hansen Eight wants to speak to Honcho Nine. Over," I replied.

In a few minutes Sergeant Major Pegram came up in the clear and we got it on. After my request, he responded, "I'll be back in one!" It seemed a lot longer than that, but as always he kept his word. The message from SOG à la Khe Sanh was short and right to the heart of the matter.

"You're to pick up your forward observer tomorrow morning at the Marine TOC. He will stay with you a few days, or until the operation is completed. Honcho Nine, over and out."

"Well sir," I said, handing the headset back to Phillips, "we did it! Now for the next problem. Who's going after him?"

"You'll go after him, Top," Willoughby said. "He can stay with you in your bunker. You have an extra cot down there, don't you?"

"It can be arranged, sir."

"Further," Willoughby continued, "you will escort him at all times, and see that he gets back to Khe Sanh when it's over!"

My team leader was definitely getting there.

"When it's over, you will brief the detachment, especially the officers and radio operators. Can do, Team Sergeant?"

"No sweat, sir. I'll lay everything on before the day is over, and I'll be there waiting on the Marine forward observer at the appointed time and place."

I decided on Peter Tiroch as my partner on the overland journey to Khe Sanh mainly because of availability. I told the intel sergeant to be ready to move out at 0800 in the morning. I fetched Lu Minh and asked him to lay on the vehicles and guards. My request was quickly attended to. And Lu Minh volunteered to accompany us.

S.Sgt. Pete Tiroch wanted to practice using his international driver's license, and Minh wanted to practice his ass-chewing techniques. Both had things well in hand when the two-vehicle convoy pulled out and menaced the interstate to Khe Sanh ville and beyond. We arrived at the Marine TOC around 0830 without incident. Everyone got out to stretch his legs but no one volunteered to accompany me into the lion's den. A few Marines sauntered down the off-center road, and the armed Bru and Minh began to receive some attention they didn't ask for.

Down in the hole I went by my lonesome and was anxious to get it over with. The clerk at the boarded counter didn't disappoint me. The hem-hawing lasted about as long as I could stand it before I flipped.

"Look," I said to the corporal, "I was ordered over here to pick up a forward observer. I've done my part, so you people produce the individual."

At that point the Marine Operations sergeant filled the doorway and we finally got something done. "How did you do it, Top?"

"Believe it or not, Gunny, it was our headquarters in Da Nang, and that tickles the shit outta me. I'm here to pick up the lucky bastard, if I can find him."

"He's finishing his packing right now and will be along directly. He's a first lieutenant and just outta artillery school at Fort Sill, Oklahoma, wherever the hell that is."

"It's where I ought to be," I answered, and left it at that. "Tell him we're outside waiting on his ass when he gets here. Good to see you again, Chief."

We waited forever for the individual, but in thirty minutes a heavily burdened first john approached our well-armed convoy, and everyone involved was shocked at his appearance. The Marine was slender, tender, and tall, with a narrow pointed chin and a long, slim neck. He looked comically pompous. His face featured large eyes with hazel glints. He had dark straight hair. And he was obviously of Chinese extraction. I helped him unload his field pack and placed it in the back of the jeep. He was somewhat embarrassed at the attention he was receiving from the jabbering Bru in the back end of the truck. I nodded at Minh and the distractions ceased.

I finally got around to saluting the very leery officer and introducing him to his guardians for the next several days. Marine Lieutenant Ching surprised me by being equipped with his own PRC-25 radio, and I was in for another jolt: he took to Lu Minh as soon as the introductions were completed. Immediately they were both jabbering in Chinese.

"Would you like to ride in the three-quarter with Minh, sir?" I asked.

"That will be fine, Sergeant. Are we ready to move out?"

The singsong Chinese folks got in their truck, and Tiroch and I in our jeep then led the way to the gate. The trip back was smooth, and even I was not as nervous as usual.

Upon arrival at Lang Vei, I introduced Ching to our SF officers, Willoughby and Wilkins, and listened patiently to them over the noon snack. With that protocol out of the way, we moved Ching's belongings into my underground hooch and I left him to get organized. Without Lieutenant Ching having said a word, I knew from his eyeballing of my bunker that he was impressed. It beat hell out of a squad tent.

I went to the radio room and gave them the call sign of the Marine artillery that we would employ the next day— Jacksonville. I also surprised them with Jacksonville's frequency. We were then closer to having real live artillery fire support than Lang Vei had ever been. Minh and I spent the rest of the afternoon showing the very interested Marine around the perimeter. It appeared to me that both of them were having a ball. That night, after the Marine retired safe and sound under twelve inches or more of reinforced concrete, I pulled my four-hour shift of watch and tell. When I retired around two in the morning, my bunker mate was dead to the world.

After breakfast, Ching briefed me on how we were going to spend the day.

"We're going to put concentrations in every part of your

area of operation. They'll be plotted by you and me as we go along. All your people have to do on an operation, for instance, is to call for the concentration by name. They can adjust from that as long as they know the name of the concentration and the grid coordinates. Do you have any questions before we get the show on the road with Jacksonville?"

"No questions, and I like the idea, sir. We have an operation out in this vicinity"—I pointed to the map—"and they're not due back in until day after tomorrow. How will we work around that?"

"Can you contact them before we start and tell them it will be this afternoon before we get to their area?" Ching said. "At what time do your people select a night location, Sergeant?"

"Usually, around 1600, sir. I'll call them and tell 'em we'll be in touch at that time. Will that be okay, sir?"

"Sure, Top. After that we'll begin, if it's okay with you?"

SFC Ronald Knight and A-101 Dr. Holt were out with twenty-five Bru, and Phillips made radio contact easily. I informed them to select a night location by 1600 and report in; we would have something exciting for them. I also warned them to be as exact as was humanly possible about their location.

We positioned ourselves by the TOC and the lieutenant went into a lengthy explanation, most of which I could have done without.

"We'll call in white phosphorous as a marking round because it's easy to see. Then adjust from there."

"It's also very inaccurate, sir!"

"Okay, Top, where do you want concentration SF One?"

"Where the road from Lang Vei crosses the Sepone River," I replied. "They have to come from there if they're in force. Okay?"

"Jacksonville, this is Spike One, are you ready to fire willie peter? Over."

"Waiting for coordinates, Spike. Standing by."

We both checked the coordinates on our map and Ching

called in the eight-digit location. The familiar "On the way" warning was not long in coming. We stood on the high ground to the left of the TOC and heard the PRC-25's warning. "WP is on the way, Spike." Damn if it wasn't!

I was born under overhead fire at Fort Sill. I survived some overhead near misses the Chinese cooked up for us in Korea. Yes, I'd been on the wrong end of it in Laos and Vietnam as well. Therefore, when I heard the loud fluttering of the round, I hit the deck and took Ching with me. The round fell only about a thousand meters short.

The misguided missile hit just short of Highway Nine and very close to the team house. The smoke covered the entire camp. If a WP round isn't a direct hit or particles do not hit you, it just smokes up the area. Immediately the cooks and the Bru were out of their confines, obviously terrified. I rose with Ching and surveyed the damage while he counseled Jacksonville on its short round. When I returned, I reported to Ching that we had suffered no injuries, but that the near miss hadn't done much for the people with dysentery. I let Ching talk to my team leader before we started again.

Jacksonville offered no explanation for the short round. After Willoughby got our people under cover, Ching and I were ready to try again. I attempted to make Ching feel better with a shrug of the shoulders. "Shit happens, sir! I've got confidence in you and will stand out here if you will."

The forward observer agreed, so that made us not only the only dummies standing in the open, but the only ones without overhead cover as well. He gingerly contacted Jacksonville once again. When the PRC-25 shouted "On the way," we were rather nervous.

The WP hit in the trees and almost in the Sepone divider. I couldn't help but join Lieutenant Ching in hysterical laughter. He nodded at me before ordering Jacksonville to "Fire for effect."

The high explosive rounds were right on target as well. I watched and shuddered when I thought what would happen to anyone in the area of concentration SF-1. The HE rounds continued to hit the trees, breaking the steel rounds into hundreds of small pieces that slammed into the ground below. Lang Vei and Khe Sanh took a long stride that day and, except for one location, we were finished by 1600.

I spoke to Ron Knight as promised. After he repeated his coordinates, Ching was ready to register our last concentration, or SF-8. I gave Knight our lay and jokingly told him to keep his head down. Ching checked his data one more time before he laid it on Jacksonville. When I heard "On the way," I switched my radio frequency to Knight's. I spotted the WP round doing its thing and knew I didn't have long to wait. The young NCO came in loud and clear.

"Spunky Hansen Eight, this is One-one. Over!"

"Spunky One-one, Eight. Go!"

"Spunky Hansen Eight, One-one. You're right on target. Go get 'em. Spunky Hansen One-one, standing by. Over!"

I smiled at Ching as he awaited the verdict. "You're right in there, sir. FFE the hell out of 'em." The HE rounds rattled South Vietnam near the Ashau Valley, and the firing ceased.

"Spunky Eight, this is Spunky One-one. Roger dodger on the marksmanship. Can I use it if I get in the shit?" Knight asked.

I glanced at Ching but knew the answer before he shook his head.

"Negatory, Spunky One-one. It's not available at this time. Do you have anything else? Over!"

The registration of artillery fire for A-101 by Marine artillery was over. It marked a great day for the detachment. The Marine Corps and the unconventional arm of the U.S. Army had finally coordinated a positive effort. No mean feat, considering the service rivalry that continues to this day.

Despite the accomplishment, the relationship between the Combat Base and A-101 would grow worse before it got better.

CHAPTER 13

December 1967 would be an exciting month for A-101. The first of the month was a total loss for Cookie. We missed a hot breakfast one morning and had to drink coffee and eat C-rations. Captain Willoughby wasn't satisfied and made sure I knew why we did without. I followed him and an interpreter behind the serving line into forbidden territory. The Spoon saw me, his face lit up, and we came to a halt in the kitchen. I looked around at the GI field stoves I'd seen nearly all my life but was none the wiser.

Willoughby spoke up, using the interpreter. "Show him the broken part, Cookie!"

"Here, Trung Si. We have tried to fix it but no can do," Cookie said.

I looked over the unfamiliar part, which I knew nothing about. "In other words, you have no spare parts for the field kitchen stove, Cookie?" I guessed. When he agreed, I rushed on. "Sir, our supply orders from Da Nang are taking weeks to fill because of the weather. You don't want to wait two weeks to eat a hot, do you?"

"No, Team Sergeant, I thought you might have a few ideas on how we can get some spare parts."

"I have no more ideas than anyone else, sir," I replied. "Khe Sanh ville or Khe Sanh Combat Base is our best bet. Why not send someone over there now to, ah, requisition one? I'd like to eat some hot chow tonight, if possible!"

"Well," Willoughy exclaimed, "you're the old Khe Sanh

expert, how about doing just that? We have some supplies on the line to be picked up also."

My face reddened some before I took a few deep breaths to control my temper. "Sir, isn't it about time you officers got your feet wet in the Khe Sanh area? Why just us NCOs? I do have limits, too, you know."

Willoughby was ready for me and sounded off, or headed me off at the pass, I never knew which. "Just what I was thinking, Top. I'll send Lieutenant Wilkins with you, he needs to improve relations with the jarheads as well as to brush up on his scrounging techniques."

"Shit," was about all I could counter with at the time. Everyone smiled when Cookie pressed the part into my hands. Willoughby was an infantry officer, and I wished I could choke the assholes who had taught him how to con the NCO Corps. A deuce-and-a-half-ton and a three-quarter-ton truck without canvas would follow the jeep that I drove while the team's executive officer enjoyed the scenery.

First Lieutenant Miles Wilkins was a likable, intelligent person who, as best as I can remember, was at the camp when I arrived. He was about twenty-four years old, and to the best of my knowledge, on his first trip to Khe Sanh. That pissed me off to no end.

But we passed the time pleasantly enough on the short trip and were fast friends by the time we arrived at Khe Sanh ville. I talked to a MACV sergeant, but only briefly, before we moved out to the Combat Base.

"Yes, we have no field kitchens in Khe Sanh village, sir!" the sergeant said. "Let's load up on supplies before we move to the squad tent/mess sections of the Combat Base, sir."

"Whatever you say, Top!"

I showed the lieutenant where the supply line was along the airstrip. I also pointed out the Air Force NCO with the clipboard and noted that his purpose in life was "to keep us from stealing everything stacked up along this front. We've earned our reputation the hard way, sir!"

I supervised the Bru loading plan. All supplies fitted neatly into the larger vehicle, so we loaded our security into the smaller truck and set out for the cantonment area. A few minutes later I sighted the line of Marines by the mess halls. I tried to make a point with the XO but wasn't sure I got it across. "This is a combat zone where you make sixty-five dollars extra a month for combat pay. Shit!"

Wilkins noted two long bumper-to-bumper chow lines along the dirt road and parallel to the tented dining facilities. I had the trucks stop just before we reached the lines and park behind the mess halls. I left the keys in the jeep, and Wilkins handed me the defective stove part only after I unloaded.

"I'll go in the back of the kitchen and talk to the mess sergeant. Shouldn't take long, sir!" I said. It didn't!

The kitchen portion of the makeshift feeder was very busy, so busy that everyone ignored my entry. I waited and watched the Marines go about their chores. Finally, an older mess-dressed type stopped in front of me. I spoke up quickly.

"I'm Team Sergeant Craig from Lang Vei Special Forces camp. Are you the mess sergeant?"

"Yes, Sergeant, and I'm very busy. You people are not allowed in our mess facilities. I must ask you to leave. Those are orders from the top, Team Sergeant."

"But all I need is a part for a field stove, Sergeant," I said. "Surely you can spare that."

"I'm sorry, Top, you'll have to go!"

I left the tent one red-faced, pissed-off Army NCO. We served the same country, for God's sake! Wilkins saw me coming and, not being color-blind, knew it hadn't gone well. I threw the part in the back of the jeep before taking the wheel. I started the jeep and with a wave of the hand told the trucks to follow me.

"Goddamn, Top, what happened?"

"Later, sir, I'm still too pissed off just now."

We slowly passed the chow line, all the while followed by catcalls and derisive remarks. I'd about had all I could take for one day. "Sir, I'm gonna stop this jeep at the head of the line. When I do, you unass and call them assholes to attention. Then we'll move out of here."

Wilkins just muttered before I stopped the vehicle. But the young officer got out of the jeep and made me proud I was in the U.S. Army and Detachment A-101. His call to *"Attention!"* could be heard for a mile or more. Silence enveloped the area. Wilkins mounted, and I put the jeep in gear. I wonder even today if anyone ever gave the starvin' Marvins an "at ease."

Still on the base's premises but about a mile down the road, I stopped the jeep and used the PRC-25. Special Operations Group put me through to Sergeant Major Pegram ASAP. He gave me the information I needed to accomplish my mission, but I had an inquiry or two before signing off.

"Okay, it's the last tent and there's no guards?" I asked.

"Not the last time I checked, Bill."

I led the trucks to three squad tents near the SOG perimeter. Unscrewing the lock's latch took only seconds, and the Bru had a field-kitchen stove loaded before Wilkins had figured out what we were up to. I leaped back into the jeep and waved the smiling thieves forward with a "Follow me" hand-and-arm signal. We were on our way to the back gate of Khe Sanh, avoiding as much foot and vehicular traffic as possible. Wilkins was kind of proud of me even though we hadn't got the spare part at the mess tent. What the hell, now we had a new stove that would provide us lots of spare parts. Only one more obstacle to overcome and we'd be home free. The back gate!

I slowed when we approached our final obstacle, knowing the Bru and the Viet SF were guarding the stolen merchandise with their lives. You couldn't ask for any more than that. The jarhead stood in the middle of the road with his hand in a halt attitude. I stopped short of his menaced ass and he came to my side quickly.

"We'll have take a look in the back of the three-quarter, Sergeant, if you don't mind," he said.

I started off slowly but gained momentum as I traveled. "I do mind, Marine." I turned my head. "Lock and load!" Twelve bolts clacked home in the three-quarter. Things became mighty quiet around the guard shack.

The Marines stepped to the side of the shack and waved us through very smartly.

The first week of December had almost slipped away, and I was in the TOC initialing the incoming messages when the call came from Company 104 through an interpreter. Phillips held the headset and cocked his head in my direction. I continued my studies until he spoke loudly. "Company 104 have GIs coming from the Sepone to their front wire, Top."

"How many and how does he know they're U.S. GIs?"

"He sees about five through his binoculars. What do they do now, Top?"

"Tell them not to shoot unless they're shot at. Stop them at the wire gate and I'll be there very soon!" Phillips and McMurray were grinning as I put on my ignorance and soft cap.

"Being a team sergeant is the pure shits, sometimes," I said. "Mac, you're getting a big kick outta it, you and the interpreter put on your gear and follow me!"

We approached Company 104 and my ol' pal Viet SF Team Sergeant Minh was waiting for me. I smiled and waved before greeting him and his interpreter. We strolled down the road to the gate and received 104's version of the confrontation before we reached the swinging portable gate. The intruders had been waiting for us, and the apparent leader stood up. The blond well-constructed Caucasian wore no hat, but his face was streaked with camouflage greasepaint and his Marine green fatigues cinched his identity. I waved and he returned my salutation before I spoke loudly while the other people, or Marines, remained prone.

"Come forward, Gunny, and sling arms that damn M-14!"

I said. He motioned for his people to remain prone while Minh shouted at the Bru not to fire.

The tired Marine did not stop until he was a few yards from our party. He grinned and we all returned the favor before he spoke. "I'm Sergeant Johnson, Force Recon, United States Marine Corps, from Khe Sanh. We were on a classified mission, and on the way back, we became disoriented. But I'd seen this place from the air previously, so we headed for it. Sorry about that."

"You got some form of ID, Chief?"

His grin never left his face. "Only a taped dog tag. How's that?" he asked.

"As long as it says Johnson on it, you're welcome to Lang Vei and Detachment A-101, C Company, 5th Special Forces Group, Airborne!"

"Fair enough," Johnson said, handing his locked and unloaded M-14 to McMurray. I verified the ID and handed it back. I didn't think I had to prove there was a war on to this intelligent individual but I still played the game by the rule book.

"Have your people come through the gate with unloaded weapons, one at a time, Johnson, and you're home free."

Gunny Johnson nodded and McMurray kept his weapon while he returned to his Force Recon teammates. Johnson came back shortly and proved to us that he knew how the game was played.

"There's seven of us, Top, and I'll ID them when they come through, one at a time." The short ceremony was over before I asked Lu Minh to have one squad or two check the area from whence they came. He nodded and Lang Vei's new Force Recon team began its short journey to the team house.

Gunnery Sergeant Johnson and I talked of many things during the ten-minute stroll, including recon duty in Korea during the war. By the time we reached the team house, we were the best of friends. We entered the dining facility only to find that

Detachment A-101 had devoured all of Cookie's cuisine. Figuring I owed the shock troops a stove, at least, I talked to Cookie, who assured me that enough food for the reconnaissance people, Mac, and myself, would be ready in fifteen minutes or so. While our guests were downing coffee and the like, I left Mac to keep them company. Because Willoughby was on operation, I thought that it was only appropriate for Wilkins to welcome them, and I told him so. Then I hurried to the TOC.

I wrote the message out to Phillips and waited until he approved my note to Jacksonville before departing. He read it back to keep down any misunderstanding. "TO: Jacksonville FROM: Spunky Hansen. Marine Force Recon Team from your location recovered at 1100 hours. Request transportation your headquarters ASAP. Spunky Hansen sends. Out."

"I don't see how the Marines can misinterpret that, Top. I'll send a runner to let you know when we receive an answer," Phillips concluded.

In the meantime, Wilkins had come and gone before I could get behind the food Cookie had amassed. Detachment A-101 had eight new friends by the time the meal was over. Cookie was also grateful to the Marines for not eating the tables. When we lit up, I had to furnish the smokes as well. Damn, but that stove got expensive. By the time I'd finished my after-dinner delight and coffee, an interpreter paged me from the door.

"Trung Si Phillips has a message for you, Top!"

I waved at the Marines then walked over to the commo shack. Phillips sat in front of his equipment. He held the message in my direction but said, "You're not going to believe this! Khe Sanh says, 'Tell the Recon Team to get back here the same way they got there! Over and out.' "

"You're shittin' me, Phil." I took the message and went up the stairs to rejoin the other orphans. The Marines treat their special units just like the U.S. Army does, I said to myself.

The laughing and joking quieted when I entered the diner. "They say for you people to get back the same way you got here. Shit, I still don't believe it, Gunny."

Gunny Johnson said, "It may surprise you, Top, but not us. I thought you knew we were about as popular with the Marines as you are with the Army. I figured SOG might have told you. Assholes! Hell, we've wasted enough of your time and resources; reckon we ought to be on our way. Would you notify the rough puffs at Khe Sanh that we're coming down the road? Fuck it, it don't mean nothing!"

"You know that ain't gonna happen, Gunny," I said. "McMurray will lay on the transportation and the Vietnamese team sergeant will lay on the security. Be ready to move out and load up in about fifteen minutes. I'll see you before you go."

And that's how the Marine Recon Team got back to Khe Sanh in December 1967. While Khe Sanh Combat Base's popularity dropped in some quarters, Lang Vei won over at least eight of their contingent.

The month of December ended with the same old good news, bad situation. The good news was kind of slim pickings, but in our isolated situation, who could be choosy?

While A-101 had its problems with camp strength and its allies at Khe Sanh, the NVA was not idle. When the Old Man and I read the summary submitted by the detachment intel sergeant, we were shocked. He concluded that in and around the Khe Sanh Combat Base there were two divisions, the 325C and the 304th, both of which showed a preference for the area, as did the 68th and 164th Artillery regiments and some armor.

I checked with Peter Tiroch for confirmation.

"That's what my indigenous laid on me, Top," he said. "They believe it, and are getting a little shaky; I hope they don't desert the ship."

"Don't worry about them, Sarge. Hell, they're playing both sides against the middle. This is pretty hot, but hell, the Marines won't believe it anyway, so we'll send it in on the first available aircraft. I don't want that CW radio net tied up with that shit."

That was the summary of the report that went to C-detachment via one of the team members who took a three-day break in Da Nang.

The artillery portion jibed with what FOB-3 at Khe Sanh had told me previously, that an unidentified artillery unit was digging into the base of the Co Roc mountain chain in Laos, which faced Lang Vei and Khe Sanh from the west. The message wasn't distributed really well before we were furnished some proof that the good times were all but over.

The team leader and I believed the information would be acted on only if confirmed by other sources. We did what we could to counter the intel mill but it didn't amount to much. We pushed our recruiting of Bru warriors and kept patrols out in our area of operations. We also permitted Sergeants Tiroch and Hanna to give us rookies some classes on the 4.2-inch mortar in the center of the inner perimeter just a few yards from the underground TOC. The classes always ended with the firing of at least two or three rounds into Laos for harassment and interdiction (H&I) purposes. According to the U.S. Marines, and probably United States Army, Vietnam, that was a no-no. But neither of them was 1,800 yards from the Sepone River.

December would not have been complete without a visit from the commander and the C Company sergeant major. The three helicopters that transported our celebrities were actually a welcome sight. The mail, Pork Chop's rations, and the rations our funds ordered always brought joy to the detachment and our smiling Bru cooks.

Although the visit might have caused some anxiety among the officers, it bothered the NCO Corps not an iota. We were doing everything possible under the circumstances. If a person could come into an unfamiliar situation and teach us or point out something we'd overlooked, the noncommissioned officers hadn't been paying attention.

The first day went swimmingly, but the second day was unrehearsed warfare as it really is.

Sergeant Major Hodge and I had just returned from the old camp after observing two A-101 NCOs and Minh's Viet SF giving classes to our thirty hard-earned recruits when 82mm 122 mortar rounds began hitting in or near the hilltop perimeter. That presented a problem if you were in the open. Hodge and I retreated to the TOC while the other U.S. went to their alert positions. I notified Jacksonville from the safety of the commo shack deep inside the TOC.

Tiroch and his crew gave the NVA a taste of the 4.2 rounds, all our fire directed at the base of the Co Roc Mountains because we knew the U.S. Marines' 105 artillery pieces could not fire into Laos. Why? According to MAF, it was a neutral country. The crux of the matter was that we had no idea where the rounds were coming from. We had an operation that was to go out the next day, but nothing patrolling the area of operations at the time. Thirty minutes later a high-flying Forward Air Control pinpointed the enemy mortars in our AO. I was quick to give the coordinates to Jacksonville at Khe Sanh, and they fired only a salvo or two before we shouted "Cease-fire." The Marines did good apparently, and the firing ceased. The high-angle fire attack would prove to be a blessing in disguise for the fortress as a whole, but for some it signaled some hard times.

SFC Ronald Knight was in charge of the twenty-five-man operation that was to depart before sunup the next day. Knight ate early and got with his Viet SF and Bru command party in time to beat the rising sun, then their situation deteriorated into chaos for some reason. I had seen similar situations in other A camps and did not fall apart over the incident, but the honchos, Lieutenant Colonel Schungel and Sergeant Major Hodge, were having a hard time living with it. The eventual 0830 departure had Captain Willoughby near cardiac arrest; he knew he would take some of the heat, and unjustly so. Only prior experience kept me aloof from any form of panic. As it turned out, Knight's operation would be of short duration, but the reluctant Bru were in their night location by 1700 hours the same day.

Hodge and I talked of the incident and I attempted to explain SFC Knight's side of the disruption while seated in a secluded nook in Cookie's temple. I knew I wasn't talking to a newbie, but I had to explain the situation clearly to protect the innocent. "I know what happened this morning upset the colonel, and it bothered me as well, but for different reasons. I would like for you to think about what I'm about to say."

"I'm hanging on to every word, Bill!" Hodge replied.

"It is very possible that something is going on that concerns this camp or our area of operation. Why were we shelled yesterday? The Bru sometimes know why and want to stay away from involvement for fear of reprisal or death. In other words, Top, they want the NVA or VC to know they will be in the area and hope like hell the NVA will avoid them. I know the stalling was planned and there was nothing Knight or any other American or the LLDB could do about it. I do not hold the U.S. responsible for what happened this morning."

"Okay, Team Sergeant, I'm glad you got it off your chest," Hodge said.

The next day was business as usual. Willoughby and Lieutenant Colonel Schungel visited all the understrength companies with Lieutenant Quy, the Viet SF team leader. Knight's operation was moving toward A Shau and had negative sightings during the daylight hours. The operation was in its location near a prominent trail when, around 2000 hours, someone began whispering into the command radio net and I was summoned from my nightly beer in the team house.

"It must be our operation, Top, but they're whispering and I can hardly make them out," Phillips said while handing me the headset.

A metallic voice on the PRC-25 interrupted. "Spunky

Hansen, this is Spunky Hansen Ten, how copy now? Over!" Knight said, loud and clear.

"I've got you five by, Spunky Ten. This is Spunky Eight. Go!" I replied.

"Spunky Eight, we just had a battalion-size unit double-time down the trail by our positions. They're on a ninety-degree heading and have cleared this area. Over!"

Knight's transmission was attracting the officers but I became too involved to worry about it. I sat next to Phillips and covered the mouthpiece with the palm of my hand. "Phil, get Jacksonville on the line for a fire mission."

I removed my hand from the transmitter and spoke to Knight. "Spunky Ten, were there any shots fired? Over!"

"Negatory, Eight. It would have been suicide to fire, but we were not detected as far as I know. Over!"

"Roger, Ten, hold what you've got. H and I fire will be on the way shortly. Let us know if we come too close. Over!"

Phillips explained the moving target to Jacksonville and they fired for twenty minutes with all rounds on or near the trail and well short of our operation. Schungel and Willoughby nodded their approval and the tactical operation was quiet for the rest of the evening. I heard no comments or reactions from Schungel about the large sighting, nor did I expect any.

Schungel and Hodge were leaving the next day, but the sergeant major had a few things to impart to me before his departure. "The colonel wants Knight relieved, so have him on the first available after he returns from the operation." I was stunned.

We were standing on top of the TOC next to the fifty-five-gallon drums filled with rocks and dirt, which ringed the apex. "What for, Top? He's done nothing wrong that I'm aware of."

"The colonel holds him responsible for the operation being two hours late leaving the compound!"

My explanation fell on deaf ears. I did make one point clear before Hodge departed the camp. "I'll do as I'm ordered, but I do not agree with the decision and I'm going to make that point clear to Knight. I'm not relieving him, you and the commander are. Okay, Top!"

"Have him on the first available. Tell him what you must. Good luck, Bill. You people are doing a good job."

After conferring with my team leader and upon return of the operation, I did just as I was instructed. But not before I made sure that Knight knew it was the commander's idea and certainly not mine. SFC Knight finished his Army career, not only in Special Forces, but an E9 sergeant major. I was right, sir!

Increased contacts by our patrols and most of all, the intelligence from our net and line crossers from patrols across the border by Command & Control's outlaws brought December to an end on a note of expectancy. Then, with little warning, a Mobile Strike Force Company from C-detachment arrived. The airborne-qualified Mike Force came, 196 strong, with six U.S. SF leaders and a ton of combat experience. They would need every ounce of both assets if they were to survive the "good deal" they had inherited from the bureaucracy in Da Nang. The Mike Force company was commanded by 1st Lt. Paul Longgrear, and his Montagnards were used as relief forces or shock troops for the A-detachments in I Corps.

Through my time in Okinawa, I was acquainted with about half of the U.S. contingent: platoon leaders SFC Earl Burke, SFC Charles Lindewald, S.Sgt. Harvey Brande, Sgt. John Early, and Medical Specialist James Moreland.

The Mike Force natives were composed of mountain folk from the Hre tribe recruited from the Darlac Province area of Ban Me Thuot. It only took me a day or so to discover the unit had a smattering of Rhade and Jarai Montagnards to boot. The four platoons and small headquarters squad boosted the morale of the Bru paranoids no end. Unfortunately, the Hre, like all the other Yards I ever came into contact with, looked down on the Bru because of their poor reputations as fighting men. Therefore, there could not be any mingling of the two forces. They could not be sent on patrol together or even occupy adjoining positions.

Lieutenant Longgrear, who appeared to be the all-American boy, was informed that his U.S. troops could eat at our mess hall any time they desired. When not on operation, the Mike Force would occupy an outpost north of camp on or near Highway Nine. We believed that northern approach to be vital to the defense of Lang Vei as well as to the interstate. We also pledged to supplement the Mike Force U.S. personnel if and when they were short or felt fatigued. In December 1967 I believed that, thanks to these reinforcements, the NVA would not enjoy a cakewalk once the flag went up.

CHAPTER 14

We Americans at the Laotian gateway, Highway Nine, to I Corps of South Vietnam did not celebrate the coming of the New Year of 1968; we thanked the powers that be that we were alive, and kept driving, trying to keep abreast of our many activities. That year Tet, the New Year celebrated in the Far East, was to begin January 31. It was still twenty-nine days away. The Bru of our four companies still had a ways to go, and we would spend the entire month trying to hold down their planned celebration.

While permitting the Mike Force to dig in and get its business together, I decided it was my turn to take a patrol outside the gate. I had no new or fresh personnel who needed breaking in, and everyone was busy attending to the myriad details involved in getting an A-detachment fully operational.

Viet SF Team Daddy Minh and I were inspecting the camp defenses the next day before moving on down to the outpost line. The outpost line positions and the Mikes were not ignored, nor was the patrol that was to leave base camp two days later. When I told Minh that the Americans were overwhelmed with work, I fibbed a tad and said that I might take out the operation by myself. He was shocked at the bold-faced lie. "I no like, Topper. I no trust Bru that much. I go with you. What you think, Bill-son?"

My plan had worked perfectly. "I can get around Da Nang and the two-man Special Forces rule, Minh, so let's do it! I'll send you a copy of the operations order tomorrow. It'll be thirty Bru from your pets, the One-oh-fourth Company."

"Yes, Trung Si, just so we no cross Sepone River, they do okay!"

We were checking S.Sgt. Harvey Brande's positions when I received my second surprise of the day. Because I hadn't been briefed on the Mike Force's tribal background, I wasn't ready for it. Brandy, whom I'd known on Okinawa as a specialist five, and I were talking about the good times on Okinawa when we stopped to examine the communication trench under construction.

The dark-skinned Rhade squad leader spotted me about the same time I saw him. When the Rhade smiled, revealing his gold tooth, I knew I had my man.

"Trung Si!" Goldtooth shouted before he grabbed me in an embrace. Brandy and Minh brought their weapons to an on-guard position but I waved them away.

"Why ain't you at Buon Mi Ga, Goldtooth?" I asked after disengaging.

Goldtooth continued his deceptive smiling while he told me how he joined the Mike Force in Ban Me Thuot a few years back and why he had done so. A cold-blooded killer—and Goldtooth was certainly that—only has two reasons for such a decision: money and more action. After ten minutes or so I bid Goldtooth farewell. Minh, Brandy, and I sauntered to Brandy's platoon headquarters bunker.

Lu Minh and I concluded the Mike Force visit. Besides, I had an operation order to write that concerned my partner and me. I bid Minh farewell before I walked the steps of the TOC and went to the Operations room next to the communications shack.

Writing and mapping the order took little time, but I did not have the RTOs send it to Da Nang until after I showed it to the team leader, who, of course, objected because there were not two Americans on the mission.

"I know what the standard operation procedure says sir," I

told him, "but I just don't have any U.S. who are not vitally committed. Believe me, Da Nang will not say a word. They will think it's a good idea, Minh Lu and I are that close. I'm asking you to trust me on this one." To my surprise, he gave in without further struggle.

The plan was to parallel Highway Nine for a few days to an abandoned village close to Laos. After checking out the area, we would closely follow the Sepone River back to Lang Vei. The operation went well, and Lu Minh and I practiced our languages on each other for five days and nights. We also followed the SOP that stated that the two Americans would never be asleep at the same time. We made no contact but did have Tiroch fire the 4.2 mortar into Laos at some road noises that began late one night. Staff Sergeant Tiroch's 4.2 rounds hit right on the money. The rumbling ceased. The advantages we accrued far outweighed any C-detachment rules we might have violated. The two SF detachments—U.S. and Vietnamese—became closer because of the operation, but that kind of joint mission never caught on in the other camps in Vietnam, so Lu Minh and I were ahead of our time.

Spec. Four William McMurray left Lang Vei around the middle of the month for Da Nang and the States. He was replaced by Spec. Four Franklin Dooms, who Sergeant Phillips had working out like a pro in a week or less. But Mac was like MacArthur: he would be back.

On January 19, 1968, the headquarters personnel at Khe Sanh proper found out the hard way that there was, indeed, a war going on. The intense NVA shelling only reinforced what we already knew. As the history books would point out, the NVA warmed up for Tet on January 20 with Hills 881, North and South, the recipients of their practice runs. The Marine line units reacted the way Marines are supposed to, and repulsed the forays. The Combat Base as a whole did not fare so well.

Once again the artillery from Laos waited until Cookie was ready to holler *"Chow"* before they began to test the dug-in

152mm artillery pieces at the foot of the Co Roc mountain chain in "neutral" Laos.

At 1700 hours the large rounds hit the Khe Sanh airstrip vicinity while a few were simultaneously trying to home in on Lang Vei SF camp. I departed the TOC for chow call but stopped in the 4.2 mortar pit with Tiroch and SFC Kenneth Hanna. While the radios in the TOC were searching for the NVA frequencies, we began firing the large mortar at the foot of Co Roc, looking for the same personnel. People not gainfully employed above ground were in bunkers with overhead cover. The Bru line companies and the Mike Force were alerted for a ground attack that never materialized.

Tiroch gave me the easy task of cutting the charges and attaching them to the rounds while he and Hanna performed the manual labor. The 152mm artillery rounds from Laos were hitting our base camp by then, and if they were simply zeroing their weapons, we hoped their artillery forward observer would cease fire, 'cause he did good. Our commo personnel relayed the coordinates to Khe Sanh of the enemy weapons locations, through their 105 Artillery Battery Headquarters, Jacksonville. Jacksonville, in turn, informed us that they were receiving 152 rounds as well, and in large numbers. We all knew that they would not fire their artillery into Laos but were too busy to worry about it. In thirty minutes or more the barrage ceased, and it was the best thing that had happened all day. While we were cleaning up our mess, Dooms came from the TOC with a smile on his face and made our day, such as it was.

"You did it, you did it! You got one, you lucky bastards!"

"We got one what, Dooms?" I asked.

"You lucky bastards hit one weapon, destroyed it and killed twenty-five NVA redlegs. Not bad for a bunch of rookies."

We cheered, and the rest of our team began assisting in cleaning the mortar pit and vicinity. Dooms continued relaying the information about the 152 artillery pieces deployment. They were dug into the side of Co Roc, rolled out to fire and drawn back into cover and concealment when the mission was completed.

"The B-52 bombers could help us some there," I said, before Dooms and I departed for the TOC.

Phillips was relieved to see both of us. "Jacksonville wants something, Top. Why don't you talk to 'em?" Phillips asked.

It had not gone unnoted that the 152s' cease-fire pertained to Khe Sanh Combat Base as well as to Lang Vei. I called the Marines and they came up quickly and in the clear.

"Read you five by five, Spunky Hansen. Give us your casualty report! Over!"

"Roger, Jacksonville, stand by One. Over!" I already had the negative report on U.S. losses, so I called Minh and he rounded up the Viet SF and Bru casualty figures for me. I didn't have too long to wait. I passed our report on to Jacksonville.

"Would you repeat that, Spunky Hansen? Over!"

"I say again, Jacksonville. One WIA, treated and returned to duty. Copy? Over!" I was telling the truth, but Jacksonville was judging everyone by their own standard so they refused to believe our figure.

It turned out that one Bru had jumped in a commo trench while heading for his bunker when the barrage began. He injured his ankle upon landing and had to crawl the remaining yards to his overhead cover. That was our casualty. It would take a few hours for A-101 to learn that Khe Sanh had lost forty-two KIA.

A horrible lesson. The headquarters area, such as mess facilities and replacement living quarters, lacked overhead cover, not Hills 881 North or South. A painful lesson, but this war was different, and for some commanders the solutions were not always absorbed in the classrooms or on Highway Nine.

The Marines on Hills 881 North and South gave classes to the NVA the next day, classes that were just as painful as the ones the 152s had inflicted on the Marines the day before. The prepping artillery fire did a job on the rear of the Khe Sanh Combat Base, but didn't get the job done where it counted.

A few days later Staff Sergeant Tiroch told me that the .50 caliber machine gun had been air-dropped with no spare parts kit, and worse, no timing gauge. "I can adjust head space by the WAG [wild-ass guess] system, Top, but I'd rather not!" Tiroch said.

"Don't, Pete," I said. "It's too dangerous. A crew in my platoon in Korea did that and blew the cover off and put the gunner in MASH with eye problems that were never solved. We'll get a timing gauge somewhere, somehow! Do not fire that .50 in any manner until you have the proper equipment, Pete. That's an order. I'll get to work on the solution ASAP."

Sergeant Major Pegram, my most infamous scrounging contact, said, "I can't help you, Bill, but I have some information that could solve the problems for you. I can't give you the scoop over the air, so come on over, haven't seen you in a while, nohow."

It was time to pick up rations at the Khe Sanh air depot, and I decided to go with the men I knew. Sergeant Dan Phillips, A-101's new demolition man, hadn't yet visited the Combat Base, so I placed him in charge of the convoy of two three-quarter-ton trucks and a jeep. I conned Minh into riding shotgun for the jeep and to help break in Phillips. I allowed Sergeant Phillips to drive the jeep and explained my plans to both on the way to our destination.

"I'll take the jeep after we reach the airstrip and go to SOG headquarters. Sergeant Major Pegram thinks he knows where I can scrounge a timing gauge for our .50 caliber machine gun. When I'm finished, I'll be back after you all. You can drive a forklift, can't you, Dan?"

"A little bit, Top," he said. "Why?"

"It'll speed things up loading the equipment that's stacked on pallets, Sarge," I replied.

"Hell, us Combat Engineers can drive anything, you know that, Team Sergeant."

Sergeant Major Pegram met me at the gate of SOG's dug-in, fortified encampment. "Here's the skinny, Bill," he said. "Some new people have moved into Khe Sanh and are digging in, I hope, on our perimeter. One of the units is a heavy-weapons company and they're across the road from the gate entrance. I don't know if they'll help, but you have nothing to lose."

"I'll let you know how I make out," I told him.

When I approached the gateway, I noted jeep tracks leading into the second growth and small trees adjacent to the main thoroughfare. I followed it only a minute or two before I spotted a group of Marines involved in varied activities. The first pair I encountered directed me to their headquarters tent. I wasn't surprised, but assumed it was only temporary. I walked into the death trap and saw the first sergeant at a desk surrounded by small cabinets and several other GI desks. He looked up at my unannounced entry and stood. I was happy that he was approximately my size and build. I spoke before he could.

After the introductions, I relayed my reasons for the visit. To my surprise, he came back with unrelated inquiries. "You're the team sergeant of that Special Forces camp down the road a piece, Sarge?"

"Yes, First Sergeant, and I learned in Korea not to fire a .50 caliber machine gun without proper timing, like with a gauge!" Still, he shied away from my plea.

"How long have you been in Vietnam, Team Sergeant?"

"Four and a half months this time, Top, but two and a half years before this. Can I help you?" I asked.

"Would you wait here while I get the captain? We might be able to help you. Wait one!"

He departed and left me muttering to myself: "That Marine is being nice; he's up to something. Shit!"

The company commander was also my size. He sported short red hair. He was also smiling. *Beware!* The saluting and handshaking were over before the commander spoke.

"I understand you need a .50 caliber machine gun timing gauge, Team Sergeant. I've got a deal for you. I have an extra one in my footlocker that's yours if you'll talk to us for a few minutes."

Beware! "Be glad to, sir. Whatcha wanta know?"

"We're new here, as you know. If you would, tell us what you can about anything that pertains to us, Khe Sanh Combat Base, and the vicinity."

I sealed the deal before the two could back out, and had the gauge in my hand to motivate my mouth. We moved from the death trap to where the company was busy building mortar pits, living quarters, and barbed-wire obstacles. I started my lecture with the intelligence briefing on the area and moved to their present location as quickly as I could. I started the localized briefing and was only interrupted once before the conclusion.

"Regardless of your prior briefings, there is a war going on over here. Believe it! The North Vietnamese Army buildup around Khe Sanh has ballooned and has been reported through channels. I hope everyone realizes that by now. While building your defensive fighting bunkers, make sure they have overhead cover and connect every position with communication trenches. That applies to all living bunkers and your orderly room as well."

"Team Sergeant, we're hurting for overhead material unless you know something we don't know," the first sergeant said.

I pointed to the perimeter front that was covered with trees and second growth. "You need to cut some of those trees for line-of-sight purposes. They'll make excellent roofing material when covered with sandbags. As a last resort, steal or borrow all the perforated steel planking you can lay your hands on. The air field's throwing it away anyway."

"Team Sergeant, we were told that the district chief allows no cutting of timber. How do we get around that?" the Marine commander said.

"Funny, I've never been told that, sir. Anyway, the district chief will never know unless you or your headquarters tells him. They won't know, and who gives a shit if they do? Don't play politics, sir, play war. You could get around it easy enough by saying you didn't order it done, and by the time you found out it was too late. That's better than going to those damn memorial services. Think war all the time while you're over here, and disregard the people who are playing politics. I've survived and I hope the hell you will, too," I concluded my lecture.

Lu Minh and Dan Phillips watched me drive up and could see from my face that I had done good.

I was breaking Phillips in as fast as I could to his surroundings. Phillips was my first and only bunker mate, and for two reasons. It was his first trip to Vietnam, and he began his Special Forces career just the way I did, as a 12B demolition man. We pulled enough watch after dark that I didn't get to talk to him as much as I would have liked to.

The next afternoon we received some 82mm mortar rounds, but they hit only on the top and the crest of the hill. Everyone was under cover quickly and we took no casualties. The outpost occupied by Staff Sergeant Brande and the Mike Force spotted the criminals and reported same. After Phillips passed me the coordinates, I was in a bind.

Staff Sergeant Tiroch, A-101's best high-angle-fire expert, was on operation, and Hanna was in Da Nang for a couple of days. So Phillips and I got out the map and I adjusted the M 1 sight on our 81mm mortar. The mortar pit was next to our sleeping bunker, and was our alert position as well. In about ten minutes we believed we were ready and notified Brandy of our counterfire plans.

Brandy was a ready teddy. "I've got my glasses on 'em, Top. Fire when ready."

Phillips removed the bore-riding safety pins and dropped three rounds down the tube rapidly. I did a repeat performance, then waited for our forward observer to give us some guidance.

"You're about four hundred yards off, Top. Before you try again, Sergeant First Class Charley Lindewald should be at your location. So wait one! Over!"

"Goddamn, why didn't I think of that," I blurted into the PRC-25.

"Who's he, Team Sergeant?" Phillips asked.

"Dan, he's the best mortar man in Special Forces, at least by reputation. I'd forgot he was with the Mike Force. Shit!"

"You don't need me then, Top. I've got to go on first watch at the TOC. I'll be listening." Phillips grinned.

I had two white phosphorous spotting rounds ready for Lindewald when he walked up, greeted me, and took the map and compass. After a few pen-and-ink changes, he adjusted the M-1 sight and squared the bubble. "We're in business, Top, give me two WP rounds and let Brandy adjust!"

"On the way, sir," was all I could offer. I dropped the WP rounds down the tube one at a time. The short, heavyset heavy-weapons specialist watched for the smoke while I monitored our FO. He came up so excited that I couldn't make out what the hell he said. "Say all after 'Mike Force Five.' "

"I say again. Cease-fire! Your willie peter rounds hit right on the button, knocking out the mortar and its crew as well. You lucky bastards. Mike Force Five, over and out!"

"Need anything else, Team Sergeant?" Lindewald said.

"I still don't believe it. But, yeah, Charley, place the mortar back on SF One, on the Sepone River approach. I've never seen any shit like that before," I said truthfully.

In only a few minutes Lindewald was waddling back to the Mike Force, but buoyed up my sanity with his departing state-ment. "That was pure luck, Bill!" It would be the last good "luck" for Lang Vei or Khe Sanh for a while.

Errors in judgment on January 21, 1968, caused the Marine commanders to lose not only Khe Sanh village and Lang Vei, but also their link to the most valuable property in their area, Highway Nine. These same commanders also proved, at least to me, that counterinsurgency just wasn't their cup of tea.

The village of Khe Sanh, like Lang Vei SF campsite, sat astride the interstate that led to the coast of South Vietnam. A moot point apparently to the I Corps commander and the Quang Tri Marines in charge. We closely monitored an all-day assault on Khe Sanh village on January 21, following it on our frequencies and the NVA's. The village compound was defended by a team of U.S. Army Advisers headed by Army Captain Bruce G. Clarke, a Regional Force Popular Force company, and a squad of U.S. Marines. In addition to the Bru rough puffs, the village housed American missionaries and French plantation owners.

To the surprise of the NVA, and Detachment A-101, the compound held out all day and all night. The NVA took an ass-kicking from the outnumbered force. Lang Vei was elated, but, like Captain Clarke and his crew of heroes, not for very long. When Clarke radioed for the relief force from Khe Sanh Combat Base, his request was declined. Then the Marines Corps compounded its stupidity by ordering the squad of Marines out of Khe Sanh village. Lang Vei came out of shock long enough to offer the Mike Force troops as reinforcements, but the Marines refused our offer.

Interservice rivalry reached an all-time low at that point in the Marines' next act. Helicopters were sent to evacuate the Marine squad, but the Army personnel and their indigenous company had to walk the three kilometers to the Combat Base. Thank God for SOG, at FOB-3, or the GIs under Captain Clarke would probably have been turned away. The indigenous rough puffs were!

January 22, 1968, sealed the fate of the Lang Vei Special Forces camp and A-101, at least in my mind. Why? The Marines' reaction force refused to carry out its assignment or contingency plans, sealing the fate of the rough puffs and the Bru population in general. The Bru now understood that they had sided with losers and that they, not the Americans who had abandoned them, would pay the ultimate price for their misplaced loyalty.

The word of the refusal to allow the rough puffs into Khe Sanh Combat Base was all over our line companies in twenty-four hours. Well-thought-out desertions began immediately. The Americans at Lang Vei felt the guilt, guilt that was none of our doing. Finally, the Marines' despicable behavior hurt the entire effort in the highlands of South Vietnam, a piece of land that afforded the support of over a million people.

The damage was done and our lifeline to the Khe Sanh air field, and our supplies, was severed. Any and all supplies would have to be air-dropped to ~~Dien Bien Phu~~ all over again. Try recovering airdrops with personnel who, after the U.S. has abandoned them, steal fifty percent of the material for themselves.

The day after the surrender of Khe Sanh village, reconnaissance aircraft were fighting the fog over Khe Sanh Combat Base when another fight broke out. The 33rd Royal Laotian Battalion at Tchepone reported they were being overrun by NVA tanks and infantry. An FAC aircraft and two fighter-bombers went to Tchepone, Laos, but never got off a round because of the fog. Did our intelligence believe that? Yes; armor had been reported in the area twelve miles west of Khe Sanh, inside Laos, previously.

On January 24 Captain Frank Willoughby was in Hawaii on R&R and Lieutenant Miles Wilkins was the acting team leader. Major George Quamo called for Willoughby from FOB-3, but I took the call in the TOC. He told me he had a fixed-wing recon aircraft available and would pick me up at the air field at the old camp of Lang Vei ASAP. I knew Quamo and did not doubt that the mission was important. The old camp, across the road from A-101, was secured for the light aircraft and I had Dan Phillips drive me over in a jeep.

The conversation that ensued in the spy flight would live with me forever. Major Quamo was about to become a hero to one E7 team sergeant in the U.S. Army.

Three of us filled the observation plane to capacity. The Vietnamese pilot was too busy following his dangerous assignment flying us in and out of Laos and I Corps to follow the conversation.

"You know the 33rd Laotian Battalion abandoned Tchepone and are headed your way down Highway Nine?" Quamo said. "That's why we're here!"

"Shit no, sir, I'm still pissed off about the Khe Sanh village fiasco," I said.

"I know that, too, Bill. This flight was ordered by MACV to confirm or deny that the battalion is crossing over into Vietnam. It's an international violation, you know! MACV has advised FOB Three to tell A-101 not to embarrass General Westmoreland."

I was furious. "I'm just worried *sick* about Westmoreland! He sure as hell ain't worried about Lang Vei, sir! Nor is Khe Sanh Combat Base, for that matter."

"Here they come," Quamo interrupted. The pilot nosed down a tad, and sure enough, a column of ducks was waddling down Highway Nine just inside the Vietnamese border. The *tahans* (Lao for "soldier") from Laos were well-dressed and all had weapons. They looked tactical except for the families that were tagging along behind them. They even had the audacity to wave and smile at our aircraft. I had my mouth open in amazement but noted that Major Quamo was staring at me and not the misplaced persons. He said what was on his mind.

"What are you gonna do, boss?"

"I'll figure it out, sir, but they're not staying in camp with us. We can handle it. Fuck the 33rd. I'm worried about us."

"Just do the best you can, Bill, is about all I can offer."

"We will, sir, but the Marines won't help us. I hope some of us make it out alive."

"We'll get you out, Bill. Count on SOG."

Major Quamo was true to his word that day, and I believed everything he said. We landed on the old strip and Phillips rushed me back to Fortress Lang Vei to await the arrival of the invaders from Tchepone, Laos.

CHAPTER 15

The TOC was a busy place when I finally sat my ass down in the operations room. Dooms continued to decipher the CW messages, but SFC Emanuel Phillips was awaiting my arrival. I beat him to the punch. "Get me the Mike Force honcho, like yesterday, Sarge!"

Mike Force One knew something was amiss and boomed back. "Go, Spunky Hansen! Over!"

"Stop the Lao on the road and have them take a break. Bring the commander to this location. Do not get nervous, they're friendly. Will explain when you arrive." Longgrear rogered my request.

I wrote out a message to the C-detachment but told Phillips to wait until after my meeting with the Lao before he sent it. The message read: "Lao battalion in old camp; awaiting your instructions."

Dooms got on the emergency frequency and told the aircraft in our area, if any, to hold their fire. All I had to do now was wait on Longgrear and Lieutenant Colonel Bao, who I had not seen since Savannakhet in 1961. Air America's Art Wilson, with my assistance, had saved the 33rd with our airdrops a time or two. I knew in my heart that Bao would defecate when he saw me, if the Mike Force didn't grease him by mistake in the meantime.

Longgrear interrupted my train of thought. "We're at the back gate. Your location in five. Over and out!"

I met Minh and Lieutenant Quy by the team house and saw

six or seven fatigues approaching. The Lao were dressed in OD jungle fatigues formerly issued by MAAG of Laos, so they were easy to distinguish from the camouflage jobs worn by us and the Mikes. Lieutenant Colonel Bao spotted me from six yards away, and a stunned look was quickly replaced by a wide-toothed grin. Mike Force Lieutenant Longgrear introduced the Viet SF and saved me for last. When Bao heard the "Team Sergeant" part of the introduction, he grabbed me in an embrace. Everyone present was startled, and Longgrear came to "on guard" before I waved him off. I greeted Bao after the entanglement in my best Lao, which surprised everyone again. The time was 1630 and we had no time for war stories.

My briefing went something like: "Your battalion will file through Lang Vei on Highway Nine and they will not leave the road for any reason. They will be identified by a commander at both the back and front gates. Their destination is the old camp you see across the highway to your front. There are two Americans and two Vietnamese Special Forces NCOs awaiting your arrival. They will show you around and you can set up before dark. Weapons will be unloaded at the back gate and not reloaded until you are outside our compound. Your defensive positions are left to your discretion. The commander of C-detachment will probably be here tomorrow, and I'm sure he'll have further instructions. Coordinate any communications with the Vietnamese on location. Good night, sir!" The farewell was in Lao. By dark the commander of the 33rd was in the old camp with little ammunition, food, or any sympathy from me. A million messages awaited our return to the TOC.

Because of the conversation with Quamo, I felt that Detachment A-101 had fulfilled its mission in relation to the international upheaval. We might well suffer some inconveniences due to their deployment, but I felt there would be no recriminations over our handling of the crisis. In the meantime, the most powerful sergeant first class, E7, in the world read one message that took some of the weight off my shoulders: "Major

Hoadley and support personnel for 33rd Battalion your location tomorrow." I should hope so, was the feeling that concluded the long, unbelievable day.

I had a night's sleep without any guard watch to think over Bao's story about the tanks running the 33rd out of Tchepone, Laos. Did I believe that NVA tanks had run the 33rd Laotian Battalion out of Tchepone? Yes, I believed it, but I also believed the story Bao told was slanted toward his unit. I was a believer because of some battles and occurrences that happened six years ago, not because a lieutenant colonel in the Lao Army told us what supposedly happened.

The 33rd was having its problems in 1961 and 1962, and for the same reasons they had an overwhelming confrontation in January 1968. Tchepone occupies a vital overland route to the Ho Chi Minh Trail and points south, east, and west. The 33rd was surrounded, out of food, and damn near out of ammo and weapons in 1962. Air America and a dumb paratrooper from Savannakhet came to their rescue then. Art Wilson, the poor man's Earthquake McGoon, got his C-47 down so low I couldn't miss the small fort with watchtowers on all four corners. The 33rd welcomed my bundles as they were slowed by cargo chutes. The village was surrounded for weeks at a time during my TDY tour in Laos. But the 33rd never backed down before the Pathet Lao, NVA, Chinese, whatever. Why, only six years later, should the same unit suddenly break and run, weapons, family, et al.?

Bao and his unit knew the tank-led attack force was coming, and coming in large, well-organized numbers. The 33rd waited until it was convinced that it would be the first target in the eight-year war to be hit by NVA tanks and infantry. What convinced them, I don't have the slightest idea, but they moved out bag and baggage to avoid the showdown. It was too obvious to me that they had not been in a life-and-death struggle for survival. Where were the wounded? Why was there no blood on their uniforms from treating the wounded? The tank saga convinced this old soldier of the presence of tanks, but not of the details of the struggle. My theories were disregarded by the Marines, and even my team leader, but I would be as busy as a bee in a bucket of honey for the next few weeks, too busy to even worry about it.

The next day Major Hoadley and crew flew in from Da Nang by Chinook helicopters. The *tahans* were no longer the tactical or logistical headache of Detachment A-101. Major Hoadley, the heavyset executive officer of C-detachment, was to try to motivate Lieutenant Colonel Bao into a more warlike response to the Pathet Lao. Hoadley brought along his own split A-detachment (half an A, or six men). Among the newbies was 1st Lt. Thomas Todd, an engineer officer sent along to survey the airstrip at the old Lang Vei camp because the one at Khe Sanh Combat Base was inaccessible to us by road.

The enlisted personnel were headed up by SFC Eugene Ashley, an older black GI with plenty of on-the-job training in conventional units. Doing his bidding would be two proficient young medics, Sgt. Richard Allen and Spec. Four Joel Johnson. Last and least of all was Spec. Four John Young—a weapons man? Gimme a break! Sergeant Major Hodge and I had words over this one young man, but things were desperate in Da Nang as well, I reckon. No E7 has ever won an argument with an E9.

A fixed-wing Army Caribou also delivered barbed wire, food, ammunition, and medical supplies to assist the third country nationals. In addition to Hoadley's bringing in a ready-made group of SF "force expanders," Team Leader Captain Willoughby returned from R&R as well. I was very glad to see him; we had a ton of work to do and talk about. But, just in time, we settled on a few SOPs: Major Hoadley was the boss at old Lang Vei, we still ran the show at A-101; there would be no Laotian operations in our AO; Lao listening posts were authorized within sight of the old camp, but only with my and Ashley's approval.

Like the abandonment of Khe Sanh village, news of the tank attack got the attention of the Bru line companies. This served to speed up the desertion rate among our warriors, despite the airdrops a day after the armor stories ran through the communication trenches. Lang Vei, or A-101, had the weapon to stop the thickest armored tank in any army in the world, the 3.5 rocket launcher; a weapon that evolved during the Korean War from the smaller 2.36 rocket launcher of WWII days. Still, the Bru line soldiers pictured themselves straddling the road with carbines going full blast as the cannon on the PT-76 Soviet tank blew them to paradise.

Captain Willoughby or someone in the C-detachment—and I never knew which—ordered one hundred light anti-tank weapons (LAWs) that were air-dropped on or about January 25. The relatively new rocket launcher came with a disposable plastic tube. All team members were required to test-fire at least one of the LAWs before the week was out. Without any assistance, I then proceeded to make the biggest tactical mistake that I would ever own up to: I gave away the 3.5-inch rocket rounds, tubes included, to SFC Ashley for his Laotians.

Why was that such a big mistake? The 3.5-inch rocket ammunition can be fired without the launching tube, electrically or nonelectrically, by using commo wire and a blasting machine or a time fuse. Even the E7 ambassador to Laos can make a mistake. A mistake that I have never forgotten to this day.

Regardless, we were now, supposedly, ready for the tanks from across the Sepone River.

Lt. Miles Wilkins was out on operation and the month was closing quickly. On the third day of his five-day stint, he was in a night location along the peaceful Sepone River only about two miles from camp. Fortunately, for convenience' sake, I was on watch at the TOC around midnight when they were probed from across the creek. I woke the Old Man while Wilkins raved on; that he was excited only proved he was human.

"Calm down, Spunky Hansen Two, help is on the way," I

said over the PRC-25. Their location was plotted on our large wall map, so I had no problem reading the artillery concentration.

Khe Sanh's artillery came up quickly. "Enemy sighted and firing from SF Two, Jacksonville. Give us willie peter and we'll adjust. Over!"

I changed frequencies and calmed Wilkins down with my information. "Be ready to adjust, Spunky Two!"

Jacksonville was right on the money, and Wilkins called for FFE, like hurry up! Jacksonville fired for effect. In five to ten minutes the 105 artillery rounds had quieted the North Vietnamese invaders. While dozing off in Dan Phillips's and my underground home, it dawned on me that the operations were now making contact closer and closer to our hometown. Considering recent events, I doubted that would change right away. Wilkins's next radio contact would not be until first light, so I slept well and without interruptions from Spunky Hansen Two or Jacksonville.

The next morning we gave Wilkins's patrol their marching orders. They were not to return home, as the Bru would have liked. We called out the coordinates that amounted to a safe trip home—the road that led to camp from the Sepone River would be their address until such time as the patrol was terminated. We certainly didn't expect any trouble so close to home.

While I was playing out my role as team sergeant of A-101, I was learning more about administrative chores than I really wanted to know. This particular day, our Group Personnel in Nha Trang taught me how screwed up the Army can get over its paper shuffling. When Dooms handed me a bulletin hot off the wire, I flipped out.

A few weeks before I had submitted all members of A-101 who qualified for the Combat Infantryman's Badge. The medical personnel, Holt and Fragos, were to receive the Combat Medical Badge. The request was kicked back because I had left off someone's—and I can't recall whose—social security number. The reason I omitted it was because he was on operation and we didn't have a file clerk, or a file cabinet, for that matter. Besides, I'd concluded, isn't Nha Trang's 5th Special Forces Group (Airborne) where our personnel records are kept? It would not be tough for them to look it up. My message to the sergeant major of C Company was rated X but it got results; CIBs and Medical Badges got moving real good before Tet. Now that I'd made my long day, I woke my roommate so he could take over watch at the TOC, but as it turned out, I wasn't going anywhere near my rack for a while.

The small arms fire that awoke the entire camp came from the Sepone River and Wilkins's operational area, therefore I stayed in place. Wilkins calmed after his initial vocal outburst, and Jacksonville was on-line by that time. "Okay, Spunky Two, if they're across the river, pull back toward camp and we'll let Jacksonville take over. How copy? Over!" I said.

"We can't pull back, Spunky Hansen, our casualties are too great. I'll need some of them evacuated first! Over!"

Wilkins was right. If they tried to pull back carrying their dead and wounded, it would result in a rout of sorts and more casualties. The twenty-five-man operation just wasn't up to it.

"We'll have some transportation for your casualties, Spunky Two. Move your wounded to the rear and we'll be there shortly. Stand by!" I handed the transmitter to the team leader and asked the team members present who would go with me in the jeep and trailer to bring back the dead and wounded. No one spoke up, so I did.

"Let's go, Phillips; this won't take long!" We secured our weapons and web gear and were in the back of the TOC quickly. I drove the jeep and trailer out the gate and turned right toward the Sepone River and the noisy firefight. By not turning on the headlights, I finally did something smart during the evening. The night was not pitch-black and the flares really gave us more exposure than we needed, or wanted, for that matter.

As we neared the firefight I slowed and two individuals

stepped out onto the road and motioned us off. The interpreter and a Viet SF began helping us with the wounded. We placed their gear in the trailer and laid four of them on top of it. The other two had been placed in the backseat of the jeep, when a flare went off directly overhead. We didn't need that. We began to receive some rounds from the NVA, and we both flinched as they came closer and closer. It was time for two scared asses to move out. When we leaped into the jeep, the two Vietnamese helpers straddled the road leading to Laos. They both fired a magazine of defiance at the Vietnamese Yankees and we were gone.

By the time Phillips and I had burdened Fragos and Holt with the wounded and the dead man, Wilkins had disengaged and pulled back for the night. The team leader briefed me and said artillery concentration SF-1 was on the way from Jacksonville. After twenty minutes the overhead rounds quieted and it was apparently over. My jeep mate took over his watch and I took over the sleeping bunker for a night's rest.

The Vietnamese Special Forces team sergeant and I waited until Wilkins and his survivors closed camp before we left the next morning. Our thirty-man patrol was a thousand yards from camp before we halted and sent a squad to recon the battle site of the previous night. Using the HT-1 walkie-talkie radios for unit communications, the all-clear was not long in the making. The rest of the detail moved to the terrain by the boundary line. What we found was rather gory, but educational, in a sense. To begin with, there was blood everywhere. After about thirty minutes of search and research we believed we knew the scenario from the previous night.

Where the NVA had assembled contained fresh blood, flesh and bones. They had taken a stand under the few trees that guarded the otherwise bald bank of the Sepone River. Mistake numero uno. Mistake numero dos was really hard to swallow, but the evidence was too prevalent to overlook. Some of these warriors had tied themselves up in the trees and used the limbs as firing platforms. When Wilkins's operation pulled back out of sight, the 105 artillery rounds had easy pickings. The high explosive rounds hit the treetops and exploded, sending hundreds of pieces of steel not only into the trees' limbs, but into the people below. We never found out how many got out alive, but soon discovered how they were transported. The elephant dung was followed, along with the hoofprints, to the riverbank. If we had any surveillance on the enemy after the artillery ceased, the NVA casualties would have been higher, and the elephant population lower. Mark up a mistake for Lang Vei, but two to one ain't bad. Also considered was the unexpected tenacity of the Bru and only one KIA. Part of the credit for the last statistic went to SFC James Holt and Nick Fragos, two terrific medical people. We also had a brand-new combat veteran in the ranks of A-101 by the name of Miles Wilkins. Last but not least, A-101 also had a brave medical evacuation expert in my bunker mate, S.Sgt. Dan Phillips.

The New Year's Day of 1968 had come and gone for the Americans, but it was the day of the monkey, January 31, that signified Tet to folks in the Far East and came in like a lion. A Mike Force platoon of fifty strong drew the combat operation on that day. The operation area was west of camp toward Khe Sanh village. It would be near this city, disdained by both sides, that we would discover who the monkeys were. The combat patrol was headed by Brandy, Goldtooth, and his mountain men, so I was betting on the Mike Force. Around noon and during the "pak" period, we found out.

A company-size NVA unit selected an abandoned rubber plantation just on our side of neutral Khe Sanh village for its pak-time nap. Mistake number one. The Mike Force got into a skirmish line and rudely opened fire on Winkem, Blinkem, and Nod. While they were marching through the first unit, a second NVA company just beyond the ambush site was getting organized. The Mike Force pulled back when it met the second NVA opponent. The NVA could have bowed out gracefully during the lull, but instead insisted on pursuit. Mistake number two.

The TOC was alerted and readied. The commo personnel were monitoring the NVA battalion's frequency in a heartbeat. The NVA commander made it clear that his unit would trail the bandits and force them to pay for their misdeeds. We were setting into motion other plans to complicate the mission of the erring battalion commander.

Brandy and the confident Mike Force were loaded down with captured weapons and trying to reach the high ground on the first large, sloping hill west of Lang Vei. We called to have a Forward Air Controller (FAC) upstairs waiting on the NVA. Skyraider fighter-bombers were on the way from Thailand, and we hoped that the Skyraiders would be on line before Brandy and the Mike Force were, but that was not to be. We reminded the FAC that a war was going on, but he assured us that he was doing all he could.

The Mike Force established a perimeter on the military crest of the high ground just in time to meet the NVA's first assault wave. Everyone within hearing distance of the radio room heard Brandy say, "Here they come!" About that time, three Skyraiders made an appearance. Things were looking up.

FAC talked to Brandy during the assault. "Pop smoke, Spunky Mike, and keep your head down!" The Mike Force did, enabling the fixed-wing aircraft to divert the NVA assault wave.

The Skyraiders' machine guns and rockets more than compensated for the enemy's numbers advantage. When the NVA fell back to regroup, their battalion CO could be heard berating their effort on our monitors. He was sending more men to assist in the onslaught. We notified FAC of his plans, and FAC informed Brandy to be ready for the Skyraiders' remaining munitions. Things were going to heat up on the next NVA skirmish. Brandy asked FAC for a repeat.

"I say ag'in, Spunky Mike," FAC said, "all we have left is napalm. Keep your heads down!"

When the bombers emptied their loads, the fire and black smoke could be seen for miles. The second growth on the hillside was afire before Brandy was heard from again.

"It's all over! Tell 'em to knock it off. The fire is the only thing climbing the hill. We've got to move out."

Captain Willoughby nodded before the Mikes were told to head back to base camp. Their part of the miniwar was over. Our monitors told us that the NVA battalion commander was moving. He gave us his location, and our FAC was interested because: "We still have a dash of napalm left, Spunky Hansen. Give us a target!"

After we complied, several of us went outside and witnessed the last air assault. We immediately saw the black hillside as we looked in the direction of Khe Sanh. The billowing smoke from the battle site reeked of burning flesh. A helluva way to die. We turned our attention to the diving Skyraiders as they homed in on a location near our side of Khe Sanh village on Highway Nine, dropped their remaining loads, and headed back to their bases. By the time we spotted the Mike Force victors heading back to camp, the NVA battalion was off the air forever.

Staff Sergeant Brande was debriefed by Captain Willoughby while his victorious warriors took up their positions on the perimeter. He reported fifty-four confirmed kills and brought back thirty captured weapons. Brandy, the Mike Force, A-101, and the U.S. Air Force had combined their talents on a decisive note, resulting in the first of many ass-whippings to be administered to the NVA during the start of their Tet Offensive.

CHAPTER 16

February 1968 came in breathing fire over the length and breadth of South Vietnam. General Giap, disregarding casualties, pulled the biggest disaster in the military history of Vietnam. Yet he became a hero to his people, and even some Americans believe him to be a great tactician. I'll bet my last dollar that one generation of Vietnamese wouldn't think so. But because he had them exterminated, their opinions will never be known.

We paranoids at Lang Vei heard the reports of the Tet Offensive through our radios. Secretly, many of us were tickled that the REMFs in the resort areas were at least getting shelled from time to time. We had ourselves and our natives to worry about and really didn't give a damn. It affected the morale at Lang Vei not in the least, not Bru, Mike Force, or Detachment A-101. Why? Hell, we never believed it could get any worse. The Air Force Skyraiders from Thailand pulled Brandy's warriors through a tough situation. Jacksonville was, seemingly, always on call when we needed 'em, and you couldn't fault our beloved C-team. They had assumed responsibility for the Laotians and air-dropped supplies when the weather allowed. Despite all the assistance, the personnel of Lang Vei still believed it was SF Detachment A-101 against the world.

For two weeks in the last part of January, we were so busy supplying food for everyone but the U.S. in A-101 that the basic staples of our diet were overlooked. Even our favorite mess sergeant in Da Nang city was of no assistance. Have you ever gone without bread for three weeks? The lack began to gnaw at our palates as well as our stomachs. By this time, our food supply had diminished just to noodles two or three times a day. Our C-rations were for field duty only, so they weren't the solution. Eventually, I had to appeal to FOB-3. The radio chief just asked, "What do you need now, Bill?"

"We haven't had bread in three weeks, pal. Some bread or flour would sure be a novelty. We could use some meat, too!"

The operator sighed audibly. "I'll pass the word to the Top Soldier, Bill. Don't get fat in the meantime. FOB Three, out!"

Between FOB-3 and the NVA, several things happened the first few days of February that solved our rations problem.

Early one morning an Army helicopter hailed us over the radio and informed us that we had supplies from FOB-3. After warning him not to linger longer than necessary, we cleared him in.

The landing pad was located by the mess hall, on the east side of the crest. Like all wartime landing pads, it was strategically located by our popular two-holer. As they had in Korea, the Commies enjoyed zeroing in on that sort of thing, and visiting aircraft meant incoming rounds from Co Roc and across the Sepone River. However, unlike Korea, the enemy gunners were still only learning. The Army Huey obeyed instructions, dropped two hundred-pound bags of flour, and cut out for the friendly confines of Khe Sanh Combat Base. The NVA didn't shell the camp until after the Huey departed so we waited under overhead cover before helping Cookie's crew recover the flour. Cookie made it all worthwhile by promising bread for the evening meal.

Sergeant Major Pegram must have told his troops we were short yet another American staple, for the very next evening three choppers came from the north and reported they had a mule deer for our dining pleasure. The large deer was slung under the lead chopper, and Cookie and his mess troops were waiting. None of the U.S. troops hung around the helo pad while the cooks earned their money skinning and butchering the deer from north of the 17th Parallel. We got a meal out of it for A-101 and the Mikes. Once again the Special Operations personnel had not forsaken their own. I never found out how much of the venison went to Cookie's helpers and families, but they earned it. We were through eating before the 152 rounds and mortars tried for the rotary-wing aircraft and our two-holer. Both of 'em got off scot-free.

FOB-3 got some assistance from General Giap's troops in solving our meat shortage. If he's reading this, I hope he understands that we appreciated the gesture. It was after 2400, midnight, when the Bru from the 104th CIDG Company reported noises by the barbed-wire gate coming from the road to Laos. The American on guard fired a flare, and the ensuing small arms fire did the rest. Phillips and I put on our webbing and went next door to the 81mm mortar-pit alert position. Another flare went off as we entered and readied the mortar. The sight that greeted us was one to behold!

The wire gate had almost been destroyed by NVA sappers who now lay dead alongside their handiwork. They had been attempting to run a herd of water buffalo through the camp, but the poor creatures didn't stand a chance against the .30 caliber carbine and A-6 machine gun rounds from the starving 104th Company. The incident filled the craws of camp personnel and Cookie's refrigerator, but left me puzzled until after the coming tank-infantry assault. Only then did I understand that the water buffalo and their accomplices were probing to see if we had antitank mines on the road or in the wire. Of course, it would have been simpler for Giap's sappers to read our current standing operating procedures, which stated that no mines were to be allowed where there was a civilian populace. Please don't tell me Giap didn't have a copy of it!

The following day we were shelled periodically. Regardless, the skinning and butchering continued.

A full stomach solves many morale problems, but in Lang Vei's precarious situation that could only be a temporary relief. Because of the CIDG's desertion rate, the Mike Force had to be integrated into the camp defense perimeter. In addition, as an early warning system, one platoon of Mikes manned the outpost north of camp each night.

The first week of February another helicopter brought a surprise to the personnel of Detachment A-101. Spec. Four William McMurray got off the aircraft. Of course, we knew he had extended for six months, but we didn't understand why he'd returned to Lang Vei. It turned out to be a personal matter that I do not care to divulge. Even so, he was told that with Khe Sanh village gone, Lang Vei couldn't be far behind if the Nasty Viet Army wanted to pay the price. I finally arrived at the point of my argument: "Get your ass back on that chopper and you may live to be an old man!"

The young radio operator was unmoved; he knew I wouldn't order him to go. His team liked him, and God knew we needed radio operators; by then we were manning the net twenty-four hours a day. He was adamant, so he was given his old quarters, and his boss, Emanuel Phillips, did the rest.

That night McMurray was pulling radio watch when we received a message from a Special Forces radio station in Saigon. The illegal transmission was one I could have done without. But the SF operator and the sergeant first class who sent it meant well, I'm sure, and I forgave SFC Jason T. Woodworth in a day or two.

In essence the message said that Gil "Hambone" Hamilton, my 1965 teammate from Vung Tau days, had died due to wounds received on a Command & Control operation. That Hamilton had died in a Saigon hospital was no consolation, and I just didn't need that type of information just then. I thought about Hambone most of the lonely, dark night before I put the episode behind me, for a while anyway.

Across Highway Nine the 33rd Laotian Elephant Battalion was apparently content with their lot and the split A-detachment that assisted them. SFC Eugene Ashley called me one morning and explained his dilemma. "Specialist Young wants to go on a combat operation, Top. Can we allow that?"

I explained the situation one more time to Ashley. "The Lao are not allowed in our area of operations, Sarge. Let him go on a listening post with 'em. That's as far as they are to go out of camp. Copy, Gene?"

"Okay, Top. I'll do that, then. Come see us when you find time. Out!"

To say that Young didn't understand the circumstances would be understating the case. The only reason the Lao wanted him along was because he could communicate with American air if they made contact. Ashley got the young recruit off his case by allowing him to go to the listening post, which was not allowed any farther out than the line-of-sight to the camp. Ashley told me they would be near the base of the high ground near Highway Nine. But that mundane assignment was not exciting enough for the young rookie. Somehow, he talked the patrol leader into venturing down the interstate toward Khe Sanh village, but they didn't venture for long. As stated previously, Young didn't know his ass from Quang Tri.

The NVA ambush was short, violent, and received very little return fire from the bugging Lao. According to the survivors, Young was wounded and left for dead. Less their dead and captured comrades, the *tahans* returned to the old camp. Unknown to us at the time, Spec. Four John Young was now the NVA's problem. All we could do was rant and rave.

I visited Ashley the next day and told him what I thought about the erring recruit; which, thirty years later, I recall running something like: "If he is a POW, and if he is returned, I will press charges for disobeying a legal order. The asshole!" Young's stupidity had cost three or four lives and a loss of face with third-country nationals. The saga of John Young did not end until July 1973, five long years later. The only positive note from the disaster was that A-101 received no more requests from the split detachment to go out on operation with the 33rd Battalion.

On February 6, 1968, Dan Phillips and I started with Cookie's version of coffee, not something easily recommended to those accustomed to the real thing—then noodles and buffalo steak. Three or four mortar rounds from Laos had us scurrying to our alert position, but Phillips wanted some OJT on the 4.2-inch mortar, so he joined Tiroch, Hanna, and our new radio operator, Sergeant Dennis Thompson, on the big one.

When I reached the 81mm mortar pit, the firing had ceased. I wish they'd quit trying to hit that two-holer, I thought, peering through my binoculars at the kingdom. This time, however, peering paid off; I saw a wisp of smoke. I relayed the location, just a few hundred yards west of the Sepone, and the mortar crew fell to. They were right on the money, and no more rounds came from that location. Then it was back to the coffee shop, where Captain Willoughby was dining.

The tall team leader ate and reviewed the day's schedule. Major Hoadley joined us, and I knew he was late because Colonel Schungel, our control-team commander, would be flying in later that day to assume control of the dealings with the Lao colonel. Hoadley was happy to be going back to Da Nang, and had packed his meagers in his rucksack before dining on steak and noodles. Willoughby was happy if for no other reason than the fact that Hoadley was happy. The Mike Force and A-101 were happy because Schungel's arrival would also signal mail call.

I hadn't had a letter from my wife, or mother, in two months. If we paranoids didn't get mail over a long period, our phobias tended to worsen. Willoughby brought me back from my mental trip to Okinawa rather abruptly.

"Who are you sending on the outpost tonight with the Mike Force platoon, Top?"

"Sergeants Hanna and Lindewald, sir. It's their turn. Why?"

"Lately our operations are making contact if they even go out the gate. I think the Mike Force is getting as spooked as the Bru. Just going to the OP is bad news."

I grinned. "We have an operation scheduled for tomorrow, so let's don't tell them that."

Lieutenant Colonel Schungel arrived after pak time, and Major Hoadley loaded while we unloaded the mail. Schungel and Willoughby went to the TOC, and I assisted Dennis Thompson in processing the mail. We had set the head space on all CIDG A-6 machine guns prior to Schungel's arrival, so I departed for my hooch to read my two letters. Getting away from the Co Roc helicopter reception committee had gone through my mind also.

Nothing transpired while I digested the news from the two Okies. The kids in Kadena Circle, Okinawa, were healthy and growing like elephant grass. My mother relayed the skinny from Lawton, Oklahoma, and my far-flung relatives. By the time I had digested the letters, it was time for supper, and still we'd received no incoming from the base of the Co Roc mountain chain.

Because the colonel had brought some American and indigenous rations, Cookie went out of his way to excel. The food was well worth waiting for. I sat at the table with the colonel and my team leader rehashing our nightly plans while enjoying the fruits of Cookie's labor.

Schungel and Willoughby informed me that they would inspect the camp defenses at around 2000 hours. I told them that Minh and I had attended to the machine guns that morning. Then the Co Roc rocket brigade broke up the party. Schungel and Willoughby went to their alert positions in the TOC and I went to mine. We were not the only ones who had the suppertime ritual down pat.

The 4.2-inch mortar crew was working overtime while I lollygagged in the 81mm mortar pit with Phillips. He hauled some boxes up from the underground ammo dump below our boxed-in alert position while I checked the sandbags that formed our parapet and monitored the PRC-25 and HT-1 camp walkie-talkie. In my spare time I noted that our 4.2

mortar rounds had the range of the problem and were beginning to move left and right. Someone on the NVA side must have noted the movement also, and the rounds from Laos ceased as quickly as they had started. The overhead rounds that had been falling on the Khe Sanh Combat Base ceased as well. It was about 1945 hours. I looked over at the two-holer. It was still open for business. Two CIDG were wounded by the barrage, and Holt and Fragos were working them over in the medical bunker. Otherwise, due to the timing, the 152 rounds only caused some indigestion and that was about it. Jacksonville inquired about our status.

While Schungel and Willoughby made their inspection, I prepared for my visual guard duty. I would be the Eye from 2000 till 2400, or the eight till midnight shift. The radiomen, and there were always two on shift by then, checked the weather forecasts while I moved a field desk and other equipment on top of the concrete roof of the TOC; weather permitting, I wanted to pull my surveillance in the great outdoors.

I got the okay from the weatherman about the same time Willoughby and Schungel finished their inspection. Because the camp commander and Viet SF Lieutenant Quy had accompanied them, I was not too concerned about deficiencies. They reported that things went as well as could be expected, but that the desertions in line units had increased that day. My PRC-25 sounded off and I turned to it. SFC Kenneth Hanna called in a disturbing report.

"Okay, Kenneth, it's not your fault. The commander will be there shortly," I said in reply.

"Sir," I said, addressing Willoughby, "the Mike Force fired a few rounds at the outpost, then backed off. Hanna just informed me they are refusing to occupy the outpost. Lieutenant Longgrear is on the way to the scene."

"Tell Hanna and Lindewald that so are we," Schungel said. And they were gone, on the trail to the Mike Force position eight hundred yards north of camp on Highway Nine. I stood fast, though I didn't like a lieutenant colonel getting into our business. But as long as he didn't interfere with the way the camp was run, everything would be okay.

In twenty minutes I spotted the three officers heading up the highway into base camp. Longgrear turned left and went to his position on the perimeter with the Mikes. Looking rather stern, Schungel waved as he descended the stairwell of the TOC.

My team leader came by to keep me abreast, but SFC Kenneth Hanna had beat him to the punch. I'd answered his call before Willoughby stood next to me on the roof of the TOC.

"Roger, Spunky Six, continue to march. We'll be standing by. Spunky Hansen, out!" I replied.

"They're back on the job, huh, sir?" I asked.

"Yeah, Top, but I'm not too happy with 'em. They're really spooked. Reckon they know something we don't know?" Willoughby asked.

"Yeah, Captain, that's a possibility. Between the deserters, the Lao, and the Mikes, we're probably in deep shit. We'll just have to hang tough and see what happens."

Willoughby nodded and went down the stairs to the TOC as the starry night began to move toward the magic hour of midnight. Sgt. Nick Fragos arrived about ten minutes before my 2400 quitting time. Fragos had treated the wounded with SFC Holt and had only a one-hour nap before coming on duty again. I greeted him and turned the watch over. The night was clear and warm, so I figured he would stay upstairs, as I had. I told him who was on the outpost, U.S.-wise, and waved upon departure.

I descended into our bunker at 2400 sharp. Phillips awoke briefly, then rolled over and back to sleep. After unassing my web gear and M-16 rifle, I took off my jungle boots, massaged my feet, threw the socks in the corner, took a shot of water and lay on my sleeping bag otherwise fully clothed.

CHAPTER 17

The first 152mm heavy-artillery rounds hit Lang Vei Special Forces camp at forty-two minutes after midnight, February 7, 1968. The first barrage woke Phillips and me; the second goaded us into action. I put on my jungle boots and reached for my web gear before I spoke. "Take everything you need, Daniel, we may not be coming back down here!"

I slung extra M-16 ammunition bandoliers over my shoulders. The artillery rounds were still coming from neutral Laos when we climbed the stairs to our alert position, but the sights that greeted us immediately deflected our attention from the artillery prepping. Trip flares and illumination rounds from the Mike Force 81mm mortars lit the night. Red and green tracers crisscrossed from the southern perimeter near the road from Laos. Then a flare exposed a tank attempting to roll over the wire near the 104th Company. The Soviet PT-76 was accompanied by NVA foot soldiers to the rear and both sides. To this day I blame my reaction on stupidity rather than excitement, but I dropped two willie peter mortar rounds down the tube so quickly that I forgot to remove the bore-riding safety pins. Phillips didn't catch it and there was no time for a critique. Then I fired some HE rounds, correctly this time, before I adjusted the tube. The tank in question was out of action, but two more took its place. I had the tube almost vertical for the close-in personnel before we fired again. But even without our fire, the noise was deafening as artillery rounds were joined by mortars, also coming from our front.

After a few rounds using the adjustment, I believed us to be on target, and the NVA troops seemed to be thinning out. Not so the tanks. Then another one went up in flames just in front of SFC Holt's 106 recoilless rifle position. Holt was on our left, on the crest of the 104th Company's positions.

The return fire from the CIDG was dropping off noticeably as the tanks began to fire their 76mm main guns at the bunkers and communication trenches of the Bru, and at Holt as well. I grabbed my M-16 and emptied a magazine at the tank firing in Holt's direction while Phillips poured on 81mm rounds. I was on my third magazine before I realized I was pissing in the wind, and set the rifle back against the wall of the mortar pit. I glanced to my right and noted that Staff Sergeant Brooks was pouring on the A-6 machine gun fire from his sandbagged position on top of supply bunker number one. I dropped in another HE round. There was a blinding flash as an enemy round hit our parapet. That was all I remember from the knockdown round. Phillips fared no better than I. How long we lay on the floor of the pit is anyone's guess. I heard Dan groan before I reached up to feel my ears. My hand came back red. Phillips groaned again before I spoke. "My ears are bleeding, and I can't hear a thing, Dan."

"My eyes are bleeding and I can't see a thing!"

I think we had both been out of it longer than we thought. S.Sgt. Arthur Brooks leaped into the pit with a wet rag in each hand. When he began washing Phillips's face, we repeated our statements. Judging from his answer, Brooks had heard the remarks before.

"Don't worry about it, guys. One of you can see, and the other one can hear, so stick together. I've got to get back to my weapon before we get ate up." Then Brooks was gone and Dan and I heaved ourselves to our feet to find out that we were otherwise okay, physically, at least. My next statement probably made Phillips wonder about my mental condition.

"Shoulda wore our helmets, I guess."

I gazed across the fitfully illuminated perimeter toward

Laos as Phillips said, "Shit, Top, the CIDG stole those helmets a week ago." For some reason, that brought me back to Lang Vei, February 7, 0130 hours or so.

A Spooky flare ship (C-47 aircraft) was overhead by then, so visibility was a minor problem. Because of the situation changes and the time, perhaps Phillips and I had been out of it longer than I'd been led to believe. I responded by answering a plea from someone on the PRC-25 radio as Phillips went after more mortar rounds from below.

"Go ahead, Spunky Mike, this is Eight!" I said.

SFC Kenneth Hanna came back in an instant. "We need help, Eight. Lindewald's hit in the gut and four tanks are firing point-blank and a couple of platoons of doggies are eating our lunch. Copy?"

"Roger, Mike, we'll give you some 81 rounds. Fire your LAWs at 'em, Ken! Talk to Spunky Hansen or Spooky overhead. Good luck! Eight, out!"

Dan Phillips and I were shaking our heads as we trained the tube northward, toward the outpost and Hanna's Mikes. We'd fired all of the rounds on deck when the second nearby explosion put us down again. This time the roar came from near the TOC, where our vehicles and gasoline were dug in. As we got back up, the flames rose higher and higher by the TOC. After a few minutes they began to recede and Phillips went below for more mortar ammo while I stepped out of the pit to survey the area. What I witnessed didn't improve our sitrep any at all. Gasoline or diesel fuel was running from the small motor pool toward our position. I watched in shock as the fluid began rolling down the ammo bunker stairs that Phillips had just vacated. I shouted at Phillips to knock off the resupply and pool everything he wanted to take with him on his body. I didn't hear his question, but somehow I knew it before it came out of his mouth. Over the deafening sound effects, I managed to communicate.

"Step outside the pit and look for yourself," I said while reaching for the radio headset, and thank God I did. Someone, and I couldn't tell who, was calling for variable time-fuse artillery rounds on top of the camp!

I called Jacksonville and countermanded the request loud and clear. "Negative, Jacksonville, this is Spunky Eight. We still have people above ground at this location."

Jacksonville rogered my negatory, and because of the interruptions, and the gasoline filling the ammo dump beneath us, Phillips was becoming apprehensive. I slung the PRC-25 radio on my back and grabbed my M-16 rifle before we began a fast walk to the east side of the camp. I talked as fast as possible to Phillips. Upstairs, Spooky continued to color the night with flares. It had grown suddenly quiet, ominous, so I think Daniel Phillips heard what I had to say.

"I know people up and down this country and in Savannakhet, Laos, so whatever you do, stay with me until this is over." I was speaking of escape and evasion. The relative quiet had something to do with my mood change.

We spotted the mess hall and someone sitting astride the mounted .50 caliber machine gun on the sandbagged roofing. S.Sgt. Peter Tiroch shouted, "Over here, Top." But it was left to Phillips to tell me what he said. I placed the PRC-25 next to the living bunker closest to the team house before Phillips and I went to Tiroch's position. I told Tiroch I couldn't hear anything, so he spoke quickly and loudly to Dan and me. Some of the information I had gleaned from the radio earlier.

SFC Holt and his 106 recoilless rifle had made believers out of the NVA tank company in the 104th area. After dismantling two of the tanks, he ran out of antitank rounds and, with the CIDG's assistance, began firing flechette rounds at the foot soldiers. The thousands of tiny darts from the rounds were enough to discourage the enemy from mass travel in Holt's sector of the camp defenses.

Lieutenant Longgrear, John Early, and Thompson were in the 81 mortar pit on the southeast end of the camp in the 101st CIDG Company area when the call "We have tanks in the wire" went out on the PRC-25 to Khe Sanh Combat Base and all alert positions. They illuminated the area with flares from the 81 mortar, and saw a tank entering their perimeter hell-bent for their location. Longgrear reached for the LAWs, armed one, and fired. Nothing! Early handed Lieutenant Long-grear another, also armed and ready. Again the weapon failed to fire. Longgrear's third try finally sent an antitank round toward its target, but when the round struck the hull, it just rocketed into the milky darkness. Then the NVA tanker de-pressed the large main-turret weapon, a 76mm cannon, toward the pit. Longgrear immediately sent Thompson to Brandy's positions while he and Early headed for the tactical operations center.

At the command bunker Longgrear told Schungel about the misfires. They thought that he might have had a bad batch of ammunition, and so organized hunter-killer teams armed with the expendable rockets. But the killer teams' luck with the weapons would be no better than Longgrear's.

Captain Willoughby was having his problems with Jack-sonville, which, unknown to Willoughby, was also receiving suppressing 152 artillery fire from Co Roc. When the Marines finally believed the tank sightings were not a hoax, the artillery fired. Willoughby adjusted and the salvos stalled the attack momentarily, until the NVA moved inside the defenses of Lang Vei proper. The artillery went off the air and out of the conflict by 0230; the dispute over the VT (variable timing) fuses might have been a determining factor.

After the Mike Force outpost was overrun, the 102nd and 103rd companies repelled an NVA infantry assault on the north end of the camp, so the infantry backed off and tanks moved in, using their cannons to extinguish the resistance bunker by bunker. Despite spirited resistance by Thomp-son and Brandy, the eastern perimeter also collapsed. By that time, distinguishing friend from foe within the inner pe-rimeter was a problem. Known to be in the TOC command bunker at that time were Willoughby, Longgrear, Brooks, Emanuel Phillips, John Early, Nick Fragos, Spec. Four Dooms,

Robin Moore's camera catches the author on a break during an operation in the Central Highlands, SVN, 1965. (Author's collection)

Author (center) bids farewell to his Delta Project team-
mates in Nha Trang, SVN, in 1965. Standing, left to right:
Sergeants Dunbar, Don Hayakawa, Ray Slattery, author,
Ken Hain, Jack Smythe, Lloyd Fisher, and Larry
Dickinson. Kneeling: Frank Webber and "Small Man" Paul
Tracy. (Photo courtesy of Bill Freyser)

Special Forces trooper Garry Stamm returning from a chow run near Ban Don, SVN. His two Yard shotguns are unidentified. (Photo courtesy of Garry Stamm)

Lang Vei village in January 1968. (Photo courtesy of Paul R. Longgrear)

Mike Force patrol returns to Lang Vei after contact in 1968. (Author's collection)

A column of refugees, soldiers, and family members of the 33rd Royal Lao Battalion await movement orders on Highway 9 outside the Lang Vei Special Forces camp, January 24, 1968. Two days earlier the battalion had been hit by NVA tanks at Tchepone, Laos. (Photo courtesy of Paul R. Longgrear)

Mike Force platoon leader SFC Charles Lindewald takes a well-deserved break near Lang Vei in 1968. (Photo courtesy of Paul R. Longgrear)

The command bunker at Lang Vei before the attack. (Photo courtesy of Shelby Stanton)

This aerial photo taken after the February 7 attack on Lang Vei shows the devastation of the attack. (Photo courtesy of Shelby Stanton)

Detail of previous photo. Note the destroyed command bunker to the left front of the damaged PT-76 tank. (Photo courtesy of Shelby Stanton)

Author and family in a photo taken in Kadena Circle, Okinawa, 1967. To the right of the author are Jimmy, Kathy, and Hatsuko Craig. (Author's collection)

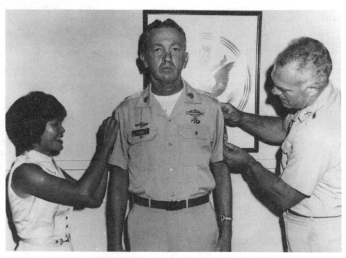

Colonel Russ McGraw and Hatsuko Craig pin command sergeant major stripes on the author at the Sergeants Major Academy, 1975. (Author's collection)

and Moreland. The South Vietnamese camp commander Quy, Team Sergeant Minh, an interpreter, and some CIDG were also there.

Staff Sergeant Tiroch and his crew fired the 4.2 mortar until the defenses collapsed, then joined the killer teams in the assault against the tanks with the useless LAWs. For some reason, they did not go to the TOC when the mission was over.

Using its spotlight to check out the terrain, a tank approached the TOC. The armor got the attention of three Americans remaining aboveground and within the inner perimeter. The spotlight hit the team house and its next victims at the same time we opened fire. If we did nothing else, at least we put out the spotlight. Tiroch swung the .50 caliber around and I assisted with the ammunition belts. Phillips was still firing at the tank with his rifle when we opened fire with the heavy caliber. The PT-76 returned fire with its machine guns, but fortunately its return fire was way off the mark.

Tiroch and the .50s armor-piecing rounds must have done something right; smoke came from the undercarriage of the PT-76. We ceased fire, as did Phillips. Then the tank's crew opened the hatch and began to climb out. The first person out was a female, but we blew her and the rest of the crew away.

Another PT-76 tank, its machine guns blazing, passed our victims before stopping on top of the TOC. Tiroch screamed for a LAW. I obliged and armed it before passing him the tube. But we had no better luck than the tank-killer teams before us; the LAW misfired when Tiroch squeezed the trigger. Pete rearmed it and tried again. No joy. Phillips handed Tiroch the last LAW on the mess hall roof. Phillips and I held our breath as Tiroch squeezed the detonator. Nothing. Tiroch threw the damn thing off the roof onto the road below. As the tank turned its attention to us, we switched back to the .50, expending a belt of ammo before the tank's lowered cannon roared. How the round missed us, I'll never know, but the NVA got the point across; we immediately vacated the team house's upper structure. The retreat was short-lived; we halted at the corner of the team house and knelt out of sight of the enemy armor. I told Tiroch we would be right back. Carrying the PRC-25 radio, Phillips and I ran to the nearby living bunker. The sound of aircraft high above the battle scenes at least stirred the inside of my aching head. I told Phillips my plan before I descended the bunker staircase with the PRC-25.

"Let me talk to 'em, we might get 'em down," I said. "Surely, they have something that will stop that tank. Stay here, Dan, I'll be right back." I was down in the living quarters' relative quietness before Phillips could agree or disagree. The Forward Air Controller came up on the emergency frequency only after I identified myself.

Yes, the fighter-bombers had napalm, cluster bomb units, general-purpose bombs, and small arms such as 20mm cannons. Identifying friend and foe within the inner perimeter had thus far precluded targets inside the camp. I gave him the location of our nemesis on top of the TOC before informing him that we would move and then get back to him.

When I came upstairs, I found myself alone. Phillips was nowhere to be seen. I was stumped, but hoped he was with Tiroch by the team house. I was still searching for Phillips when I spotted a line of people hell-bent for the emergency medical bunker. I leaned into the top of the bunker mound and emptied a magazine without receiving any return fire. As the group of soldiers cleared my line of sight, I ceased fire and changed magazines. Bag, baggage, and PRC-25, I headed at a run for Tiroch's location near the team house. He was still watching the tanks from his perch on the team house when I asked him where Phillips was.

"I thought he was with you, Top," Tiroch said. "And who in the hell were you firing at?"

I told him what I knew about Phillips's disappearance but could not identify who I was firing at; not positively, anyway. My being unable to answer the last inquiry convinced both of us we should move. We were not alone in that thought. About five individuals ran from the vicinity of the tanks to the eastern perimeter wire. Unfortunately, a flare from Spooky pinpointed them, and the tanks on or near the TOC homed in on them with their machine guns. A third tank near Highway Nine joined in, and what was left of the five people began a low crawl under the barbed wire that defined the inner perimeter. When the flares died out, so did the interdicting fire. Thanks to the defective LAWs, there was no doubt who was in charge of the inner perimeter.

"We need to get off this damn hill so we can bring smoke on those assholes," I said. "Besides, the tanks and their infantry are the only ones we can identify for sure."

"You're not waiting on me, Top," Tiroch said. "When this flare dies out, let's cut." We did just that.

We were across the road and almost to the wire when another flare from Spooky destroyed the darkness. We hit the ground and began our own low crawl when both tanks opened up with their machine guns. When the tracers came close, we froze and waited until the flare died out, then we began again. The PRC-25 on my back wasn't doing much for my low profile, but that didn't dawn on me at the time. Thoughts of Phillips's whereabouts grew more tenuous each time we played hide-and-seek with those machine gun tracers. What seemed like forever ended a few yards past that last double-apron fence at the dry creek bed. Once we reached the slight depression, the firing from the TOC ceased as well.

Tiroch and I were a few feet apart, on our bellies, facing north, and were not deceived by the noise to our front and sides. Several CIDG eased next to us and no acknowledgment was necessary. I quietly took the thousand-pound radio off my back while thoughts of Phillips ran through my mind. Four or five helmeted men approached to our front. Their steel helmets gave them away, and our M-16s were joined by the carbines of the CIDG. The noise behind the dead men prompted each of us to empty a full magazine before we ceased fire. Tiroch and I glanced at each other and waited for some return fire or a flare, but the CIDG were not in a patient mood and streaked toward the village of Lang Vei. During their move, they received no fire from our front.

We waited a few more minutes before I whispered into the radio. FAC came up and we told him the tanks inside the perimeter were fair game unless someone told him otherwise. By then it was approximately 0300 hours and activity had not ceased during our trek, but we paid little attention to the flares and tracers that we heard and saw from Lang Vei.

The PT-76s standing by the TOC fired into the command bunker door and seriously wounded Specialist Four Moreland. John Early and Paul Longgrear were knocked down by the blast also.

Schungel and Wilkins were still aboveground, and fled to the team house after the tank blasted the TOC entrance. They were on the road side of the building when a squad of NVA armed with satchel charges contested their presence. Despite their overcoming the squad with small arms and grenades, a satchel charge wounded Schungel in the right leg. Wilkins assisted Schungel to the dispensary, where they hid under the wooden flooring until daylight. Aboveground activity for A-101 ceased. It was time for the Air Force to do its number.

With white phosphorous, FAC marked the three tanks that were then firing into the TOC. From above the scattered clouds a twin-jet B-57 medium bomber dropped four general-purpose bombs at the targets. FAC reported the tanks destroyed and many secondary explosions.

With the night half over, Captain Willoughby requested the Marines to activate the contingency plan to relieve A-101 at Lang Vei. But the Marines refused. When Special Forces units in-country heard the denial, tempers flared throughout South Vietnam. But to no avail. When Tiroch and I heard this, my memory went back to my conversation with Major Quamo, but it didn't linger long on the subject because of the unruly guests to our front. While A-teams from I Corps were calling Da Nang to offer their assistance, Quamo's words became louder and louder. But the ring of steel got my mind back in place.

The NVA to our front had either heard the radio or were guessing at our location, because they began laying down a salvo in our direction. Because they were not as low as we were in the creek bed, the rounds were a foot or more over our heads. We didn't return fire but I did turn the communication channel back on. It seemed to me time to break that damn ring of steel, or try anyway. I explained our situation to FAC and he offered us what he had.

The key to using the cluster bomb units in close-in fighting is dropping them a little closer to the enemy side than to the friendly. Once the CBUs are released, they explode when they near the earth. Small lead pellets are then scattered by the explosion and descend at a high rate of speed. The only drawback is that the pellets cannot differentiate between friend and foe. Before I gave him the go-ahead, I looked at my pardner for approval or no. He nodded then said, "What the hell have we got to lose?"

The pilot confirmed and I whispered to Tiroch, "Two passes and it'll be over."

The first run by the Skyraiders was right on the button; we received no stray pellets, but screams and moans could be heard to our front. When the bombs went off on the second pass, I must have screamed the loudest. That, or I couldn't hear anyone else. A couple of pellets hit me in the ass and two struck my back near the right shoulder blade. But the one that did the damage, I felt the least.

A pellet, or pellets, hit the leather heel of my jungle boot, forcing my foot into the ground. It felt like I'd sprained my ankle, but it would be a while before I could test it out. Because of my own pain, I forgot about the man on my right. When I finally remembered him, Tiroch showed me his arm, penetration location, blood, and all. He could move his arms and I was having no trouble with mine, so the Air Force did good. The moaning and noise to our front slowly died out before the dawn arrived. We were in good shape in comparison to the crowded command bunker and some of our comrades.

SFC Gene Ashley, the head enlisted man at old Lang Vei, was heard from. He had finally convinced Lieutenant Colonel Bao to help his comrades in the command bunker. After the Marines' refusal and against his better judgment, Bao allowed two platoons to accompany Gene. After laying on two air strikes to cover their advance, Ashley notified Willoughby of the rescue attempt.

As the motley crew neared the eastern perimeter and Company 104's area, the NVA opened fire with machine guns, and the elephant soldiers broke and ran. By the time Ashley had assembled volunteers, the NVA mortar shells began to drop around them. The uproar could be heard in the command structure.

With daylight fast approaching, the NVA renewed their efforts to dislodge the survivors in the TOC. When satchel charges failed to dislodge them, the NVA threw tear gas and thermite grenades down the holes made by the explosives. Smoke from the burning of classified documents, thermite grenades, and tear gas, caused consternation and a search for fresh air. When all else failed, wet surgical dressing brought a little relief. Then a demand for surrender came from above in Vietnamese. The interpreter handled the translation for those who needed it: "We are going to destroy the bunker. Give up now and no one will be harmed."

While the scared, exhausted men stared at the door, one American answered the request. *"Fuck you!"*

To the surprise of the U.S., the Viet SF commander began to confer with his subordinates, and they agreed on a different approach. He forced the door open and led his soldiers up the stairs. One of the eight Americans immediately bolted the door shut.

The execution of the surrendering Vietnamese and CIDG was testified to by enemy gunfire just outside the bunker. So much for the Geneva Convention. Another surrender demand was preceded by a shower of grenades down the staircase. Despite being short one interpreter, the Special Forces Troops needed no translation. At 0700 the remaining Americans readied their ammo and equipment for the final charge.

At first light Tiroch and I tested our wounded limbs. We received no fire as we left the creek bed and headed back through the wire toward the team house. We were joined by four or five CIDG. Though my ass ached a tad, I was limping noticeably from the sprain, if indeed that's all it was. If so, it was the worst one I had ever suffered, but only a minor inconvenience considering the overall situation. We were through the wire and approaching the road before automatic weapons' fire sought us out from the vicinity of the command bunker. We hit the deck but could not spot our assailants from the low crawl position. After a minute or so we rose again and veered right, away from the TOC. We made it to the road when two GIs in camouflage fatigues smiled broadly and grabbed our hands. Wilkins and Schungel didn't look any better off than we did, maybe worse.

Lieutenant Colonel Schungel's right leg wound was missing a piece of meat and he was limping as badly as I was. "Come on, sir," I said, "let's move down the road to the old camp. You need that leg looked after!" With Wilkins and Tiroch following, we had limped down to the foot of the old camp before we received mortar fire. We hit the ditch on the side of the road and waited it out. When it let up, a jeep came from old Lang Vei and took Wilkins and Schungel to the old camp medics, Allen and Johnson. Tiroch and I turned toward our camp and ran into Ashley's Laotian troops, who were by then in full retreat. We slowed 'em down until Ashley came raging down the hill on the south side of camp.

Due to our pain and exhaustion, Tiroch and I did not want to go with Ashley but volunteered to assist in another assault on the bunker. Our five CIDG didn't have much choice but to follow suit, and the Lao also agreed. According to Ashley, this would be the third attempt.

Reaching the top of the dogleg hill, we formed a skirmish line facing the objective. It was not lost on me that the Lao were lagging behind, if only a yard or so. With Joel Johnson on one end and Tiroch on the other, Ashley and I urged our warriors forward from the center of the line. Our assault started well, but once we received small arms fire, the charge sagged. We returned matching fire, to make the NVA keep their heads down, and slowed our advance. We were edging closer when the enemy machine gun halted our progress. I went to one knee but could not locate the weapon. After firing some semiautomatic return fire, I looked to my sides and was immediately brought to my senses: only the Americans were returning fire; our skirmish line had broken and run. I motioned that we should cover each other as we backed off, too. Before reaching the assembly area, we began to receive mortar fire once again. We waited it out and conferred after it ceased. Most of the rounds went over our low profiles into or near the old Lang Vei campsite.

The platoon leader counted heads. Ashley's recruits were down to roughly a platoon. Through an interpreter, Ashley was urging one more try. Tiroch and Johnson asked me my opinion, and I said, "We've got to get close enough to knock out that machine gun or we'll never get there!"

I was mildly surprised when the Lao *tahans* agreed to give it one more go. Before we started, Tiroch asked me if the ankle was going to hold up. I shrugged, and off we went.

Once again we did fine until the machine gun got into our ranks. This time my ankle gave way and I went down in a heap, but my head came up and I tried to spot the automatic weapon. I thought I saw it and laid some M-16 rounds on the location. Tiroch and Johnson tried to get me on my feet when I ceased firing. "They're bugging, Top, let's go!"

With some assistance, I got painfully to my feet; the ankle had run its course, as had my confidence in the Laotians. They just weren't ready to go that extra yard. Tiroch helped me back to the assembly area, where I sat down, disgusted. My part of this war was about over. I knew in my mind that American air power was going to have to get the prisoners out of jail.

I was loaded with the wounded Lao and taken to the med bunker. There, I conferred with Sgt. Richard Allen concerning the ankle. The only way to know if it was broken would be to X-ray it, which, of course, was not possible there. Allen could tape it for the time being. The boot was doing the same thing the tape would do, but if I took it off, I'd never be able to get it back on. He put some antiseptic on my CBU holes, and I could continue to march.

The bunker that Schungel and Bao were using as a TOC was my next destination. The lieutenant colonel was glad to see me again and asked me my opinion of the rescue operation. I did not present what he wanted to hear, but he nodded in acknowledgment. I suggested having the aircraft make live runs at the camp until the NVA were afraid to stick their heads up, then about the fourth run should be a dry one, enabling the group in the TOC to make a break to safety. He said he would suggest that to Willoughby if Ashley's final attempt didn't pan out. Until then I didn't know that Ashley had talked the Laotians into another attempt.

"If you need me, sir, I'll be at the dispensary with Allen," I said. Ashley had his people ready to try again by the time I hobbled the few yards to the medical bunker to monitor the latest charge.

Things started out as before, but Spec. Four Joel Johnson had scrounged a 57mm recoilless rifle and managed to knock out the machine gun near the bunker. Then the Lao surged forward into the trenches before Ashley received a chest wound. Seeing the black soldier go down, the NVA took heart and drove the Lao into a full retreat once again. It was the closest the Lao had come to success, but it just wasn't to be. The fifth and last attempt had failed.

Tiroch and Johnson, who'd accompanied the charge, saw to

it that Ashley made it back to Highway Nine, where a jeep was waiting. They loaded Ashley on the jeep and headed for the dispensary but we began receiving mortar fire once again at the old camp. Just inside the wire, a round shattered the jeep, killing Ashley and wounding Johnson. I checked Ashley when he was brought to the dispensary, and he was dead. Still on the stretcher that had brought him out, he was unloaded and placed near the medical bunker. The man had given his all for his teammates, and you can't do any better than that.

The seven still-conscious men in the bunker were all wounded and injured. They sensed it was now or never and prepared for the breakout while Willoughby and Schungel were laying on the plans for their relief from the eighteen-hour ordeal. The overhead jet aircraft would make three "hot" runs, giving the NVA reasons to keep their heads down. After that the dry runs would follow, hopefully causing the NVA to continue keeping their heads down while they fled the scene. The group had to make one painful decision that no one relished. Moreland would be left behind because of his condition as well as theirs.

After the third hot run by the jets, they unbolted the door, climbed over the dead bodies in the staircase and filed upstairs. The enemy fire they had expected failed to materialize and they made good time in the late afternoon sun across the open ground to the east. Lieutenant Quy, the Vietnamese Special Forces officer from the old camp, met them in a jeep. They loaded and sped back to the old camp.

Schungel ordered Allen and me to organize the people in the medical bunker for evacuation. We agreed, but didn't know what the hell he was thinking about. We had to monitor our PRC-25 to find out.

Because of the battle at Hue, Westmoreland was now in Da Nang. He had ordered the Marines to provide choppers to extract the survivors of Lang Vei. The plan that evolved from the order was a simple one. FOB-3 would use a small force of Special Forces people, of course, to secure the drop zone at old Lang Vei. A large CH-46 Marine helicopter would land and take the survivors to Khe Sanh's medical bunker. While Major Quamo was getting the coordination organized, First Lieutenant Todd was finally heard from.

The engineer officer had played possum in the emergency medical bunker, and after the breakout of the TOC survivors, made his dash for freedom. He paused at the TOC, then made his way down the jumbled stairs. He was almost overcome by the stench of blood and was about to leave when he spotted Moreland. Only after determining that the young medic was dead did he sprint up the stairs, hell-bent for the open ground and the eastern perimeter. He received small arms fire at the wire but outsprinted it to the old camp.

Major Quamo, true to a promise that he made a few weeks before, was over the old camp in a UH-1B Command & Control helicopter. Three Marine CH-46 troop carriers circled, waiting for Quamo to land.

Schungel and the survivors of the TOC were loaded on the C&C ship while we waited on the CH-46s. When they landed, well-armed FOB-3 people ran off the choppers and began a semblance of a protective perimeter. I knew most of the personnel, and when I heard, "Hi Bill," I smiled for the first time in a while. Then they helped load us on the large transports. In only minutes we landed at the Khe Sanh Combat Base and were escorted to a very busy medical bunker. The physical battle for Lang Vei was over, but for many of us the mental portion would go on forever.

CHAPTER 18

As I've said before, the first use of armor in the Vietnam war by the North Vietnamese Army did not go unnoted. Down through the years since that long night and day of February 7, 1968, a number of books have appeared on the subject. There are three that I think are worth reading.

Major David B. Stockwell's *Tanks in the Wire*, by a GI still on active duty, explores not only the tactics but also the motives and personnel involved. The lack of unity between Lang Vei and the Khe Sanh Combat Base is given a hard stare.

The End of the Line: The Siege of Khe Sanh, by Robert Pisor, presents a very different slant, in my opinion, possibly because it is only a segment of his overall subject matter.

Valley of Decision, by Ray W. Stubbe and John Prados, also relates Lang Vei to the big picture. I might add that I met Stubbe, a Navy chaplain, at Lang Vei after the fall of Khe Sanh village. Chaplain Stubbe not only gave us his blessings but helped us recover one of our many airdrops. I still communicate with the chaplain, who has retired from the military but is still active in his ministry.

The question I would like to answer that the other authors cannot is: What does a participant of the conflict think about the tank-infantry attack after two decades? Keep in mind while I'm rambling that not a day has gone by that I haven't thought about it. Did the North Vietnamese Army win the battle? Yes; they accomplished their objectives. They opened Highway Nine in order to supply their Tet Offensive. The shock effect of even the thin-skinned armor of the PT-76 tank got the job done. The NVA were willing to pay the price.

What about the paranoids of A-101 and the Mike Force? Down through the years I've kept track of the personnel, twenty-five to be exact, the best I could. I have had contact with them or their relatives; and some of them I have not heard from or about. I've read about some of them in books and in the Special Forces quarterly magazine, *The Drop*. What might surprise everyone is that fifteen of them are still alive and kicking, as far as I can ascertain. What these people accomplished was apparently recognized by the Navy, or Marine Corps. As a unit, we at A-101 were awarded the Naval Presidential Unit Award (PUC) for actions at Lang Vei. With this award and the personal commendations, we became one of the most decorated small units ever in the United States Armed Forces.

Sergeant First Class Eugene Ashley, medic, was killed in action. SFC Ashley used his own initiative to obtain a relief force from the Lao 33rd Elephant Battalion. He mounted five attacks on the NVA in an attempt to free our teammates in the command bunker. Eugene Ashley was awarded the nation's highest award for valor, and the Purple Heart for wounds received in action. Unfortunately, both the Medal of Honor and Purple Heart were awarded posthumously. Ashley was known as a soldier's soldier.

Lieutenant Colonel Daniel F. Schungel, the commander of Company C, 5th SF Group (Abn), was awarded the Distinguished Service Cross for Gallantry in Action and the Purple Heart for wounds received at Lang Vei. A Special Forces team sergeant's dream, he told the team leaders, "The team sergeant runs the team and you command it." Schungel retired a brigadier general and died a few years later.

First Lieutenant Paul R. Longgrear, the Mike Force commander, was a first-rate soldier who later served another tour in Vietnam. I have corresponded with Mr. Longgrear, who became a minister in Georgia. He was awarded the Silver Star,

Vietnamese Cross of Gallantry, and the Purple Heart for wounds received in action. In my mind, he is still the picture of the all-American boy.

Captain Frank C. Willoughby, team leader of A-101, was older than most captains. He was the kind of infantry officer who thought before he spoke or acted. He was awarded the Silver Star, the Vietnamese Cross of Gallantry, and the Purple Heart. I had no contact with the captain after Lang Vei.

First Lieutenant Miles Wilkins, executive officer of A-101, came to Lang Vei an inexperienced young officer and departed a combatwise veteran. He was awarded the Purple Heart for wounds received in action. His other awards are unknown, as are his whereabouts.

First Lieutenant Thomas E. Todd, engineer officer, who was at the old camp to survey the airstrip, received the Purple Heart for wounds received in action. Todd is said to have stayed on active duty, but I have no other information on him.

Sergeant First Class William T. Craig, team sergeant, was awarded the Silver Star, Vietnamese Cross of Gallantry with Palm, and the Purple Heart. Craig retired at Fort Bliss, Texas, as a command sergeant major on November 1, 1976, with twenty-six years' service.

Sergeant Richard H. Allen, medic, assisted in the assaults to rescue the people trapped in the TOC. He also manned the medical bunker at old Lang Vei, and assisted in the final evacuation. He was awarded the Bronze Star with V device for valor, and the Purple Heart.

Specialist Four Joel Johnson, medic, was wounded in action. He also assisted in SFC Ashley's assaults. Although badly wounded, he helped in the evacuation efforts at old Lang Vei. He was awarded the Bronze Star with V device, and the Purple Heart.

Staff Sergeant Peter Tiroch, our intelligence specialist and heavy weapons leader, stayed at the 4.2-inch mortar tube until the ammo was exhausted. I watched as he knocked out one tank with the .50 caliber machine gun. He was awarded the

Silver Star, Cross of Gallantry, Bronze Award, and the Purple Heart. The last I heard of Tiroch, he was a major on active duty. A good man to have on your side when things get rowdy.

Staff Sergeant Emanuel E. Phillips, radio operator, made A-101's commo as good as any in I Corps. Trapped in the TOC until the breakout, he was awarded the Vietnamese Cross of Gallantry, Bronze Award, and the Purple Heart. In 1969 I heard through the notorious rumor mill that Phillips was shot and killed at Fort Bragg, North Carolina. After what he'd been through, it didn't seem fair.

Staff Sergeant Arthur Brooks, light weapons leader, brought me and Phillips out of it when we were knocked goofy in the 81mm mortar pit. When he ran out of ammo, and the inner perimeter was overrun, he went to the command bunker. He was awarded the Vietnamese Cross of Gallantry and the Purple Heart. Brooks and I met in a club in Bien Hoa in 1971 and we swapped tales for a spell. A career soldier, and a damn good one.

Sergeant Nickolas Fragos, medic, relieved me on watch the night of the assault and did a helluva job. He was also later trapped in the command bunker until the breakout. He was awarded the Purple Heart for wounds received in action. Fragos got out of the Army and called me in 1972 at Fort Sill, Oklahoma. He was in medical school then, where I wanted him to be. The next thing I knew he was working for the Drug Enforcement Agency and was killed in a building collapse in Miami, Florida, in the seventies. What a waste! The narcs and the country lost a good man.

Specialist Four Franklin H. Dooms, radio operator, was on radio watch when the assault on Lang Vei began. He was awarded the Purple Heart for wounds received in the action. Dooms later came to his senses and became a career soldier, a lifer. I served with him a few years later in the 1st SF Group (Abn) on Okinawa. The last I heard of him, he was a sergeant major in the 10th Special Forces at Fort Devens, Massachusetts. A hardworking, dedicated individual.

Sergeant John Early, platoon leader, Mike Force, was trapped in the command bunker after being seriously wounded. He later received the Purple Heart for his wounds. He returned to civilian life and became a writer and editor on the staff of *Soldier of Fortune*.

Staff Sergeant Earl Burke, weapons man, wounded in action, was on the 4.2-inch mortar until he and Tiroch ran out of ammo. When the inner primeter was overrun by tanks, he evaded toward old Lang Vei and was never seen alive again. His body was recovered April 13 by the 1st Cavalry near Highway Nine. Awarded the Purple Heart posthumously. A great soldier and teammate.

Prisoners of War

Sergeant First Class Harvey G. Brande, platoon leader, Mike Force. After instructing the NVA on January 30, 1968, in the science of fire and maneuver and in the proper use of aircraft support, things went downhill for this great soldier. Brande was captured with Thompson by the NVA during the battle of Lang Vei. The two escaped on February 18, but due to a previous injury, Brande couldn't keep up and ordered Thompson to go on alone. Thompson refused. They were both recaptured and were not released until 1973. Brande was awarded the Silver Star for gallantry and the Purple Heart for wounds received at Lang Vei. I have not met Brande since Lang Vei, but my informants tell me he is living in San Antonio, Texas.

Staff Sergeant Dennis L. Thompson, radio operator, was captured with Harvey Brande during the assault. Thompson's refusal to leave Brande on February 18 says all that needs to be said about his character. Upon repatriation in 1973, Thompson was awarded the Silver Star for gallantry and the Purple Heart for wounds received at Lang Vei. While attending the Sergeants Major Academy in 1974, Thompson and his wife came to my quarters at Fort Bliss, Texas, for a light lunch and heavy conversation. He looked terrific and did not seem embittered over the hand that fate dealt him. After his gradua-tion, I lost contact with the master sergeant E8. Being in a North Vietnamese jailhouse for five years apparently did not slow down this hard-charging soldier.

Specialist Four William G. McMurray, radio operator, had been at Lang Vei, both old and new, longer than anyone else who participated in the showdown. Regardless of his rank and youth, he was a reliable, combatwise soldier. He was wounded at the start of the fray and I never saw him again. To my great surprise, years later he came out on the list as a prisoner of war. He was released in 1973 from North Vietnam. I have had no luck in contacting the young man, despite numerous attempts. His awards and decorations are unknown but the Purple Heart can be attested to by the members of Detachment A-101.

Specialist Four John Young, weapons man, old Lang Vei, was seriously wounded before his capture on or about Janu-ary 30, 1968. Once he recovered from his leg wounds and was moved North, he screwed up again. He became a card-carrying advocate of the five-man "Peace Committee." Charged with misconduct after their release, these peaceniks got off the hook when charges were dismissed on July 3, 1973. The Army did something right in Young's case by bar-ring him from reenlistment. His awards and decorations are unknown.

Missing in Action

Sergeant First Class James Holt, medic, knocked out the first tank in the assault of Lang Vei. The last time I saw Holt, he had gone after ammunition for his 106 recoilless rifle. When we had to leave the mortar pit, the road from Lang Troi was awash in tanks and NVA corpses. I give Holt the credit for that. An outstanding medic and a helluva combat soldier. His awards and decorations are unknown.

Sergeant First Class Kenneth Hanna, light weapons leader, and SFC Lindewald were on the outpost manned by the Mike Force when it was overrun early in the conflict. The last I heard from Hanna was reported in the last chapter. To me, Kenneth Hanna was the type of person you want to be in the Army with.

SFC Charles Lindewald, Mike Force platoon leader, and I had served together on Okinawa. He was one of the most knowledgeable weapons men, light or heavy, in Special Forces. Early in the fray, he suffered a stomach wound on the outpost with Hanna and the Mike Force. Due to his status, his awards and decorations are unknown.

In early 1969 I was in Company C, 1st SF Group (Abn), and told to report to the NCO Club annex at Camp Kue, Okinawa, to meet Lindewald's brother. Despite not being accustomed to being in drinking establishments during duty hours, I complied. When I saw him seated at a table of the small annex, I thought he was Charley. Except for being a few years younger, he had me fooled. After introducing myself, I told what little I knew about the situation on the Mike Force outpost. Mr. Lindewald wanted to know if I thought his brother might still be alive. I told him that it was most likely that Charley had died from his stomach wound or resulting infection.

Specialist Four James L. "Wes" Moreland, the Mike Force medic, was also trapped in the command bunker at Lang Vei. He received a serious head wound early in the fray and became delirious. He was administered a painkiller that knocked him unconscious. He was left for dead in the bunker during the breakout on February 7, 1968. Although First Lieutenant Todd found him later and reported that Moreland had died, his corpse is apparently still on location and he is carried as MIA. Why his body has not been recovered and turned over to the U.S., I do not know. His awards and decorations are unknown.

Sergeant Dan Phillips, demo man and engineer, was a terrific person who wanted to get the job done. Because of his MIA status, his awards and decorations are unknown. I can attest to his having earned the Purple Heart. Godspeed, Daniel! I communicate with his mother in Florida and his cousin, William R. Phillips, from Milton, Pennsylvania. Bill Phillips had told me, and the press, that there is a possibility that Dan is still alive. Given the half-assed effort to recover the MIAs, I certainly can't refute his beliefs.

These are the men who celebrated Tet in 1968 at that lonely outpost near the Lao border. They will live in the history books forever.

CHAPTER 19

The Khe Sanh dispensary was near the main runway on a perforated-steel-plank apron and helicopter landing pad. When the large helicopters landed, the naval medics who attempted to remove our injured were assisted by Special Forces medical personnel from Da Nang. I helped remove all personnel from my transportation before I slowly followed the flood to the medical bunker. To my surprise, the bunker was fortified with logs and sandbags. The war had finally begun to penetrate the command of Khe Sanh Combat Base.

Inside the structure, corpsmen and SF medics helped the doctors, who were swamped. Among the SF people was I Corps SF Sergeant Major Hodge and a few other personnel from the C-detachment. Major Sky, my old friend and the former 1st SF Group (Okinawa) surgeon, was in the middle of the building working on a patient. I backed up against the wall of the madhouse so no one would bump into me. The wounded, still on stretchers, were all over the center of the med bunker. Medical personnel began moving people out of the shop before I woke up. Sergeant Major Hodge brought me out of it.

"Are you hurt, Bill?" he asked.

"Yeah, Top!" I said. "My ass and back have shrapnel and CBUs embedded, plus my ankle is sprained or something."

A doctor left Hodge's side and looked at my bloody shirt and pants. He said, "Goddamn, get him on the C-130 also, Top!" Hodge obliged.

We were outside before I finally realized they were loading patients for Da Nang. A jeep with two stretchers pulled up and the driver relieved Hodge of his charge. The next thing I knew, I was on a C-130 Hercules cargo aircraft that was sitting on the main runway. The aircraft was jammed with Army and Marine Corps stretcher and ambulatory patients. I found a seat near the downed rear ramp and gently sat on the canvas seating, but I had to maneuver my buttocks and the CBU fragments before I could allow my full weight to rest on the seat.

I vaguely heard the four turboprop engines revving up when Major Sky and another doctor brought a stretcher case aboard. As I watched them, mortars or artillery from Co Roc began seeking out the C-130. Still we did not move.

The stretcher case was a Marine, about six-foot-two, with no fatigue jacket on. He was easily the best built man I'd ever seen, though there was no flesh on his exposed stomach. I was watching the bloody stomach muscles go in and out when the young Marine next to me got my attention. I turned to my left in order to hear what the young man was about to say. I made it out, I think. "If they don't get this damn aircraft off the ground, we've all had the meat!"

I dully nodded in agreement while high-angle fire crept closer and closer. After what seemed like ages, the pilot and the tower finally agreed and the C-130 began to edge toward the main strip. The sun died away as the aircraft gained ground speed and we were airborne. The big Marine on the stretcher greeted the darkened skies with what might have been his last breath.

Despite not having slept for about thirty-five hours, I stayed awake and watched Major Sky and the Navy doctor attempt to save the Marine's life. They took turns administering mouth-to-mouth until the plane began its descent. I couldn't believe it when Sky covered him head to foot with a GI blanket. A shame and a waste!

The rear ramp of the aircraft was lowered and the two side

doors opened to the darkness. Naval medical personnel were immediately all over the compartment. Still, I sat. After the stretcher cases and the dead Marine were off-loaded, I tested my ankle again. My boot was holding the foot together so I took a few steps toward the slanted ramp to the airstrip apron. Before I covered the distance to the cement, my limp was worse and I wished I had some support.

I made a half right and eyed my destination. The large, three-story, modern Da Nang Naval Hospital lighted the otherwise dark area. Mortar and artillery came to mind as I passed under the foyer canopy that fronted the entrance. I was totally beat when I leaned on the counter and did the usual paperwork for a young sailor. It was quick for a change, and he nodded for me to be seated in the lobby behind his throne. "You'll be called shortly."

I found a large cushion support and lowered my body into it, maneuvering around the holes in my posterior and back. I glanced down at my filthy cammies and shook my head. Food and the image of a large bed were flashing across my screen when the sailor boy sounded off. "Sergeant Craig!"

I was briskly escorted down a hall and into a small room with a movable screen, a bed, and a frowning physician dressed in the standard white smocks. In short order the doctor removed the CBUs from my rear end. He said the shrapnel in my back would have to wait. Then he handed me over to an orderly, for a wheelchair visit to the X-ray department.

I got in a wheelchair, and John, the orderly, rolled me down a few doors then knocked. Just before he left, the corpsman said, "He'll fix you up and I'll be back by then." He pointed out the latrine as he was leaving.

While I was waiting for my photos, S.Sgt. Arthur Brooks came grinning down the hall. His black skin and white, shining teeth made it easy to spot him. He hugged me by the shoulders and I pressed his hand. His next few remarks did not surprise me, complaining about ol' Doc Sadist, but he finally said what was on his mind. "Sonofabitch, I'm a starving Marvin." We had not eaten lately.

"Shit," I said, "let's look around. You're the first one who brought up the subject." Down the hallway I saw what I think Brooks had seen before he'd seen me. The smooth-talking bastard. The good Lord was still looking out for us.

Two trays of steaming-hot food were sitting on a cart outside a room; officers, I guessed. It was just too easy. "Bring 'em both to the shithouse," I said, motoring my chair the few yards to the latrine door. Leaving the wheelchair outside, I ignored the ankle and held the door open for the tray-laden Brooks.

I carefully sat on a stool and Brooks handed me my rightful share. We were just about finished when we heard the screams, which slowed us down not at all. When the wardmaster came into the latrine, the mystery of the missing food was quickly solved.

"I guess you all were ready for chow," he said. He took the empty trays and departed, saying, "Yeah, he's in there, Doc." After my X rays, I was wheeled to a bed, and the rest of the night was a dream.

How the patients in the ward woke me for breakfast, I'll never know, but to my credit I was conscious long enough to eat. I found myself in a long hall-like ward with beds on both sides. Room between individual beds was minimal, and it goes without saying that the ward was packed beyond capacity. I drifted back to sleep and was awakened before the noon meal. The doctors and a nurse were staring me down from the foot of the bed. After administrative small talk, they briefed me on my injuries. It seemed that the CBUs lodged against my rib cage would present a delicate removal task but were not critical; they would be removed later. The ankle was broken, and after hearing of the X-ray results, I glanced at it for the first time in a while. The joint was swollen beyond recognition. For that reason, it would not be placed in a cast for a few days and I was to be evacuated from the war zone, or South Vietnam. That failed to break my heart. Otherwise, in comparison to most patients, I was not in bad shape. I was pleased that someone had bothered to fill me in on all the details.

The rest of the day was spent taking a much-needed bath and receiving visitors from the C-detachment. I did one other thing that day. I bought a carton of Lucky Strikes and wrote on it the names of all personnel from A-101. If I knew their status, I wrote that alongside their name. I still have the memo.

The very next dawn, I was transferred to an annex closer to the runway. The briefing had revealed that I would be shipped to a hospital in an undisclosed destination outside South Vietnam. I spent the rest of the day and night in deep thought over what had happened at Lang Vei, to whom, and why. I repeatedly replayed the incidents and, most of all, the personnel involved. I'm sure I wasn't the only one at the hospital annex undergoing the same mental anguish.

The following day, we were told to pack because we were departing Da Nang ASAP. That didn't take long. My ditty bag, a present from the C-detachment, was packed with cigarettes and my billfold. Just before sunset I was placed on a stretcher then put on a GI bus. The rest of the fully loaded vehicle contained jarheads and one other litter case, a Marine gunnery sergeant. There was no doubt about it, I was surrounded by 'em.

Stretcher patients were loaded first, and that usually took four personnel. The loop straps that held the supports hung from the ceiling of the GI Greyhound. When the chore was completed, my face and body were no more than ten inches from the ceiling. The tight fit was in order to give the walking wounded space enough to be seated beneath us. When I was finally as uncomfortable as possible, they brought on the second victim, and the gunny was soon hanging across the aisle from me. Then the ambulatory patients loaded and we were ready to make it to the aircraft that I assumed was on the airstrip.

"This would be a helluva position to be in, in case of a mortar attack," I said.

The gunny, apparently not as deaf as I was, overheard the remark. "Don't worry, Sarge, these are Marines. They'll take care of us," he said loud and clear.

I didn't have time to retaliate because the driver, an Air Force buck sergeant, boarded, called for our complete attention and got it before he began his dissertation on our favorite subject.

"We're going to a C-141 Starlighter that is now on the runway. In case of a mortar attack, I will stop the bus. Everyone unload and get in the ditches along the runway or the road. Make sure that you take off the two stretcher cases and place them in the ditches also."

While I was mumbling "I should hope so," the Air Force sergeant started the big conveyance and we were off, but we weren't off for long. The mortar rounds came raining down before we'd gone over a hundred yards. I'm sure, these many years later, that we were not the target, but I was not so confident at the time. The mortars, probably 122mm, were getting closer when the supervisor stopped the bus and was off first, with the rest of the ambulatory wounded not over an inch behind. That cowardly deed got my mind off of A-101 and Lang Vei for a spell. I stared at the ceiling and then, as was expected of me, began to harass my only companion, whose face was no farther from the ceiling than mine. I made sure my sarcasm could be heard and understood.

"Don't worry, Sarge! These are Marines. Damn, if they ain't. Sure lonesome in here!" I glanced over at the gut-shot gunny for some reaction.

The gunny's face was flushed red, and even in the dim light I could detect his anger. Fortunately it was directed at his ditch-digging charges.

When the negligent troops, their Air Force chauffeur in the lead, staggered back into the bus, the tirade began. I would not attempt to repeat the worst ass-chewing I'd ever heard in the forty-two years that I'd been in and around the military. Even when everyone had reclaimed their seats, the gunny never slowed. I gave the gunny an A and the students an F before we moved out, once again headed for the aircraft. I knew no one in the U.S. Army who could hold a candle to him.

After that I already knew who was going to be loaded aboard the C-141 jet aircraft first. Believe it! Other busloads would just have to wait their turn, thanks to the chastised stevedores aboard our transport. When we were secured, a white female handed me a blanket and I was asleep. I awoke just before landing at Tachikawa Air Force Base near Toyko, Japan.

We—the gunny and I—were taken off and placed in a GI ambulance that awaited us on the runway apron. It was the first time I'd been on Japan proper in a long while. We arrived at the 249th General a short time later and were both placed in a ward for our preliminary exams. Naturally, I was placed in a bed next to my professional ass-chewing buddy. A Hawaiian nurse of Japanese descent got our attention and our minds off Vietnam for a change.

I ended up in the orthopedic ward, but it was so crowded I didn't miss my ol' pal. The beds were close together in the long hall-like compartment. Tet was bringing smoke on folks all over Vietnam, and forty-two of us would be operated on that very night. The procedure would take most of the night, but considering the workload, it was fast and efficient. I remember little about it except for the long line of beds we passed while heading for some rooms in the rear of the ward. I went to the station where our wounds were prepped, then on to the mind-altering station. Shortly after I took a shot and a pill, the early morning greeted me. The medical attendant propped up my bed and I joined the breakfast crew. I noted that my ankle had been placed in a cast during the night, but I felt no pain from whatever they had done, and lit up a cancer stick after my morning meal. My neighbor to my right was a young soldier from the 101st Airborne who was in a cast from the waist up. I spoke with him and we enjoyed the camaraderie.

It was a few hours before the ward's head doctor, a major, began his rounds. He had a ton of patients to administer, and should gain a ton of knowledge, I thought, from the assignment. Before he began, he announced loudly that he would have a surprise the very next day but it would serve no purpose to unveil it at that time. No one seemed excited by his announcement.

By the time he got to my bunk, I was allowing my mind to wander and, of course, I was smoking a cigarette. The major didn't approve of either action. Everyone who smokes has heard the lecture, so I'll omit it. I gave him something to think about at the conclusion. "A few days ago I'd have paid money to live long enough to get lung cancer."

The major's diagnosis was good despite my smoking. All the lead had been removed and I was in a walking cast, but crutches came with it until I could place my full body weight on it. My favorite major then moved on to my airborne buddy. While he finished his rounds, I got my mind off Lang Vei and into the Medical Corps major; seems like I had one in every port. Why? Maybe this one would go away, I thought, but with his love for smokers, I doubted it. Oh well, do the best you can till you get twenty.

That afternoon I was issued crutches and given some walking lessons. I practiced awhile to and from the latrine before calling it a day. Being mobile eliminated my need for catheters and bedpans. I was ready for the assignment-of-duty-stations explanation promised for the next day. Time spent in an Army hospital always puts me in a negative frame of mind.

The next morning, looking very self-important before making his rounds, the major stood facing the double row of patients. To prevent another lecture, I didn't light up. He was standing at the end of the hall, so I'd rely on my airborne pal on my right if he didn't speak up loudly. Fortunately he did. He read from an order dated February 10, 1968 from the Joint Chiefs of Staff and signed by same.

"All personnel who have been wounded due to enemy action in Vietnam and medically evacuated out of the country will be recipients of the following actions. Number one: all personnel will be transferred to an Armed Forces hospital closest to their home station. Number two: all personnel, regardless of time spent in Vietnam, will be given credit for a full tour of duty."

Major Buddy paused and lapped up the cheering before carrying on. "If there are no questions, these people by my side will be at each bed, getting your desired permanent change of station move arranged."

Major Buddy had become an instant hero in the ward, but I knew there was one patient who wouldn't go for it. Why me, Lord? I was thinking as quickly as I could while the major kept advancing toward me. Maybe I was overreacting. Surely Okinawa would count as my home, though in the States, it ain't! The crew finally arrived and the clerk had his weapon in hand.

"I heard you're up and about, Sergeant. Don't be in a hurry to place all your weight on that ankle. Take it easy, okay? Where you going in the States, old soldier?" he finally asked.

I tried to keep my voice as low as possible but apparently didn't get the job done. "I ain't going to the States, sir. I want to go to Okinawa!"

The ward quieted for the first time since Major Buddy's speech. Even the field-grade officer was stunned. "I thought I misunderstood you, soldier. You have to go to the States to receive all the benefits. Now, where do you want to go in the States?"

"I'm not going to the States, sir!" I said loudly. You could have heard the pin drop once again. "If I go the States and leave my wife and kids in Okinawa, it would take the U.S. Army a year or so to unite my family. I know the bastards better than you do, sir. *No!* Hell *no!* I'm going to Okinawa, period."

The youngsters in the ward understood my reasoning, but the major was having a problem with it. He calmed as best he could then spoke again. "Where do you live in the States?"

"The last time I was there, in 1961, I was living in Lawton, Oklahoma," I replied.

He still didn't want to bend one iota. "We could send you to Fort Sill, Oklahoma. No problem!" he said.

"I'll go back to Vietnam before I go back to Fort Sill, sir," I said. "I'm Okinawa bound."

"They have no beds available in Okinawa. You damn well might go back to Vietnam."

I watched as the kid next to me got the assignment he wanted, and I was happy for him. He deserved it. Still, I failed to see why Camp Kue, Okinawa, would be any different from Fort Campbell, Kentucky, Station Hospital. Could the inflexible Army fail to see that the Okinawa solution would be a terrific money and time saver for both of us? Surrounded by a bunch of happy young soldiers, I rose and practiced walking with my crutches. I took some good-natured ribbing from my room-mates, but still I felt that they were on my side. I also felt that if I lost this battle, it could well be years before I saw Hatsuko, Jimmy, and Kathy. I paced the hall while attempting to come up with a solution to the problem. After the supper hour and before lights-out, I thought I had a plan. I knew from the major's reaction that I was not on orders as yet, so my campaign would begin at first light.

The major started the controversy again the following day. "Have you come to a stateside destination?" he asked.

"No, sir. No stateside for me. Back to 'Nam I guess. Can I visit the Post Exchange on my crutches?"

"Yes, Sergeant," he said disgustedly.

That very afternoon, after the quiet hour, crutches and all, I was off to the Post Exchange, which was no more than two hundred yards away. I visited the facility and the bowling alley next to it for the next three days before I put my plan into its final stages. I even ran into Lieutenants Longgrear and Wilkins from A-101. They both were happy about their stateside reprieve. My progress moved forward after talking to the sergeant first class hospital wardmaster in the bowling alley one afternoon. With each day, I was placing more and more weight on my ankle and walking cast. One night, after lights were out, I took out my dialing instructions for the overseas phone system. No one noted my presence in the ward office when I dialed my home away from home in Lawton, Oklahoma. My mother answered and recognized her long-lost son.

"Well, Bill, how bad are you hurt this time?" she asked.

I was stunned, but only for a moment. My mother had always claimed to have psychic power, and now even I was beginning to wonder. I went on to satisfy her that I was okay and to allay any fears she might have had in case the Army had sent her a disturbing message. It was good to hear her voice, but I couldn't tell her the real reason I'd called. When I concluded and had hung up, I had all the confidence in the world in my Edison instructor, but hustled back to my darkened bed before the charge of quarters returned.

I lay back in comfort and placed my one remaining problem in the proper perspective: From the Ward office, how was I to call in the daytime to Camp Kue Army Hospital in Okinawa? I fell asleep only after coming to the obvious solution. I'd have to observe the comings and goings of permanent personnel in the small compartment during duty hours.

My observations only took one day to complete. The magic hour was during quiet hour, that is, 1300 till 1400 each day. I confirmed my findings with the wardmaster, and the call went right through.

"Would you say again, your last transmission?" the receiver asked from Camp Kue Hospital.

"Yes, ma'am," I replied. "I'm in the 249th General in Japan and want to talk to the commander of Camp Kue Army Hospital." A lowly E7 wanted to talk to the colonel? Such nerve!

"Hang on, Sergeant! I'll see if he's busy."

The colonel couldn't wait to get on the line. "You say your wife and kids are here and they want to send you to a hospital in the States with those mundane injuries? Preposterous!" the colonel said.

"Yes sir, but they said you didn't have any beds," I came back.

"We always have room for people like that, Sergeant. I'll handle it from here on in. Name, rank, and serial number, with your telephone number attached, is all I need."

The deed was completed in about ten minutes. The wardmaster came in and saw me climb into bed with my walking cast and a smile. My part of the contest was over.

On his morning rounds, Major Buddy tried to sneak right on by, but I wasn't going for it. I lit up a cigarette to get his attention. When he started his asinine lecture on the evils of tobacco, I couldn't resist a chance to rub his nose in it.

"Sir, I'm limping only slightly now. I'll trade you these crutches for a cane, if one's available. I won't be needing them in Okinawa, sir!"

He nodded at one of his aides, who took away the crutches. "How did you know you were going to Okinawa, Sergeant?"

"Just a lucky guess, sir."

"The wardmaster will brief you later, but tomorrow you're gone. Hope you enjoy finishing your tour in Vietnam."

I wasn't convinced that he was being honest, but when you're on top, you very seldom worry about tomorrow. The wardmaster came to see me after quiet hour and gave me the skinny. The colonel from Okinawa had called and confirmed space for me in Kue and by name, pissing off the local bureaucracy. I would leave Tachikawa Airbase sometime after 0900 tomorrow for the Rock. My local transportation departed the 249th at 0800.

"Good luck, Top!" the wardmaster said to me. "One last thing, though. I think Major Buddy's right about your tour completion in 'Nam, but I sure hope I'm wrong. Take care."

I shook the soldier's hand. He had taken care of a fellow enlisted man, and I was proud of him for that.

At Tachy, as the GIs called it, I caught a WWII cargo flight home to Okinawa. I was walking well enough by then and carried only the ditty bag with me. The only medevac of five soldiers on board the C-46, I bid farewell to Japan.

CHAPTER 20

We landed at Kadena Air Force Base, Okinawa, after a box lunch on the Air Force antique. An ambulance was waiting. The medics were mildly surprised that I sported a walking cast and otherwise appeared healthy despite my pin-striped blue-and-white hospital robe. I handed them a set of orders and we made the twelve-minute trip to Kue, arriving in the middle of the afternoon. In spite of the bumper-to-bumper traffic, I was glad to see Camp Kue and Okinawa.

I was in-processed and placed on the third floor, and in a room no less. My three roommates were all in casts and conked out, so I deposited my ditty and moved out to find the NCO in charge. Knowing Camp Kue Army Hospital as well as I did, that didn't take long. He told me, in essence, to return to my room, and a doctor would brief me at 1600 on my injuries and answer any questions I might harbor. I was ready for that.

When the doctor removed the stitches and told me to continue to march, the wardmaster and I conversed privately. He told me a convalescence leave would be immediately arranged because Kue needed the bed space. With the Tet Offensive in full swing, the two thousand casualties a week were placing some burden on Camp Kue Army Hospital also. He said I could wander, being a double Oki, but to be back in my room for the 1800-hour head count. My my, it was good to be home again.

Wearing my blue pajamas, flip-flops, and robe, I was quickly in the lobby. I spotted Staff Sergeant Moyer and his wife before they saw me. I buttered up to the C Company medic before I told him my story. They were both sympathetic, so I told them I wanted a ride home. I acted like some country boy on Saturday night while we crawled from Kue to Kadena Circle in Moyer's "privately owned vehicle."

When they dropped me off at the side street to my home, I stood by the wooden gate and looked over the cement block fence. Kathy was sitting in the yard piling up the small coral rocks that constituted the green, green grass of our home. She looked at me and quickly looked back to her miniature rock pile. The two-and-a-half-year-old young lady refused to respond to a stranger. "Kathy, it's Dad, or Papa-san. Don't you know me?" A dumb question if for no other reason than I already knew the answer. I opened the gate and walked in when Hatsuko sprang, literally, from the front door of our small abode.

"Papa-san, Papa-san, Papa-san is home," she screamed, hugging me strongly. I was near tears as Jimmy came out the door behind her. I gave credit to my four-year-old son; he did remember who I was. I hugged both kids and we went into the house.

Hatsuko knew nothing about Lang Vei, therefore I relayed only how I got hurt, because I didn't think the details would serve any purpose. After some cold refreshments in the air-conditioned home, and attempting to get acquainted, it was time for me to get back to Kue. I decided to take one of the island's infamous skoshi cabs back to the hospital; hell, I needed the excitement. I was by my sack with a few minutes to spare before bed check.

Several days later I was given a complete physical exam and did well except for my hearing. The doctor gave me a temporary three-profile on my hearing and ankle. I was also given a thirty-day convalescence leave and moved out of the hospital. Getting used to family life and visiting my old unit, the 1st SF Group, was how I spent my time.

One afternoon I got a call from the hospital telling me to report back the next day. Naturally, I raised hell. For once, I was wrong. After hearing my argument that I still had fifteen days of my leave left, the NCO calmed me down. "Be here at 1400, Top, and you'll be gone by 1430. Wear a uniform, if possible, and believe me, you're gonna enjoy yourself."

The Army had me stumped again, but what choice did I have? I'd signed ten statements about Lang Vei; what else did the bastards want this time? I prepared a fatigue uniform for the outing. How dumb can you look, what with only one jump boot? The only green beret I owned with a 5th Special Forces flash on the front was in a footlocker in Lang Vei, but that presented only a minor problem. I wore an old one with the 1st Special Forces flash. Very few GIs, or anyone else not in SF, knew the difference in March 1968.

I reported in and was deported to the rear admittance office on the first floor. In the lobby of the businesslike establishment, I was told to be seated. I was not alone in the outer office. Another SFC E7 wearing a 1st Cavalry Division patch on his fatigues sat in a wheelchair with his right leg in a cast from the knee down. He nodded and I returned the greeting. We didn't have long to wait. A warrant officer came out of the office and said, "Would you two master sergeants come in the office, please?"

I looked around to see who he was addressing, but the Cavalry was already saddled up and in a gallop so I followed the in-patient. A major, no less, was standing behind his desk, and he smiled when we both halted to his front. The warrant officer went to his side and handed him what appeared to be a set of orders. The field grade cleared his throat before he began. What he read was:

Department of the Army, Headquarters, U.S. Army Medical Center, Ryukyu Islands, APO San Francisco, 96331. Special Orders Number 55 dated 14 March 1968. To be Master Sergeant (E8):

STRAIN, FLOYD S RA38497052 PSG E7 MHD
USAH RYIS
CRAIG, WILLIAM T RA25700157 SFC E7 MHD
USAH RYIS

When he finished, we snapped to and saluted. The major
returned the formality and shook our hands in congratulations.
I still didn't understand what in the hell was going on, but I
sure as hell wouldn't knock it.

I stood at parade rest while the WO handed us a couple of
sets of orders that had the black collar pins of E8s attached.
Piss me off. The ceremony was apparently over and we were
now allowed to ask questions. Dazed though I was, I had a
few, as did the soldier on my right. The major's first explanation cleared the airways.

"The new Army regulation states that any NCO who is on a
promotion list and gets wounded in combat will go to the top
of the list and will be first to be promoted. Apparently you
both were in that category and were on a previous list."

My mind went back to a promotion board for E8 held on
Okinawa prior to September 1967 and Vietnam. I remember
coming out number eighteen on the list. I just jumped seventeen of my lowly peers. Tough shit!

We both nodded. I listened for the rest of the session while
the warrant officer answered all the questions I had in mind.
"Both of your record files have been annotated and a copy
given to wherever your pay records are. Sergeant Craig, yours
are here at this time. Your base pay has risen from $452.10 to
$475.50 a month."

I congratulated the new master sergeant from the Air Cav
before departing. If nothing else, the promotion made conversation material for the next few weeks in the American Legion
and the NCO Clubs I frequented from time to time. When my
leave was up, I reported back to Camp Kue, had my cast
removed and ankle X-rayed. I was ordered to take fifteen more

days and report back to the 257th Replacement Company at Camp Sukiran for reassignment.

Lang Vei left me in good shape, so far as time off was concerned, but one thing it didn't improve was my mental state. For one thing, I didn't like to talk about the event, and would do so only with people who I knew very well and trusted. Those discussions helped my mental situation, but in a very short time the mental anguish would return. I did not know it at the time, but some of the sores would scar me for a lifetime. What was bothering me? I sincerely hope that I'm an isolated case, but I think otherwise.

Despite the advantages of becoming reacquainted with my wife and kids, and enjoying other facets of the island, all good things must come to an end. I reported and signed in at the Replacement Company and was handed my orders: I would return to the Republic of Vietnam to complete my one-year tour. Though I accepted that, I believed it would be fair if I were to be given credit for a tour and shipped to the States, or back to the 1st Special Forces Group on Okinawa. However, I was given only three to five days to report to the 5th Special Forces Group (Abn), APO 96240. Oh well, I thought, everybody makes mistakes, so I didn't get uptight about it.

The personnel sergeant of the 257th said he would be available shortly, so I rested in place. But Major Buddy must have briefed him in such a manner that he was ready for the likes of me.

"That's the way the Special Regulation reads, Sergeant Craig," he told me. "If you were evacuated to the States, you would be credited with a completed tour. You did not, so you've got six more months to serve. Good luck!"

The 257th Company arranged for my transportation, and around the last of March, I landed in Tan Son Nhut airbase in fatigues, boots, beret, and a hacked-off mental attitude. As I was moving to the terminal, a Vietnamese bag lady tried to sell me a pack of C-ration cigarettes. I needed the smokes so I took the pack and kept on walking. The illegal vendor screamed to high heaven and finally got a Military Policeman's attention and the flatfoot stopped me.

"Did you pay the lady for the cigarettes?" he asked.

"No, it's against regulations," I said, before showing him what it said on the pack of stale cigarettes. "Not to be resold under any circumstances." I continued to march and, richer by a pack of Luckies, left the cop to do his job.

I carried my practically empty duffel bag and handbag to the outside of the terminal to see if any transportation was available. Despite orders that read 90th Replacement Battalion, I was not about to report to that leg outfit. Special Forces had a replacement unit in downtown Saigon. I espied no ride, so I waited. The other newbies piled on the GI buses for the 90th Replacement. One staff sergeant asked me if I wanted a lift to the 90th, but I refused; if I reported in there, I'd end up in some leg outfit in Can Tho or someplace. I thanked him and waved when the OD bus pulled out.

About ten minutes later, and after enjoying one of mama-san's stolen smokes, I spied my ride. A buck sergeant and a captain, both wearing green berets, pulled up in a jeep and parked. Damn, it's about time, I thought. While the young sergeant was helping the officer check on his gear, I loaded mine in the rear of the jeep and stood by. The soldier returned shortly with another captain in tow. He saw me and nodded at my gear. "Reporting in, Top?"

"Yeah, young man. Reporting back in's a better way of putting it. Ready to go?"

The captain had his gear loaded by then. "Yeah," said the driver, "hop in for the usual exciting ride downtown."

"I can hardly wait," I murmured.

The small replacement unit promised to have me in Nha Trang the very next afternoon. I was in good health but I wasn't prepared for a night on the town in Saigon, so I stayed in the house.

In Nha Trang, after signing in, I was given VIP quarters with wooden flooring and siding, with a tent awning. I moved to my quarters only after being given an appointment with new Group Sergeant Major Maddox, my top kick during the DUI days on Okinawa. I was rather anxious to find out how I would spend my next six months. Sergeant Major Maddox was not only cordial but acted sincerely happy to see me again, which helped my pissed-off state of mind no end.

"We have a project here that we're trying to get off the ground and would like for you to head up, but you have to agree to it. We will not force you to take it. It's simply this: we, and other units in-country, are going to duplicate what we did in Korea; we're starting a week to two-week orientation course that will be required for newbies in-country. It's now a Group regulation. The NCO-in-charge job is wide open, and Colonel Ladd hopes you'll go for it."

I hedged, for several reasons. I needed to go to I Corps to pick up the equipment I had left up there, and to go back to Detachment A-101. Maddox just said, "We still have two weeks, just let us know in that time. Glad to see you again, Bill!" I was in a C-130 aircraft to Da Nang very shortly thereafter.

I enjoyed walking around the compound and meeting the people I knew in Company C's lash-up. The Tet Offensive had hurt Hue city, but Da Nang's Marine and Army troops had kicked Giap's ass good and proper, just like he deserved. I was convinced he wouldn't win as long as the U.S. remained in South Vietnam.

Sergeant Major Hodge took a while to lay out what he had in mind for me before I told him about the assignment I'd been offered in Nha Trang. His assignments narrowed down to two.

Kham Duc, the last border camp in I Corps, was located on the western fringe of Quang Tin Province, close to Laos. It fell under the direction of the 23rd Americal Division, and because the division was stationed on the opposite, coastal side of the province at Chu Lai, reinforcing the camp would be difficult. Hodge made it clear that I would not be forced to take the team sergeant's slot except on a voluntary basis. What other jobs did he offer? Not much really.

Detachment A-101 was going to be rebuilt in the area of Khe Sanh, but not at Lang Vei. Unfortunately, their CIDG would consist of many of the Bru who'd formed the previous CIDG force. My feelings about the Marines and the Bru weighed heavily on my mind. The sergeant major gave me a few days to make up my mind and told me that he would go along with whatever I decided to do. I did not make the decision lightly.

In the Army an experienced NCO can learn as much in bull sessions as he will from briefings, sometimes a lot more if he knows who to talk to. Seeking as many opinions as possible before I was ready to make a decision, I deployed to the club.

Kham Duc and Detachment A-105 were easy to focus on because of previous experience. I had been on the team that surveyed the area in 1962 as a possible A-detachment site. We'd rejected it due to its lack of a native population. With a beautiful airstrip, that location should have gone to the conventional forces, just as the A Shau should have. It was another case of Special Forces taking a job that no one else wanted. I concluded that its destiny wouldn't be much different from that of Lang Vei's. An easy decision, I thought. In the middle of May I would be proved right; A-105 and Kham Duc went down the tube.

In my short stay at Da Nang, I met none of my teammates from Lang Vei; those still employed in I Corps were in the distant A-detachments. Possibly because of that and my memories of building a new campsite and then seeing it go to hell, the second alternative was much easier to refuse. So, on my third day at the compound, I packed the gear I'd left behind when I was evacuated. Then, bidding my friends farewell, I went back to the rear with my gear for my last six months in-country on that tour.

When I reported back to Group headquarters, I signed on as the NCO in charge of the 5th Special Forces' first-ever combat orientation course. The cadre and the students were to be housed in the Recondo School area, so I moved there in advance of opening day. Ironically enough, I was doubled up with my old roommate in Delta Project in 1965, SFC Paul Tracy. As Tracy said, we were probably the only ones who could stand each other. I was happy with the arrangements and Paul needed the company. While he and the Recondo cadre were putting students from almost every unit in the U.S. and Korean armies through a rough, tough reconnaissance training course, I met the captain, Francis, who was to be the officer in charge of the combat orientation course. Then he and I went to the Group S-3 (Operations) office and received a very long briefing.

The captain and I took our notebooks along and asked all the right questions of the operations people. In this case, the Operations officer appeared to have all the right answers so we accomplished a ton in a very short time. The captain had a previous permanent change of station (PCS) tour to Vietnam, and he nodded and grinned in complete agreement as our briefer, a lieutenant colonel, spoke. The other four Operations people sitting across from us at the long table were happy because we were happy.

"Most of our casualties have occurred within the soldiers' first ninety days of combat," the lieutenant colonel said. "This rate is what we're trying to reduce as much as possible. All Special Forces replacement captains and below who have not already spent a six-month temporary duty tour or a PCS tour in Vietnam or Laos must go through the two-week course. The course will consist of one week in the classroom and a field training exercise.

"You, the cadre, and the students, will be housed in the Recondo School complex in wooden, tent-roofed hooches. The classes will be held in the outdoor pavilion by your quarters and in the GI theater located in the same area. All course support, excepting only instructors, will be furnished by Group

Operations assisted by Recondo School. We expect the first class to be on line and in the classroom in two weeks.

"The classroom portion of the curriculum will be written by Captain Francis and Master Sergeant Craig and lying on my desk in one week. Do you have a problem with that?"

Our head shakes spurred the colonel on. "Your instructors, in addition to yourselves, we need to talk about. Especially how they're selected and what their job titles will be."

During a smoke break outside near the wooden complex, we agreed on the first point rather easily. We needed one each SF job title or military occupational specialty (MOS): medic, 91B; heavy weapons leader, 12B; light weapons leader, 11B; combat engineer, 12B; and a radio operator, 05B. I would be the 11F, operations and intelligence NCO, and Captain Francis the team leader. The second issue took the rest of the break before Francis conceded. That the selected individuals had to have two years in-country rankled Francis, for some reason. Only after I assured him that there were sufficient personnel with two years in Vietnam and/or Laos did Francis surrender. The fact that I had three and a half years in-country already might have helped sway him. I didn't believe it would serve any purpose to tell him the reasoning behind that request, simple though it was to me. What I wanted was instructors from the 1st Special Forces Group because they were the most experienced SF people in the Far East and, as best I could recall, that's where we were at; not Central America, and certainly not Europe. We put 'em in the butt can and went back to the briefing room.

The Operations people went along with our request for one NCO per MOS in each enlisted field in an A-detachment for instructors. But the second request caused some mouths to drop, and the colonel said, "You might find people with that much experience hard to come by, Sergeant Craig!"

But I had rehearsed my comeback outside, so I could handle it: "They come in grooves from the 1st Special Group on Okinawa that have two years or more, sir. But if we have a problem getting them with two years, then we'll lower the requirement to a year. Let's start it off that way, sir. It'll work!" Without waiting to hear whether I'd won or not, I double-timed past the instructor qualifications. "How long before we'll see any of 'em, sir?"

"The information will go out on the wire first thing tomorrow to all control detachments. So, I'd say a week or less. Fast enough, Top?"

Captain Francis and I used a Recondo School office the next day, and before the day was out I was a clerk-typist again. The first week would consist of map reading, physical training, basic medical courses, patrolling, A camps in Vietnam, instruction via an interpreter, calling in and adjusting artillery and mortar fire, and radio procedures. The FTX, field training exercises, would be no larger than twenty people and would be of four days' duration or until contact was made.

The instructors arrived before the first class, but not by a helluva lot. I wrote the lesson plan on the A camps and would give the first four-hour class of each two-week session. At the very least, Lang Vei had qualified me to speak on the fortified A camps in Vietnam in 1968.

The instructors were all friends and acquaintances of mine from the 1st Special Forces Group on Okinawa and Fort Bragg. With this caliber help, I foresaw no problems accomplishing the mission. Their experience in the host country and Laos was most impressive. The medical NCO, SFC Hugh Hubbard, had numerous six-month stints in Vietnam and was now on a PCS move. SFC Burl Wilson, light weapons leader, also had time in Laos and was now on a PCS move to the 5th SF Group (Abn). SFC Wilson had been on Detachment A-4, the first A-detachment I was ever on at Bragg in 1960. SFC William Bush had accumulated similar experience, and the weapons leader completed the cadre with expertise that would impress any student that might come our way. This group ensured that the first class of approximately forty students was in and out of its Vietnam orientation in good shape, ready for the real world.

When I was not instructing, I assisted the principal instructor. If coordination was needed with the 5th SF Group, Captain Francis or I would attend to that. The Group Operations shop monitored the first class very closely. Their reports reflected that they were as pleased as Captain Francis with the instruction. Complaints were few and trivial. Who were the students and from where did they come? We looked that one over only after our first class was dispatched to complete their twelve-month assignments.

Despite only one class having run through the orientation, the student class makeup would vary little, if any, during my stay as NCO in charge. The officers were captains and below, with few exceptions fresh out of the Q course at Fort Bragg. The NCOs were another matter, however. The majority would be fresh from the Special Forces Branch Training Group courses at Fort Bragg, but to my surprise some were old SF hands. How had they managed to miss a war that had been going on for six years and more? Apparently, permanent change of station moves to Panama; Bad Tolz, Germany; and Fort Bragg had been taking up their service time. Okinawa had not been included in their PCS moves because if you were on the Rock, you were going to Vietnam, previous tours be damned. The fact that SF operators normally specialize in one area of the world also helped to account for this phenomenon.

While Recondo School was churning out reconnaissance people from every combat unit in Vietnam, the COC course managed Class Two without mishap. Class Three would prove to be a wee bit more exciting. Considering our eight-till-five office hours, maybe the students—and the cadre—needed an eye-opener. The incident occurred on the course's graduating exercise in a rice field near the resort city of Nha Trang.

The student patrol was in its night location in a deliberate ambush awaiting the enemy. Due to the variable cloud cover, visibility was far from unlimited; even so, the NVA troops made their way along the long axis of the ambush before a young lieutenant stepped on his necktie. As the patrol leader was exerting pressure on the claymore clacker to initiate the ambush, a lieutenant violated instructions by taking his M-16 off safe. The resulting *click* could be heard for miles. An NVA troop whirled and fired into the trap before he was cut in half by the ambush. Several AK-47 rounds went into the mouth of the errant officer, ending his PCS move to Vietnam and his life. Even so, the NVA suffered another horrible defeat. The enemy's weapon-and-body count numbered thirteen, and the COC troops lost one killed in action (KIA). We cadre were jubilant that things had gone so well with our charges; not so Group Headquarters.

Francis and I were invited—ordered may be a better word—to a meeting at Group Operations before Class Four began. The one casualty had rattled some cages with the REMFs in Group HQ. From the beginning of the conference, headed by the same lieutenant colonel who had directed us to write the two-week schedule, I felt the COC course was being admonished because a lieutenant had made a horrible mistake and paid the ultimate price.

At the end of the first hour, the lines were drawn. It was Group Operations against Captain Francis and me. My only contribution to the discussion caused considerable officer-NCO resentment. So what else was new? "This is not Fort Bragg, North Carolina, nor Bad Tolz, Germany, for that matter," I said. "Mistakes in Vietnam are often dealt with very harshly. If we're gonna knock off the FTX, we might as well let 'em sit around Group Headquarters for two weeks. Besides, it was a helluva victory for our side. One of the Viet Cong casualties was a province chief. Finally, if the U.S. casualty had been an enlisted man, we probably wouldn't be sitting here." I felt no regrets for my remarks; it was about time someone brought it out in the open for all to see. Even the master sergeant representing Group was aghast at what I believed to be the case. Big deal!

The session was concluded only after the lieutenant colonel in charge promised to forward our recommendations for no changes to the Group commander. We must have won the encounter. Only after I rotated was a change made in the course—the entire operation would be moved to Hon Tre Island, just off the coast of Nha Trang. I do not concede that I was wrong. Combat orientation should not be like Bragg, safe and secure.

The four months I spent as the NCO in charge of the COC course, called the "Cock Course" by the wits, went by swiftly for several reasons. First of all, we never had it so good. We stayed busy all day, every day, and the NVA were ignoring us almost completely. At night the Recondo Club furnished entertainment in the form of beer and bull sessions that were amusing as well as educational. I learned many things doing these nightly endeavors, some of them I wasn't too happy with. For one thing, the few officers assigned to Recondo would drop in for a beer from time to time. Many of us knew this was wrong, but we could do nothing about it. If an altercation had occurred between an NCO and an officer, the NCO would have bought the farm. Fortunately, that possibility did not occur until after I departed. From past experience I knew that alcohol, NCOs, and officers do not make a healthy concoction.

All good things must come to an end, and in August 1968 my orders for the 7th Special Forces Group (Abn) at Fort Bragg proved that. The directive to return, bag and baggage, to the USA rattled my cage. It shouldn't have if for no other reason than I had completed seven consecutive years in the Far East and CINCPAC.

At that time, the regulation governing time spent overseas stated that six years was the maximum in one overseas command. I had been in Okinawa, Vietnam, Laos, Taiwan, and Thailand for seven consecutive years. All of these locations came under Commander in Chief Pacific, or CINCPAC, quartered in Hawaii. I was therefore a year overdue for a stateside assignment. The director of personnel in the Pentagon, Ms. Billye Alexander, was only doing her job—and doing it very well, in fact. Simple, right? Wrong! There were no provisions in the orders for a foreign-born wife and two small children to accompany their sponsor. I was going to prove the old axiom that if a person wanted to, he could justify anything. Off I went to the 5th Special Group Headquarters Personnel shop. The Personnel sergeant was an understanding sort, and in twenty-four hours my orders read the 1st Special Forces Group, APO 96331 on Okinawa. Things were looking up by the time my replacement arrived from Fort Bragg.

I did not know the master sergeant E8, and he didn't appear to want to know me, so I handed over the reins of COC in quick time. The date was on or about September 1, 1968, leaving me twenty-five days to go on my PCS tour. No problem, GI, I thought. I'd just go off to Group Headquarters to negotiate a two-week "drop" from my PCS tour. This time I received some unexpected opposition from the Personnel shop, and ended up in the Group adjutant's office standing at parade rest. The major wasted no time or words on my presence.

"The command in Vietnam is very stringent on any drop time in relation to a twelve-month tour, Sergeant. Special Forces follows their directives to the letter. Your request for a two-week drop is therefore denied. Unless you have some other subject to discuss, you are dismissed!"

That night over a beer, I found the solution to my unwanted two-week vacation at the Recondo School facilities. After hearing my problem, my old friend SFC "Small Man" Tracy asked me, "Who is the assistant group commander, Bill?"

"Hell, I don't know, Paul. Who is it?"

"A lieutenant colonel who is completing his tour after a few months in the hospital for his wounds suffered at Lang Vei. That should be clue enough, William!"

"Schungel?" I said. "Tell me I'm right, Paul!" My ex-roommate grinned. "I'll be on my way in a week, ol' pal. Just you wait and see!"

The next day the Group adjutant wouldn't budge from his perch on high. I raised my voice, in order for it to penetrate the closed door of the 5th SF Group executive officer. The ploy worked. Colonel Schungel, my C-detachment commander at Lang Vei, opened the door aggressively before shouting, "Get your ass in here, Team Sergeant!" But only after casting a few last aspersions at the confused adjutant did I comply. I stuck out my hand as I neared Schungel's complex. He grabbed it and pulled me inside, smiling broadly and shaking my hand repeatedly after closing the door.

The reunion took at least ten minutes to conclude before we came back to 5th SF Group Headquarters in September 1968. Only then did I bother to explain the situation. "Therefore, sir, I have a replacement, and in turn have nothing to do but drink beer and squander my time. I'd rather be on my way to Okinawa, sir."

"Seems pretty minor to me, Team Sergeant. Give me a copy of your orders, and on your way out tell that major to report to me. Come see me before you depart Nha Trang, Team Sergeant!"

I relayed the message to the shook-up major. In my soul, I wished I'd had permission to witness the ass-chewing, but you can't have everything. Three days later, very early in the morning, I was to be on my way to Cam Ranh Bay to catch a flight to my adopted homeland—Okinawa.

CHAPTER 21

The 5th Special Forces Group had dispatched a jeep to take me to Cam Ranh Bay at 0900 hours. The night before, I had placed my belongings in a duffel bag and shined my Corcoran jump boots for the flight home. I also prepared the only Class A uniform in my possession, taking pains to see that it was up to snuff. The khaki uniform included all awards and decorations upon my chest, as the song goes. Awards be damned, the thing that would get us to Cam Ranh Bay on time was the patch on my right shoulder.

Then, as even today, your present unit patch is on your left shoulder, your unit combat patch on your right shoulder. By the book, the golden thunderbolts with the blue background on an arrowhead was on my left shoulder; the 45th Infantry Division Thunderbird patch of the Korean "police action" was on my right. SFC Paul Tracy complimented me on my appearance as I threw my duffel bag in the rear of the jeep. I would be hard to piss off that morning, and my decor reinforced my positive attitude.

"To Group Headquarters, Paul, and no pit stops!" I said. SFC Tracy obliged and we made the mile-o-more without a hitch. Tracy went the extra mile by rounding up my Vietnamese-driven jeep while I detoured to Group HQ to thank Colonel Schungel once again for his able assistance. When I returned, my bag was loaded and Tracy and I bid each other farewell.

My Viet driver took the coastal route toward Cam Ranh Bay, thirty minutes or so away. To prove he knew his business, the driver even missed a hole or two along Highway One. To my surprise, in about ten minutes the picnic was over. Vietnam was a harder place to depart from than I really wanted to believe; a South Korean tank blocked the interstate, leaving us without viable options.

The tank unit was deployed on the highway, and no traffic was coming or going. The Korean captain eyed us after we pulled off the blacktop road. I returned the favor between glances at my stolen GI wristwatch. In the distance I heard the Koreans brutally interrogating some Vietnamese. When fifteen minutes went by without any movement, I decided to do something even if it was wrong. I figured the South Koreans owed me a favor. I told my Viet driver to cool it then walked toward the Korean officer. The captain watched me approach, very warily, of course. When he spotted the 45th Division patch his face changed expression completely. To preserve my spit-shined boots, I was stepping cautiously through the road dust and vegetation. When I stopped within hearing distance of the U.S.-made tank, I was greeted in perfect English—but only after I had saluted. After, once again, consulting my time-piece, I had a few words my own damn self.

"Sir, I'm leaving this asshole place at one o'clock if I can get to Cam Ranh Bay air terminal. What's the holdup?"

The Korean officer again glanced at the patch on my right shoulder. "When were you in Korea, Sergeant?"

"In 1951 and 1952, sir!"

To my surprise, the captain climbed down from his throne and, after shaking my hand, did an about-face. He spoke to his radio operator in the armored vehicle before he began motioning all tanks off the road. When he finished, he turned to me and spoke an encouraging word. "You're free to go, Sergeant. Good luck, and thank you."

We made it to the air terminal in good shape, and I checked in my duffel and had time for a smoke. Four of us were going to Okinawa on a four-engine C-141 cargo jet. We reported just outside the terminal at the appointed time, to find the pilot awaiting our arrival. Standing alongside the aircraft, he said, "We have one engine that is strapped down and inoperative. We're going to fly to Kadena Air Force Base on three engines. The only inconvenience is that it will be low and slow. Those who still want to fly to Okinawa, get on board. Any questions?"

Of course, I had one. "Are you flying it, sir?"

The U.S. Air Force major nodded, and I boarded. I was the only passenger on the C-141 late that afternoon. With my duffel bag over my shoulder, I exited the busy Kadena terminal in September 1968. Being a good Special Forces soldier, scrounging a ride to the 1st Special Forces Group Headquarters complex was a minor problem. The Okinawan gate guard stopped our vehicle and I dismounted, thanking the GI for the ride to Bishagawa. The uniformed Security Police called the staff duty NCO and a jeep was prompt in arrival.

I presented a few copies of my orders to the NCO before I signed in on the dotted line. He was preparing to call a line company for quarters when I held up my hand. "Don't waste your time, young Sergeant, I live here! Just give me a time tomorrow to in-process and I'll catch a ride to my home in Kadena Circle. I own a house there, furnished with a wife and two children."

I was told to report to Group Personnel (S-1) at 1000 hours the next day. Within fifteen minutes I was stopped in front of our cement-block, two-room mansion. My wife was overjoyed at my unexpected arrival, but my five-year-old son and three-year-old daughter acted rather annoyed at the interruption. After all, a perfect stranger was intruding upon their nightly routine at 2000 hours. Nevertheless, we all survived the homecoming, and we were enduring a home-cooked breakfast when I brought some joy and excitement into their humdrum existence.

"Yes, Hatsuko, Jimmy, and Kathy, you heard me right. Make sure your passports are up to snuff. We're all going to the USA in a week or so. You two are going to your homeland not only to see Oklahoma, but your grandma as well. How does that grab you, Jimmy?"

"What's a grandma, Daddy?"

After talking myself out of that one, I quizzed Kathy in order to see if she needed some stateside duty. "Where does milk come from, Kathy?"

"The commissary, Daddy!"

I was finished with in-processing by 1400 hours the next day. The very sharp, black S-1 master sergeant E8 called me into his office before I departed to my new old unit. "I don't know, or care, how you did it, but you're on shaky ground and I think you know it!"

My answer was innocence personified. "What are you getting at, old soldier?"

"You've been in CINCPAC for seven years and you're assigned to Okinawa for three more? You know the limit in one command is six years. Miss Alexander doesn't make mistakes like that, Sergeant Craig! I hope your scheme works out for you, but don't bet on it. We won't say nary a word, so that will delay her reaction for a while."

"Thanks, old soldier. I've got a few more things to distract Ms. A. with before I'm ready to throw in the towel. Thanks for your help," I concluded.

I cranked up my 1956 Ford convertible and, briefcase and all, was on my way to my "Chargin' Charlie" Company assignment at Site Yara. My presence would furnish C Company with a surprise, but they had a few in store for me as well. I was welcomed home by Sergeant Major Kralick, a friend from before the PCS move to 'Nam. The next day I would confer with the commander, a Lt. Col. Lawrence Trapp. Trapp was the team leader of the area assessment team out of Da Nang in 1962–63 TDY, when he'd been a captain. Despite being a lowly E8, I seemed to be receiving a gob of attention.

Like my sergeant major and commander, I was in the duty uniform, jungle fatigues, boots, and beret. The briefing and assignment conference would be held in the small room located behind the ol' man's office. The colonel insisted on a briefing about Lang Vei, and I complied, but stated only the facts that had been reported in the news media; I did not want to become emotionally involved. Sergeant Major Kralick inquired about my wishes concerning my present assignment.

"I'd like to find out what family life is all about, for one thing," I said. They grinned. "The next thing I need to accomplish is to take two U.S. citizens to their homeland. My children have never set foot on American soil." Again they smiled. "And I wouldn't mind finishing college at the University of Maryland, here on Okinawa. And that's my final goal."

Both men looked at each other before the colonel took charge. "How many days will your leave consist of, Bill?"

"I've put in for forty-five days, but I'll be back in less time than that, sir!"

"Good!" Trapp said, glancing at his sergeant major. "We've already discussed a job that will enable you to accomplish your goals. The slot should be open by the time you're back on-island."

"Yeah," the sergeant major inserted, "by the time you return, we'll mash it on you."

"Have a safe trip home, Sergeant," were the words that left me in the dark about an assignment, with no time to worry about it.

I finished in-processing with an on-post housing request. I was informed that housing had been taking up to ninety days to achieve. Because of the forty-five-day leave and the time it could take to sell my place at Kadena Circle when I returned, I lost no sleep over it. Why did I want to move on-post? I figured that the more it would cost the Army to set up proper housekeeping for me and my family, the better chance that the Department of the Army would overlook the horrendous mistake it had made keeping me in one command for seven years. I didn't have anything to lose or gain but a stateside assignment that I didn't particularly want, now or ever. A few days later my forty-five-day leave came through. The orders had my wife and children's names and passport numbers on them. We were ready to visit the land of the big PX.

On a weekday morning nearing the last day in September 1968, Sergeant Major Kralick picked us up at Kadena Circle and we were soon at the large Kadena Air Force Terminal. I signed us up for a space-available flight to the States and we went to eat in the cafeteria. Kathy had just celebrated her third birthday a few weeks earlier and probably thought all the moving about was part of the festivities. Jimmy was five and curious about the unusual activities and the talk of the faraway land that he was a citizen of. By 1700 we were lollygagging in the terminal when Kralick returned to check on our progress.

He was not happy with our situation, and told us so before moving to the large terminal counter. I just watched as he talked a mile a minute to the booking personnel who were dressed in Air Force blues. Squeaky wheels must get the grease; within an hour our names were called. But I knew we were in trouble as soon as I spotted the C-141 cargo aircraft. The four jet engines were idle as we loaded. In my opinion, the squeaking wheel, Kralick, had gotten us an undeserved shaft. A luxury liner was a little more what I'd had in mind for the long flight.

Few passengers were competing for a rough-riding trip on the C-141. After fastening two children and Hatsuko into the first aircraft they'd ever set foot on, I looked around. The C-141 was hauling a jet engine that fit snugly in the rear. I knew that could only make for a rough flight. How the wife and kids were going to stand up to it worried me. Of course, I'd be lying if I said that this was my first inkling that sergeant majors were not always right.

Hatsuko had brought some motion sickness pills to combat the rough journey, but the kids were another matter. It was not lost on me that they were the only children on the manifest. After we reached cruising altitude, I went to the crew chief for burp bags for my dependents. Before the long flight to Hawaii's Hickam AFB was over, they had put the bags to good use, along with their mother. The only consolation we had was that the C-141 cargo jet-flight would terminate in Hawaii.

At Hickam AFB we proceeded to the Air Force dispensary. I don't know what the medic administered, but in minutes the wife and two children were eager to resume the journey. The NCO at the check-in counter promised me there would be no more rough cargo flights for us. An eight-hour flight awaited, to land at Travis AFB in California, but the booking NCO kept his word; in two hours or less we were on a U.S. Air Force 707 jet. At Travis AFB we were processed through U.S. customs before proceeding by taxi to San Francisco's International Airport. The cab fare was expensive by Okinawan standards, but the money I'd saved while in 'Nam would see us through any financial contingency we could possibly encounter in the land of the big PX, even having to pay airfare back to Okinawa. I called my mother after we ate and she said she'd make arrangements to meet us in the west-side air facility in Oklahoma City. That night a Caucasian male, an Asian lady, and two *hanbun hanbun* (half Caucasian and half Oriental) children who wondered how they would be accepted by their countrymen and relatives slept on the hard benches in the civilian terminal, awaiting an early morning flight to Oklahoma City.

The flight to the great Southwest was uneventful, but the reception at the state capital was another matter entirely. My high school chum and best friend, Fray Palmer, had taken a day off from his booming pawnshop in Lawton to drive my mother to the classic. While I chatted with my curly-haired pal, my family was busy being adored by my mother. Fray Palmer finally got the chaos organized and we were driving south in no time a'tall. Fray and I talked of personalities and days of yore in the front seat of the four-door Buick while my mother was getting acquainted with the rest of the story— and for the first time—in the rear of the luxury liner. By the time we'd driven the hundred miles of State Highway 277, everyone had been accepted into the clan. My mother was very impressed with her daughter-in-law and her beautiful grandchildren. I was no less impressed with the fact that I still had friends in the States who would sacrifice their time and effort on my behalf. The visit would get better before the leave was over.

After we were settled in on the west side of Lawton in the house I had purchased in 1953 and turned over to my mother, suppertime had arrived. My stepfather, John Cotton, came aboard, and Hatsuko relaxed while my mother cooked the Oklahoma special. The chicken-fried steaks with cream gravy and mashed potatoes were devoured with little or no lost motion by the family. Then John Cotton, I, and the two off-spring retired to the living room to watch American television. Another first for my children. Hatsuko chatted with Mom while they washed the dishes and cleaned up the kitchen. Everything was new to the children, so they were easily enter-tained. I brought my stepfather up on the news from Asia, and he returned the favor concerning Lawton, Oklahoma, and the country as a whole.

My folks took pains to ensure that the latest additions to the Craig family were entertained. Joe Bob, my youngest brother, was teaching school in Lawton, but found time to visit and get acquainted. My sister Jean, whose husband was sta-tioned at Fort Sill, also came by. My oldest sister, Pauline, a nursing supervisor in Phoenix, Arizona, traveled the thousand miles to get acquainted with her relatives by marriage. Only my brother Peter missed the golden opportunity. Apparently, his New York City (a naughty word in Lawton) business could not be adjusted to meet emergency situations like the sudden arrival of a new family.

Sue Firman, a naturalized U.S. citizen from Okinawa, also helped make Hatsuko feel welcome to the melting pot. Sue was a hairdresser in a beauty shop that my mother frequented. During one of Mom's visits, Mrs. Firman learned of my mother's Okinawan connection. The Firman friendship and concern was a boost to Hatsuko's morale and confidence in the American way. The friendship flourishes even today.

While my kinsmen made sure that Jimmy and Kathy never endured a dull moment, I made a lot of personal visits. Ramey's pool hall and Fray Palmer's pawnshop were my hangouts downtown, and I had no real problems locating pals of Korean and pre-Korean days, and the catastrophe of Lang Vei was never mentioned because none of my old friends even knew of the event.

The fate of Vietnam and the U.S. GIs was still a concern to the people of Oklahoma, much to my pleasant surprise. Despite knowing that Oklahoma was a "My country, right or wrong" state, I protested fighting the war with only regulars, or professional soldiers, and draftees. My conclusions often went over like breaking wind in the front pew. But I still enjoyed having the opportunity to spout my viewpoint.

The dialogues usually went something like this: "Let's call in the National Guard and the Reserve units like we did during the Korean conflict. They have been drawing that state and federal pay for lo these many years. Ain't it 'bout time they earned it? Besides, it would do several other good turns."

"Such as what?" was always the comeback.

"For one thing, it would take some heat off the eighteen- to twenty-six-year-olds. That damn age limit for the draft should be raised to at least forty!"

"A forty-year-old draftee couldn't cut the mustard, Bill. Get serious!"

"I'm as serious as sin, gentlemen. I know all of you are veterans, but give me some credit. I just came back from Vietnam and I've just turned forty-two years old. That alone should prove you wrong." Of course, the opposition refused to budge. They had little use for experience!

"You're an exception," was one cop-out. The next one got me excited, and was therefore not pursued to any lengths. "You're an E8, you don't have to hump those hills anymore!" That line went down the tube rather easily. But about all I ever accomplished in our bull sessions was to enable my friends to visualize an alternative to the "youth-prosecution" draft law. And that was my purpose to begin with.

Thirty days, give or take, passed all too quickly. By the time the middle of November 1968 rolled around, we all had had the chance to learn some things. Hatsuko now knew that she could survive in her children's homeland if the occasion—or the necessity—presented itself. The boy and girl now knew firsthand that milk came from cows and not the commissary. They, too, fell in love with hamburgers and all the rest of the goodies that the medical profession said were not good for your health. They appeared to have enjoyed themselves immensely. Then it was time to use the other half of the round-trip commercial airline ticket to San Francisco International.

Leaving my mother in tears, we sadly boarded the Greyhound and solemnly rode north to Oklahoma City's air terminal. Several hours later we were en route by cab to Travis AFB from San Francisco International. I checked us into the Space A flight desk at Travis but was told to return tomorrow, as the only Far East flights that night were booked solid. Finding the transient billets and retiring for the night came only after we had eaten the Travis terminal cafeteria into a possible food shortage. The next day was spent in the Travis terminal. That night we again retired to the transient sleeping facilities. The children were restless and my wife apprehensive the next day in the Space A waiting room. We still had plenty of time left on my forty-five-day leave, but I was becoming irritated as well.

After a light lunch, things did an about-face. A full-bull Air Force colonel entered the overflowing waiting room and began questioning the staff sergeant in charge of booking and scheduling. I overheard all I needed to hear to boost my morale. "Are all of these personnel waiting to get outta here, Sergeant?"

"Yes sir! We just haven't had the Far East flights, sir."

"Put on an extra aircraft and get 'em on their way," was his reply.

That night we spent far and away from the Travis AFB

guest house on a luxurious Air Force airliner. After stops in Anchorage, Alaska, Hawaii, and Tachikawa AFB in Japan, we landed at Kadena AFB. A short taxicab ride to Kadena Circle, and three U.S. citizens and a green-card Okinawan mother were home again. I alternated sleeping and wondering what the next three years on Okinawa had in store for me. Once the family and I were rested, I signed in from the stateside leave to find out.

CHAPTER 22

Company C, 1st Special Forces Group (Airborne) and Sergeant Major Wally Klink did their best to enlighten me after I reported in at Site Yara, a mile or so from Kadena Circle. "Take a few days to get moved on-post, Sergeant Craig!" He handed me my orders. "When you've completed the move, report back here to become the operations sergeant of Company C, of the 1st Group."

I was not too surprised, but thanked the top soldier while glancing at my orders for on-post quarters. "Sukiran, huh, Sergeant Major?"

"Yeah, Bill, it's a nice area, even if it is next to the Marine barracks." He grinned. "Have you sold your house yet?"

"No, Top, but I have a solid offer from an Air Force NCO that I'll take if he comes up with the cash."

"What are you asking, Bill?"

"I'll take $4,500 for it, old soldier. Hell, I paid $4,200, so I'm not too far out in left field."

"Report back in when you're finished moving on-post. Good luck, Bill!"

In a week the Okinawan moving crew, assisted by the guiding hands of Hatsuko, had our new hilltop quarters shipshape. The two-bedroom duplexes consisted of a kitchen and dining area, latrine, two bedrooms, and a spacious living room, in addition to a screened-in porch that overlooked Buckner Bay. Only two blocks from the back gate of Sukiran, this would be our home for the next three years. We had spent some of the cash flow that had been going to the American Express Bank, but when our house in Kadena sold for the asking price, I had more money than I'd ever dreamed a mere master sergeant E8 in the U.S. Army could legally assemble—around eight thousand dollars to be exact. My monthly check would keep that amount from diminishing much over the next three years.

I was now an E8 with over eighteen years' service. The ever-present $55 jump pay and $21 overseas pay combined with my base pay added up to $541 a month. We could survive on that without Hatsuko going back to work. Taking care of two children, a house, and a husband would keep any woman gainfully employed.

The new home of Company C, headed up by Lieutenant Colonel Trapp at Site Yara, kept me gainfully employed after a few weeks of on-the-job training as operations sergeant. I was confident about being able to handle the job, which consisted of coordinating operations with Personnel and Headquarters up and down the Army, Navy, Air Force, and Marine Corps chain of command. By the time I became familiar with the procedures, my two NCO assistants were on board as well. Staff Sergeant Sterling Smith and SFC Ratchford Haynes were young, compared to me, and sharp as any NCOs I had ever worked with during my time in the Army. The job procedures were easily defined and we all learned as we performed; it's the only method I have ever learned and retained in doing a chore for any length of time.

The subordinate detachments, A and B, were responsible for their training and scheduling it. Only if outside help or coordination were needed would we come into play. Air, water, and ground clearances were our responsibility, and we became proficient at getting them. When our unit went off-island, the Group Operations (S-3) took charge.

The Company Operations S-3s consolidated training and provided the needed coordination and support. The training consisted of the basic Special Forces subjects: weapons, demolitions, tactics, map reading, medical procedures, airborne training, intelligence training (to include escape and evasion), operations, and radio procedures, including sending and receiving Morse code. The schedules were consolidated and sent forward to Group S-3, where they would be consolidated with the A and B Companies' output and forwarded to USARYIS Headquarters. Although we were always learning, the Group S-3 shop was equipped to advise the subordinate detachments in all fields of training.

In 1968 and 1969 unqualified replacement personnel were being shipped to the 1st SF Group not only from Fort Bragg, but from other units in the Far East. Their training fell upon the shoulders of the deploying unit, 1st Group. This was no mean feat because 1st Group was also keeping Vietnam supplied with TDY teams to assist the 5th in its monumental tasks of defeating the Viet Cong, North Vietnamese, Jane Fonda, and the news media.

I wound up each day with my personal physical training program: forty to fifty minutes jogging on the Site Yara road that led to the Air Force's police dog compound and the wooded area behind it. It drove the dogs berserk but it got the job done. About March 1969, Colonel Robert "Bob" Rheault, the commander of the 1st SF Group, developed a program that would someday in the distant future get the entire over-forty-year-old Army personnel off their duffs. When Colonel Rheault's staff broke the news of the physical training test for the elders, I was a ready teddy. Unfortunately, many of my peers had let their physical conditioning go to hell after reaching forty or so because in 1969 PT testing was no longer required after that age. The good old days for the Over the Hill Gang went by the board in the Fighting 1st Special Forces Group, thanks to one of the better commanders who ever wore a beret—or any other Army headgear.

Colonel Rheault's last innovation before he left for Vietnam was to test whether forty-year-old personnel that sported berets and an S prefix were willing and able to pass the same physical training test as that required for jump school in 1959. The 1st SF Group also was the guiding light of Staff Action Force Asia (SAFA) that included leg units such as the 539th Engineers (which, in a civic-action role, often supplemented A-detachments sent to Vietnam), psychological warfare, and medical units. Some of the personnel of those units, too, would be found wanting—at least physically.

I ran every afternoon before 1700 and had no misgivings about the worth of the colonel's idea. I did not know Colonel Rheault personally, but some things about the full-bull (0-6) colonel, and commander of the best unit in the U.S. Army, were common knowledge. The colonel was in good physical condition, lean and mean, and over forty years of age.

Colonel Rheault led off the activity one humid afternoon in March 1969. Station One was push-ups, twenty-five standard being the magic number. No problem, GI! Station Two was my favorite exercise, sit-ups, and the goal was thirty-two in under two minutes. The last exercise, the one that would prove or disprove anyone's physical condition, was the mile run, which had to be completed in under eight and a half minutes.

As usual, I had a well-thought-out plan. For stage one and stage two I planned to accomplish only the minimum because the scoring was simply pass or fail. But I wanted to lower the time for my mile run, so the colonel would know that some of the older enlisted were also in shape. I knew *he* would not just try to get under the wire, and I had a few things to prove my own damn self.

When I finished Station Two, the sit-ups, the colonel was on his first of the five laps around the Bishagawa compound. I'd watched him only a minute or so before I concluded that I couldn't beat him. Still, I was determined to give it a bloody go, so as not to embarrass the NCO Corps. My first two laps constituted an airborne shuffle, only a little faster than a brisk walk, or about a nine-minute mile; I planned my last lap to be a little different.

I increased the pace and then stopped jogging completely before the last 250 yards to the finish line. I had my breath under control and sprinted the remaining distance. I therefore concluded the seven-minute mile rather winded, shall we say. Colonel Rheault and the timers witnessed the mad dash. While I was walking it off, I suddenly found the colonel strolling by my side. I continued gasping for air as he spoke. "How come you screwed off until the last two hundred yards or so, Sergeant Craig?"

"I had to sir," I gasped, "so I wouldn't embarrass you field grades!"

Colonel Rheault had enough field-grade left in him to ream out one fat medic who was being treated at the finish line after only his third lap. The colonel's words rang in my ears while I was preparing my sweaty uniform for the trip home to Sukiran.

"If you don't pass the test the next time, your jump-status days are over. Do you understand, Sergeant?"

The prostrate fat-boy mumbled something while I grinned all the way to the parking lot. I sure hated to see Rheault leave the best outfit in the Army and take over the 5th SF in Vietnam.

Colonel Robert "Bob" B. Rheault (pronounced Row) assumed command of the 5th Group in Nha Trang, South Vietnam on May 29, 1969. In my humble opinion the best CO the 5th ever had, Colonel Rheault didn't have a long wait for the beginning of the end of his career.

Special Forces was furnishing most of the military intelligence in the country when the colonel took charge. Before the summer was over, the quality of some of that information took a severe dive, and the reasons came as no surprise to the old hands: a Vietnamese Special Forces (LLDB) officer had become a double agent and was disrupting the allied information channels. The U.S. intel specialists—career NCOs, some of whom were not SF qualified—who discovered the treason should have bowed out of the picture at that point. But instead of having the traitor shipped to an A site and then forgetting about the incident, they asked the SF archrival, the CIA, what they should do about the snitch. Why they did that has never been explained. They followed the CIA's direction and executed the traitor themselves before dumping his body in the China Sea. The word eventually got to General Creighton Abrams, and he was in hog heaven over the opportunity to bring some smoke on people he otherwise had little control over. Colonel Rheault then made a mistake; he followed the basic leadership principle, the one that states, "Take care of your people."

An Article 32 (pretrial) investigation was ordered by General Abrams, and Rheault was stockade-bound to the Bien Hoa hoosegow. Naturally, the pro–Viet Cong press of the U.S. was having a field day. The "Green Beret Murder Case" filled voids in the U.S. papers. But in what other unit in the U.S. Army, Marine Corps, Air Force, or naval forces could you kill a double agent and be court-martialed for it? Army Chief of Staff General William Westmoreland finally ordered the fiasco terminated, and the three-ring circus was almost over. I have the following information by word of mouth from one of the few rumor-mill sources that I place any faith in—the Special Forces NCO Corps.

After his release from Bien Hoa, Rheault asked that he be reinstated in his command position. Abrams refused, and was apparently backed in that decision by the Pentagon. Rheault chose to part ways with Abrams and the Army rather than give in to the leg commander. On September 29, 1969, Rheault requested retirement. One of the best officers that I had ever served under sacrificed his career for his unit—and became a hero to many of us lifers.

Abrams, consistent if nothing else, then appointed a bona fide leg (nonairborne personnel) as commander of the 5th SF Group (Abn)! Nobody could be that vindictive, we thought. But, yes, a Colonel Lamberes was the first leg to be assigned as the CO of the 5th Special Forces Group—or of any other SF unit that I was aware of. But when he donned the green beret, the sergeant major of the 5th came to our rescue. "You'll have to become qualified before you're authorized to wear that headgear, sir," were the heroic words attributed to Sergeant Major Ron Bowser. Heroic acts such as that feathered my ambitions to be a sergeant major someday. Abrams eventually found a qualified colonel he could trust. On or about August 31, 1969, Colonel Mike Healy, an old SF trooper, became his man. I would meet him as a general years later at Fort Bliss, Texas.

In the meantime, back on Okinawa, things were perking up. I had the Operations chores narrowed to where I could handle them. In addition, I had completed two three-hour courses at the University of Maryland that counted toward a bachelor of arts degree with a major in Far Eastern Studies and a minor in Education. I had completed twelve hours of foreign language in 1967, and that eased my load considerably.

In order to complete the requirements for a degree before rotation time in 1971, I had to take thirty-six hours of courses, including fifteen hours of Far Eastern History, or five upper-level courses. Given my Ops assignment, I foresaw no problem, except bowing my neck and getting with it. I can only speak of the University of Maryland in relation to night school, and the following description will only be of that institution. A regular institution's semester lasts four months. Therefore, a three-hour course is attended three times a week for sixteen weeks, totaling forty-eight classroom appearances. A night course at my alma mater met for three hours a night, twice a week. At the end of two months you have a semester of attendance. There were four or five semesters in a school year on Okinawa, and taking two night courses in a semester at Maryland was strongly advised against. I did it only two or three times, to find out why the institution advised students not to attempt such an asinine endeavor. Also keep in mind that when you miss a night of school, you have just missed a week of school.

My new routine would find me rising before the sun in order to be at work for the 0730-hour work call. Physical training preceded a day's labor at Site Yara. At 1600 I was en route to my Fatima housing facilities in Sukiran to change clothes and eat. My keeping Jimmy and Kathy occupied would allow Hatsuko to prepare the evening meal. Most of our classes were in U.S. facilities on post in Sukiran so travel time was minimal. Before 1830 (six-thirty P.M.) I was in an upper-level class that would consume the next three hours.

In all fairness, the instructors were terrific. Of course, the usual ten percent of near misses in the teachers' ranks affected the University of Maryland just as it does every school in the world. Twenty-one thirty, or nine-thirty P.M., found the class on its way home. In my case, I often made a stop at the Habu Pit, the snake pit that was the Marine NCO Club only a few city blocks from the Fatima housing. Despite drinking a few beers to wash down the day, I would be home by closing time, or 2300 hours, whichever came first. That was the weekday routine I followed during my last hitch in Okinawa. Thanks to the common sense of the profs, homework was normally assigned for weekends only, the student body being ninety-five percent working folk.

Homework usually consisted of term papers, so Saturdays invariably involved research in the Sukiran library. The remainder of the weekend was free time, which I used to become acquainted with my wife and children. I enjoyed my family to no end, although I often denied the fact to my hard-core unaccompanied teammates.

We usually ate out on the weekends, and the children, along with their mother, appeared to enjoy the NCO Club atmosphere and cuisine. By then Kathy and Jimmy were four and five years old, respectively, well-behaved, and a pleasure to be around, even in public. What few paddlings they received obviously got the job done, or else they inherited an inner discipline from their mother's side of the coop. I recorded some of the more memorable incidents that are hidden in that portion of my memory's deposit box.

Hatsuko was a professional housekeeper long before I met her, so she had no problems on that score. Like most on-post families, she hired an Okinawan papa-san to keep the small front and rear yards mowed and immaculate. The cost was minimal so I concurred rather than do it myself. Her second request I went along with also, but it took me a while to fully understand it; Hatsuko wanted to hire a housemaid. I didn't really understand why, and only after looking at the pros and cons did I consent.

In addition to the usual maintenance of the living room, kitchen, bathroom, and bedrooms, the children came in for some attention due to their varied activities. And like the yardman, house help was so affordable that it was hard to resist, especially on a master sergeant's (E8) pay. Hatsuko had become acquainted with Kiyoko Yonaha while I was PCS to 'Nam, 1967–68. Kiyoko lived with her family in Kadena Circle and was six years younger than my wife, about twenty-eight at the time. The situation jelled from the start, but as I was to learn later, it had some drawbacks.

Kiyoko was a good-looking, well-put-together Okinawan lady, who was leaving the home, normally, when I was arriving from work. No problem on that score. However, she spoke little if any English, a drawback because that meant my children—Americans, you know—heard no English all day until I arrived home about five o'clock. Sooo? So, it caused some English-learning problems for the two young U.S. citizens.

Hatsuko got up every morning, made coffee and went back to bed after I finally rose at five. Jimmy often got up and drank milk with me then went back to bed. One morning, much to my surprise, Kathy joined us. I served her some milk on the kitchen table that bordered the screened-in porch overlooking the lights of darkened Buckner Bay. After I resumed drinking my coffee, Kathy mumbled something that went over my head. When I asked her to repeat it, she did, but in the Okinawan dialect. Perhaps, though I doubt it, if she'd spoken in Japanese I could have grasped what she wanted. Finally, I said, "Kathy, I don't understand. Try saying it in English, please?"

The comeback was in Okinawan. I threw up both hands. Fortunately, Jimmy came to the rescue in passable English.

"She wants some cereal, Daddy!"

I complied with her request, and while sipping my coffee, realized I'd have to take steps to correct what might become a language problem. On a Sunday afternoon while watching a two-week-old NFL football game at the club, I decided to buy a small portable television set that the ladies could use during the day to watch Japanese TV programs, and the children could watch the U.S. Armed Forces station to become familiar with their native tongue. I foresaw no problem for them to learn two languages. I did my part by watching the Andy Griffith show with them at night when not in school. Jimmy also took to American football, and Kathy liked the cartoons, so both children's English began to improve. I was more than pleased with the results. The next problem created by their environment was a little different.

Japanese culture dictated the roles of children by gender, and young boys and girls were treated very differently in the family. Boys are looked upon as the coming masters of the family, and the future breadwinners were very selectively punished, if at all. Young girls were taught to grow up to please males. Hatsuko and Kiyoko did not differ from this pattern, but one master sergeant in the U.S. military did.

Whenever I caught Jimmy treating his sister in a demeaning manner, I tried to correct the situation. To make sure that I was educating the guilty party, I often went to Hatsuko after the children were tucked away for the evening and talked to her about it.

Hatsuko was quick to agree, but she said that following the traditions of their culture was not an easy habit to overcome for her and Kiyoko. Despite our discussions, the matter came up again and again in 1969 and 1970.

The first time I saw Jimmy misbehave in this way, I talked to my son, out of earshot. The lecture was short and to the point, but the young soldier did not seem to take my warnings as seriously as I thought he should have. "Jimmy, it is the brother's job to protect his sister from others," I told him. "Men do not strike the weaker sex. You are not her boss, nor is she your slave. At the very least, treat her as your equal. You got that, son?" No response; the ol' family counselor continued to march.

"Do you love your mother, Jimmy?"

I finally got a rise out of him: "Yes, Daddy!"

"Okay! I'm sure you know that your mom is a female, or girl." 'Nuff said, I hoped. It wasn't.

A few days later I came home early after my five-mile jog at Site Yara. While I was preparing for school and supper, Jimmy again struck his sister. A short lecture was preceded by the topical application of a GI belt to the largest muscle in the body. This dismayed Kiyoko Yonaha, who became sullen. I took no notice of the reaction at the time and continued my chore. I finished supper and headed for the University of Maryland classroom at nearby Kubasaki High School. After three hours, I returned home. I was in for a shock.

Hatsuko and Kathy were watching *Mission Impossible* on the Armed Forces TV station. After I put away my books, it dawned on me that someone was missing. I inquired as politely as possible about my son's whereabouts while Kathy's innocent look remained in place on her sweet face. "Is Jimmy already in bed, Hatsuko?"

"No, Papa-san," she replied. "Kiyoko wanted to take him home for the night, so I said okay."

It was not lost on her that I went into the first stages of shock, while managing to respond. "Why would Jim want to stay at Kadena Circle instead of his own home?"

"Because you spanked him, Daddy. He didn't like it and Kiyoko does not believe little boys should be reprimanded in that manner, if any. You know how the Japanese and Okinawans feel about that. Don't you?"

I counted to ten. "James J. Craig is an American citizen, Hatsuko," I said, "and will be raised as such. We have talked about this before, and I thought you were coming around to my way of thinking on this issue."

"I am, Bill. But Kiyoko is another matter, and another culture. She means only the best for Jimmy, so try and see her side. Please!"

I allowed myself to calm my temper before replying. "Okay. I'll not say a word about it, but you inform your maid that I run this family. In other words, she needs my permission before she keeps Jimmy overnight. The issue is closed."

I lay back in the recliner and Kathy snuggled up to her mom while Robert Stack was still trying to solve some problems of his own on *Mission Impossible*. He's got it made, I concluded before slumber took over.

Not having matured to perfection even then, like most husbands, I was prone to mistakes. Shortly after the "kidnapping," I apparently blew it again. Hatsuko had graduated from damn near every cooking school on the island and was by then involved in Okinawan sewing classes. The members of the doll-making class met twice a week to work on their Japanese dolls. Our quarters at Fatima housing was the doll-making classroom from 1300 until 1600 on those afternoons. The participants numbered six or seven, and all were Japanese or Okinawan women married to GIs stationed on the island. Evidence of Hatsuko's involvement can be seen even today, more than two decades later, in a living room in southwestern Oklahoma where lifelike dolls of ancient Japanese rulers, geisha girls, and imperial ladies inhabit a glass case adorning our front room. How did I screw up this time? It turned out to be relatively simple. I used no secret formula to accomplish the mission.

One slack afternoon at Site Yara, I finished my run by 1420 hours and called it a day. Sergeants Haynes and Sterling Smith grabbed the reins of the Operations shop as soon as I departed.

Dressed in bloody, sweaty, smelly fatigues and jungle boots, I arrived at my hooch around three-thirty P.M. The stares and

Japanese remarks I received when I marched through the "classroom" were shocking even to a military professional—and that's pretty shocking. But Kiyoko, Jimmy, and Kathy greeted me in a friendly manner from the screened back porch, and that was gratifying. I was glad someone still loved me. By the time I cleaned up for chow and night classes, the assembly room had been vacated. After Hatsuko gave me a verbal thrashing for the manner of my interruption, the episode was over. Like a good soldier, I promised I wouldn't make that mistake again, and believe me, I didn't.

On Okinawa military school buses picked up dependent children each morning to transport them to school. One bus stopped on the street in front of our quarters. Every day, Kathy and Jimmy watched the children form up and board the bus. They were fascinated by the activity. At the ages of three and four respectively, they began to complain of inequity. As they grew older, so did the complaints. At least once a week I attempted to explain away the problem. The explanation bounced off their pretty heads, but I endured.

"You must be five years old to begin preschool, or kindergarten. Furthermore, the age of six will see you into the first grade. Now do you understand?" I think they understood; they just wanted to get on that school bus with the rest of the kids. Several times Hatsuko had to remove them from the line of students. The bus drivers thought it was hilarious, but it brought back memories to me that I'd just as soon have forgotten.

My first experience in school was marked by the cruel taunts of my classmates because of my slurred speech and nasal tone. I had a surgically repaired harelip and a cleft palate; over the years, I gradually trained myself to avoid all traces of the nasality that helped make my childhood especially difficult. I was secretly pleased that my children viewed their coming attendance at school as something to be looked forward to; and for both of them, it would turn out to be just that. They rejoiced when they could bring home books and other material they could pore over the same way they'd seen their father do, weekend after weekend.

The first few school years went swiftly. Jimmy began nursery school and kindergarten in 1968 and '69 at Camp Boone, located near Ojana on Highway One, not far from the capital city of Okinawa. In 1970 until March 1971 he attended Camp Mercy Elementary as a first and second grade student. The second grade would be his slot when he finally reached his homeland in March 1971. Kathy followed in her brother's footsteps in 1970 and '71. She would be a first grader upon enrollment in a stateside school in 1971.

Meanwhile, I finished my last University of Maryland course in late November 1970. I was scheduled for graduation in January 1971 in Tokyo, Japan.

CHAPTER 23

In December 1970 I had many hurdles to clear besides the Tokyo graduation. My stay on Oki was drawing to a close. Although my wife and children were looking forward to the stateside environment, I was *not*. I only had to look at the Far East situation to explain my side of it.

According to the news media, the Armed Forces were rife with rebellion and insubordination. But on Okinawa there seemed little evidence to support that claim. The 1st SF Group (Abn) was as strong and well-disciplined as it had ever been, and I saw no problems with the Marine Corps and Air Force units. Dope? I doubt that there was any on the island, anywhere but the pharmacy. The local penalty for illegal drugs was not as harsh as Malaysia's death penalty, but it was severe enough. I couldn't really vouch for the situation in Vietnam, due to my two-and-a-half-year absence. And Vietnam, tactically and politically, was another matter entirely.

By late 1970 the draw-down of U.S. personnel in Vietnam was well under way. General Creighton Abrams had been handed Westmoreland's position to do just that. That being the case, the commander-in-chief of all the Armed Forces in Vietnam was efficient as "Speedy" Gonzales. The draw-down was devised by the U.S. politicians for vote-getting purposes and to appease a vocal minority of riffraff in the U.S. Abrams wasted no time gutting Special Forces projects. The Civilian Irregular Defense Group had been turned over to the ARVN Rangers and phased out by August 27, 1969. The 5th SF

Group (Abn) was scheduled to be down to zilch by March 31, 1971. There was no doubt that the general's vendetta would reach its goal on his timetable. Unfortunately, the quicker Special Forces rotated, the quicker the South Vietnamese would go down the tube, making our years of sacrifice appear wasted.

The remainder of the combat troops were hanging in there, as best I could tell, continuing to march in a military manner. By that I mean they continued to punish the North Vietnamese youth who composed the failing North Vietnamese Army, as very few generations had ever been punished, before or since. Their casualties, thanks in the main to our uncontested control of the air, were simply unreal. Even I felt sorry for those kids; Jane Fonda and Ho Chi Minh knew best. Most of our combat troops would be out of South Vietnam by the time I rotated, so I was fairly confident of a stateside assignment. After all, I had been in the Pacific Theater almost ten years by then, in continued violation of the six-year limit. I only hoped the wife and kids would like Fort Bragg and the Fayetteville, North Carolina area. Unfortunately, my calculations were off base in more respects than I'd imagined. In the first part of January 1971, a thunderbolt worked its way down through channels to my unit of choice on Okinawa.

The Company C sergeant major handed me my orders, and I exited the orderly room to the Operations hut, where I read them in disbelief. "Individual will proceed on Permanent Change of Station as indicated." The indication was U.S. Army Vietnam Training Support Headquarters, APO San Francisco 96240. Any SF soldier on Okinawa knew that APO 96240 was Nha Trang, South Vietnam. No mention of what to do with a wife and two children was noticeable. I knew Ms. Alexander had a ball having these orders cut and distributed. Payback is hell, I again reminded myself before returning to the orderly room.

The orders were classified, but the unit sergeant major gave me the lowdown, to hell with the classification. "The Military Assistance Command, Vietnam, is taking over the training responsibilities of the 5th Special Forces Group, which will depart Vietnam shortly for Fort Bragg, your old hometown, Bill. A total of 240 SF people will PCS to fill the slots. All of the 240 must be SF qualified, and you are apparently one of them. You'll report to the headquarters in Nha Trang, the old home of the 5th Special Forces. Where in the hell you'll go from there, it's hard to say. But it'll be the Long Hai, Chi Lang, or Bien Hoa training centers. I know that much."

"Who are they training, Sergeant Major?" I asked.

"At Nha Trang they're training the ARVN Rangers and LLDB [Viet Special Forces] who have taken over the border camps, or A camps. At Long Hai and Chi Lang, they're training Cambodians to send back into Cambodia. Why, I don't know. But there you are, Bill. Any comments, old soldier?"

Why me? came to mind, but I skipped over it. "I've spent forty-nine months in that region and have no desire to return," I said. "I guess that cuts no mustard. Huh?"

"I've studied your records, Bill, and all but one year of that time was temporary duty from Okinawa and/or stateside assignments. They don't count that as time spent in-country. To the Department of the Army, you've spent one year in Vietnam. Sorry about that."

I knew that, so I switched tactics—to no avail, of course. "What about nine years and four months consecutively in one overseas command?" I tried.

"The Department of the Army knows you pulled a funny there, somehow. You're already in violation of the six-year rule, so what's another twelve months going to matter? You might as well get ready for the assignment. Where you gonna start?"

"I'm going to Group Personnel and initiate orders for my wife and kids to move to the States. Thanks for your time. Haynes and Sterling Smith can handle the Operations shop while I'm out-processing. I'm off to the 'Nam again, but I goddamn sure don't have to like it. Screw D.A.!" (Department of the Army.) I inserted the last remark to let the top soldier know I hadn't changed any.

I revved up my newly purchased Datsun four-door sedan and headed for Fatima housing in order to begin the processing. I secured the needed documents while Group Personnel awaited my arrival. The orders were in my hands in five working days. Hatsuko, James, and Katherine would be on their way to the USA on or about March 10, 1971. To be exact, the orders designated 2820 G Avenue, Lawton, Oklahoma, as their new home of record. Doing my night chores, I made sure my mother was aware that she would soon have three new room-and-boarders in her mansion on the west side of Lawton, near Cameron Junior College. The telephone calls home were well worth the expense, and the entire family enjoyed them tremendously—including my lonesome. If nothing else, I got a charge out of watching and listening to Jim and Kathy talk to their newly rediscovered grandma. It was a riot. In fact, it helped take my mind from my assignment in South Vietnam.

I did not officially notify my alma mater that I would not be at the Tokyo ceremony, but mentally made note of that fact. This didn't forbid the *Pacific Stars & Stripes* from making a big deal out of it, much to my delight. The January issue listed the names of the participants, their units, and military rank. Nor did the fact that I was the only enlisted scum go unnoticed. My unit commander and the Group commander sent me Letters of Commendation that noted the spectacular achievement. In reality, I owed my unit, for allowing me to stay in one place long enough to accomplish the mission. A hearty thanks went out to all concerned. The only sad note was that Ms. A.'s revenge would prevent my live participation. Hell, you're gonna lose *some*!

In February 1971 Hatsuko and the packing crew from USARYIS stowed our furniture. Practically everything would go to a storage facility in the United States. With our bags and baggage, we moved into the transients' quarters near Hatsuko's old place of employment at Sukiran—the Coral Hill NCO Club. I liked that arrangement because it offered me an opportunity to drink a few beers and practice my farewells to my favorite unit in the U.S. Army. I was only sorry when the long Okinawan chapter was closed by a luxurious Class A airplane flight to my other home. At Travis AFB we were presented with a U.S. Air Force bus ride to the San Francisco International Airport. I can't tell a lie; I enjoyed the Armed Forces waiting on us hand and foot.

After we paid our fares to Oklahoma City, the wife and kids settled in the uncomfortable airport arrangements for a night's rest. I called my mother and asked her to meet us in the civilian air facility the next day around noon. I strongly suggested that Fray Palmer, my ol' high school pal, might once again furnish the transportation if approached in a motherly fashion. She said she would try.

I woke the wife and kids in their new country in time for a late breakfast and an early flight. To the relief of my mother and her chauffeur, Fray Palmer, we arrived safely in Oklahoma City at around noon. The hugging and handshakes consumed some time, but with baggage accounted for and loaded, we were soon in a new Buick on our way to Lawton via State Highway 277. I sat in the front with the driver, while Hatsuko again had a chance to admire the flat Oklahoma terrain from the rear. All the while, Grandma Katie talked with her good-looking, well-behaved grandchildren, also from the large rear compartment.

Upon arrival at our destination and after Fray's departure, my mother showed us the living arrangements that would prevail during my absence. Hatsuko had a room and double bed to her lonesome. Kathy and Jim had a room with small single beds. I was satisfied they would make do during my year's absence. A few days later I saw to it that Jim and Kathy were enrolled in Cleveland Elementary School. Since the school was four blocks from the house, transportation would not be a problem except during weather extremes. My stepfather's car would fill in during those rare periods.

On March 20, 1971, I escorted my children to school for their enrollment. They were delighted to be going back, and I was delighted to find out that the school principal was an old St. Mary's School acquaintance of mine. Principal George Steuver welcomed me to his office as the children continued the enrollment process. We laughed and talked for twenty minutes before Jim and Kathy were done. They were then ushered into Steuver's office. He had a chance to study the two only briefly before Jimmy said, "Why can't we go to classes today, Daddy?" Steuver was mildly set back, but I shoulda known it was coming.

"Because I wasn't thinking, Jimmy. I see no problem, if it's okay with your boss," I said, pointing to Steuver. "I'll go home and get your lunches and you can pick them up here at noon. Okay, George?"

The astonished school administrator granted my request before I continued. "I'll see the two of you when school is out and we'll walk home together. Okay?" My mother was also surprised, but Hatusko fixed sandwiches without any display of emotion. Two students who loved their work were in their first day of school in their native land.

All my bank savings, except the overseas savings deposits that were drawing ten percent interest, were transferred to a bank account in Lawton. My mother's house payments continued to be paid by an allotment from my monthly paycheck. Except for the administrative chores, I enjoyed the three weeks with my family and friends. Before I departed Lawton, I was assured by my brother and sister, Joe Bob and Jean, that Hatsuko and the kids would not want for support, and Sue Firman also promised companionship and support for my wife and children. I did get some respite from all the mental anticipation my assignment had brought about. Hatsuko informed me a week or so before I left that she was indeed pregnant . . .

again. We had wanted the third child desperately and were
both overjoyed with the news.

All I had left was to complete my last tour in-country, a tour
that would forever change not only my life, but my family's
and others too numerous to mention.

CHAPTER 24

Nothing good lasts forever. I was shortly on a commercial flight from Oklahoma City to Travis AFB, California. At Travis, the system wasted little time loading my duffel bag on a C-141 cargo plane for Nha Trang. I stood in the boarding line adorned in jungle fatigues and jungle boots for a luxurious ride to Vietnam. A similar aircraft was on a runway facing the opposite direction, and I recognized almost everyone in the line for that plane, even at a considerable distance. They waved and grinned when they saw my beret. When I spotted the colors of the 5th SF Group waving in the cool breeze, I responded to everyone who wanted to listen. "Them assholes are going to Bragg and I'm taking their place with 239 other dummies. Someone don't like me." The tour would prove me correct for a change.

After refueling stops in Alaska, Hawaii, and Japan, my C-141 landed at Nha Trang AFB, South Vietnam, on April 2, 1971.

I was the only GI aboard who sported the green beanie that Abrams and MACV loved so. I was also the only one who waited for a ride to U.S. Support Headquarters. Nha Trang AFB was located on the west side of the resort city, and the old 5th HQ was within spitting distance of the hangar where I impatiently waited for transportation. I didn't wait long. I hailed the first jeep driven by a U.S. Army soldier and ordered him to take me to the 5th's former stomping grounds. He appeared happy to transport an unhappy master sergeant to his new duty station. The short trip culminated when the driver stopped in the center of a cluster of one-story, framed, sandbagged buildings. I unloaded and sincerely thanked the young man, but he only smiled and drove off. I stood on the side of the road that split the complex, and turned to face the old headquarters building. But before I could load up and saunter into the building I knew so well years ago, a staff sergeant came by and squared me away.

"No, Top, that's a classroom area now. The new headquarters is the large building east of the NCO Club."

I did an about-face and looked at the building he spoke of. "I'll be damned. That was a briefing hall back in 1968."

"Correct, Top. They've done some remodeling since then. Just walk in the front, and Sergeant Major Darcy's office will be right in front of you. Good luck!" Before he walked away, I noted a flash in his beret that I'd never seen before.

I proceeded, bag and baggage, to do as instructed. I knocked, and I heard Sgt. Major Paul Darcy's voice for the first time since 1961, at Fort Bragg: "Come on in!"

I left my luggage outside and walked in hat in hand. Darcy, slender-tender at six feet five inches tall, smiled, stood up, and shook my hand. We exchanged amenities before he invited me to be seated in front of his desk. Unknowingly, I started the conversation with my jump boot in my mouth; not unusual for me. "Damn, Paul, when was the last time I saw you? In 1961, I believe—when we returned from Laos in civilian clothes. Where in the hell have you been, anyhoo? I've been in Okinawa and here for ten years!"

Darcy blushed before replying. "I've been at Bragg and the 8th Special Forces Group in Panama, Bill."

"You haven't been back over here since Laos, Sergeant Major?" I asked in astonishment.

"Nope, I've been too busy in other areas, Bill," he answered, with a rather hostile tone. "What can I do for you?"

I presented a copy of Ms. A's revenge and became a little hostile my own damn self, not knowing at the time that it was something I'd better get used to. Darcy had prepared me to meet a herd of them before my life in the Army was finished.

Darcy handed back the orders except for one copy before he spoke. "Damn, I didn't know you were coming. I'll look at our outlying camps and see what openings we have." Darcy then briefed me, and it came out about like the briefing by Sergeant Major Klink about a month prior in Okinawa. He then briefed me on the local layout, which I still knew better than he did. Come time for departure, we both lied. "Good to see you again, also," he said before I left.

In-processing filled the rest of the day, and I came out clothed in camouflage fatigues and floppy jungle hat. I was booked into the VIP quarters and had a comfortable wood-plank room sandbagged waist high. At the evening meal, I met SFC Melvin Englebrecht, who had been my running mate at Bragg and for a while on Okinawa. I told him my plight and promised to meet him at the NCO Club after dark. Except for Englebrecht, I was otherwise in foreign territory in the Nha Trang mess hall.

That night in the large one-room club, we sat at a round table a short distance from the bar and sipped our brews. We spoke of the Laotian days with Darcy et al., and of our days in Okinawa before and after we both got married. Engelbrecht married a movie star of Japanese descent who sang in the clubs and honky-tonks on Oki. She had decided the redhead was her cup of tea, and they tied the knot about the same time we did. His wife and two young girls were now in the States with his folks. We finally homed in on the present situation. Mel was instructing some class but was also up to his neck in his love of the crafts. He made training aids for the other instructors, a job he'd mastered over the years. I promised to come see him and some of his work the next day. He couldn't help me much on my assignment, but I did get the impression that being away from his family was driving him out of the Army. I'd seen that enough in Special Forces not to become too alarmed about it at this stage of my career.

I left the club for my bunk and, because of what I'd seen and heard the first day, never once worried about mortar or sapper attacks after dark. First impressions are often wrong, but I was willing to bet my life I was right—at least as far as the Nha Trang area was concerned. General Vo Nguyen Giap, the idiot who supposedly never lost a battle but had succeeded in losing a generation of northern troops trying to win one in South Vietnam, had sense enough to fall back, regroup, and wait until the U.S. deserted the sinking southern ship. I was sure of that, and most NCOs believed just as I did. Despite what author Peter Macdonald would write years later, I always believed Giap to be a loser. He won at Khe Sanh? Gimme a break.

I reported to Darcy for the next four days and was turned away jobless each time. I was beginning to believe two things about my ridiculous assignment: (1) I was surplus; (2) the people who had earlier avoided 'Nam resented me. After yet another negative progress report by the sergeant major, I spoke my piece: "The Department of the Army obviously screwed up. That, or their math is second rate, Top. There's no assignment for me here, so I suggest you say so and ask them for a further assignment, like stateside."

I had my sergeant major's attention. He blushed openly and moved nervously behind his throne before replying. "I don't have the power to reassign you, and by the time D.A. got around to it, your tour would be over. However, I have an idea that might help us both. Do you remember Johnnie B. Miller from the old Lao Task Force?"

"Sure, Sergeant Major, we ran around together from time to time at Bragg."

"Well, he's the Operations sergeant major at Chi Lang in 4th Corps, and I'm sure he can find a slot for you down there. They're training Cambodians, so there's always plenty to do. Let me contact him, and I'll get back to you tomorrow."

Much to the relief of Darcy and me, Miller agreed to put me to work at Chi Lang. The next day I was on a C-130 cargo plane to the large Bien Hoa airstrip the U.S. Air Force maintained thirty kilometers south of Saigon. A small encampment there was a logistical arm of MACV Training Support Headquarters and run by a Sergeant Major Ferguson. I stayed overnight in the III Corps Tactical Zone and former home of the old Bien Hoa Stockade that Colonel Rheault had made famous during his stay.

The next day I was awaiting a ride to Chi Lang in my usual habitat. The club was small and ill-lit, but a black friend of mine found me. Staff Sergeant Brooks, formerly of Lang Vei and A-101, greeted me loudly when he saw me sitting at the small bar. We moved to a booth to talk, and we homesteaded there until closing time at 2300, relating our experiences before and since our last meeting at the Da Nang Naval Hospital. The meeting of an old bloody reminder of Lang Vei left me with a thought that still exists twenty-six years later: Lang Vei will never mentally go away in my lifetime.

The small fixed-wing aircraft hummed out of III Corps the next day with me and three unknown SF operators aboard on a Chi Lang heading. Chi Lang, in the IV Corps Tactical Zone of Vietnam, was located south of Bien Hoa and the Parrot's Beak, near the Cambodian border.

Sergeant Major Johnnie B. Miller, from Carrollton, Ohio, stood five-ten and weighed in at 175. He'd been about thirty years old when we first met in the 77th SF Group (Abn) in 1960 at Fort Bragg. While training with the Lao Task Force before departure, Johnnie B. was in another A-team that would deploy when we did. Englebrecht and I lived then in the wooden barracks but often met the ol' blue-eyed married man in the main NCO Club or Annex Eight for a few beers before he deployed to his wife and kids. I thought I knew the congenial, brown-haired Miller until he became the hand-to-hand instructor for the "trash force," as it was vulgarly known. He was the best I'd ever encountered in this Special Forces physical subject. Until I endured his instruction, I'd always believed that hand-to-hand fighting was a way to get your point across before you got sewed up by the doctor, or had your victim sewed up. The last hour of each day in the trash force with Johnnie B. as my instructor changed my outlook on fighting. Fun it wasn't, but hard work it was. That was often the conclusion I came to, bruised and panting, after the classes.

After we returned from Laos in 1961, Miller and I went our separate ways, only to meet again in the Delta Project in 1965. Fortunately, I was leaving the Delta snoopers and poopers for my new family life in Okinawa, while Miller was just beginning his Delta tour. He survived and returned to his family in one piece; many did not. On June 29, 1969, the smiling 111.B4S light weapons man fared no better than many of us did at Lang Vei.

While serving in the II Corps Mike Force, he was gut-shot attempting to relieve an A camp in the coastal city of Qui Nhon. The AK-47 round nicked the esophagus before it entered his stomach. The same helicopter that brought him to the ill-fated encounter removed him to the Saigon hospital. There, he was under the knife within the twelve hours allowed for that type of wound. With a scar that ran from his crotch to the center of his rib cage, Johnnie Miller survived the experience and recovered in Womack Hospital at Fort Bragg.

The sergeant major of Chi Lang met our light aircraft on the small Chi Lang airstrip in the middle of April 1971 at 1500 in the afternoon. After the usual laughing, long-lost friendship was renewed, I piled my equipment in Johnnie's jeep, but only after the other operators had departed in a three-quarter-ton truck. I felt fairly comfortable for the first time since I had received my orders months before.

Chi Lang SF Camp was, as I recall, a three-street layout separated from a large ARVN camp by a north-to-south parade field and an east-west dirt road. We turned left into the second street and saw a few permanent wooden buildings and a ton of squad tents with wood flooring and sides, sandbagged in the appropriate manner. After the turning maneuver, I asked, "Where am I gonna stay, old soldier?"

"With me, of course. We'll talk and then I think you'll understand why. Okay!" We stopped on a road in the center of camp, and I put my ditty bag and duffel bag in the top's tent. I noted that my bunk was already made with sheets, GI blankets, and a pillow. The foot tour started with the mess hall, on to the small club, both catty-corner from our quarters, then to the A-detachment's quarters, which were like our own. The Cambodian quarters were surrounded by communication trenches and overhead cover facing a dry rice paddy. During the tour, I received a personnel briefing as well. Because Miller and I spoke the same language, I had no problem understanding exactly what he meant.

The commander of the modified B-detachment, or Command & Control detachment at Chi Lang, was an Engineer officer with no prior Special Forces experience. Natch!

During supper—excellent cuisine, I might add—and a few beers in the club before bedtime, the sergeant major continued to fill me in. We finally arrived at my assignment. The Chi Lang Operations sergeant was a master sergeant E8 who had been in the slot since its inception. Miller admitted to me that he was doing an excellent job. "The major has asked that I not replace him with you. I know this may not set well with you, but hear me out.

"This Special Forces qualified individual needs no indoctrination to the Cambodian training program because he has been with it since the beginning. That's why I kinda go along with the major on this one. You can assist him, and when you have slack time, you can assist me. That's about the best I can do, Bill. Hope you go along with it."

That's where I stood in my Chi Lang assignment. I really was surplus in Vietnam, but someone was determined that I would do my year regardless. I went along with it, not that I was ever given a choice in the matter. I got along very well with the Operations sergeant and helped him along when my experience warranted it. Sergeant Major Miller had many coordinating tasks that required travel to other camps in the vicinity, so coordination took up my time and little else. My relationship with the other SF people remained aloof. Why? My relationship with Miller and resentment of my previous Vietnam time was all I could ever figure. Many of the GIs at Chi Lang were of the variety of military hippies I'd heard about on Okinawa and in stateside newspapers. In retaliation, I became more unpopular by correcting gross uniform and behavioral violations. As far as we could see, Miller and I were the only ones who did so. I made myself even more lovable in the club one night by professing my thoughts very loudly.

Miller was unpopular for another reason. Any Special Forces camp, or MACV compound, for that matter, was off limits to prostitutes, and you were not allowed to cohabit with women inside any SF camp I had ever been in. It's only common sense. What if you were falling in love, momentarily, of course, with the camp commander's wife? That could cause a problem, or a killing, if the locals became aware of the situation—and in a camp, hiding that kind of liaison is almost impossible. Miller enforced this commonsense approach at Chi Lang. The enlisted troops didn't like that, and for a reason I'd never encountered in Vietnam or Laos. It only took me a month to discover that a few U.S. officers did not go along with the nonfraternization policy, a policy enforced in the U.S. Army since before the Civil War. I went to their small officers' club one night to confirm the rumors. They were so obvious that even a dumb master sergeant came away shaking his head. I guess my thoughts on officer promotions were correct—anyone who breathes long enough can make major. I confronted Sergeant Major Miller with my undercover work the very next day. He acted ashamed, but damn if I know why—it wasn't his doing.

"I've warned the major about it, but he's a liberal, I guess. I run the camp, but apparently not the officers, Bill! It's the new hippy Army you've read about. Do you have a solution?"

Three months into my twelve-month farce, I finally got to earn some of my "combat" pay of sixty-five dollars a month. I was happy about it, but not over the way it came about.

Despite the fact that by 1971 the SF tours were R&R in themselves, the troops were still authorized to take the official Army-sanctioned rest and relaxation for six days. A team sergeant's R&R to meet his wife in Hawaii came at the same period as the graduating FTX for his Cambodian troops. What a coincidence. I got my verbal orders for the exercise from J. B. Miller.

"The major said for you to take Master Sergeant Hula's place on the operation with his unit tomorrow."

In a way, I was happy, but in a way, I was shocked as well. I never knew the major's motives, and still don't. I met with the rest of the team that night in their makeshift team house near the south end of the camp. Captain Biggs (not his real name) was a stocky, muscular youngster in his late twenties or early thirties. He introduced me as the team sergeant for the exercise. His XO, a thin young lieutenant of the grade school variety, was not too thrilled by my presence, nor were the rest of the unknowns in the detachment, but the captain appeared pleased, and that was all that mattered to me at the time.

The Cambodian battalion would move out in broad daylight at around 0800 the next day. They would never be too far from Chi Lang, and would operate as companies. The unit would circle Chi Lang and be back in five days if everything went as planned.

I would be second in command and remain with Captain Biggs and the battalion staff, such as it was. I was pleased with the briefing, but was also secretly pleased that I had worked out almost every evening since my arrival to maintain my physical condition.

The appointed time found our command party—composed of the battalion CO; the executive officer, Biggs; an SF medic; an indigenous RTO; an interpreter; and me—centered securely in the march order of 2nd Company. The unit moved slowly and the men were well-disciplined. Disciplined enough that they avoided open terrain, skirting the flat rice paddies for the concealment of the brush and trees on the outskirts. We surrounded an abandoned village, searched, seized, and secured it by 1600. At 1700 we were in our night location under the humid dry-season sun.

By C-ration time the captain and I had our sleeping gear ready near an abandoned bamboo hut. We had our canteens refilled and agreed on the fifty percent alert arrangement before the dark, star-filled night took over. I was curled up on my winter sleeping bag when the first rounds hit the nearby huts and got my complete attention. I rolled over and had my M-16 facing the outer perimeter in a military instant, the Captain being only a few yards away in the same alert attitude. The firing from both sides of the perimeter continued for what seemed to be a long period, but was probably only ten minutes in reality. If any rounds or ricochet rounds approached our command crew, I was unaware of it. While the battalion CO observed, the RTO worked out on the PRC-25 radio. When he ceased, the Cambodian interpreter took over and we got the poop. All U.S. personnel had checked in on our net before we were briefed by the interpreter. Our village had been probed by a platoon-size Viet Cong unit. Because of the interlocking return fire, the enemy withdrew.

The company had only one serious casualty and no KIAs, but damn if I know how. All I could surmise was that with no high-angle mortar support, the VC must have been inexperienced and firing high. The wounded soldier was being brought to our location, so I called our U.S. medic over the HT-1 walkie-talkie. The young, very serious SF doctor and the chest-shot stretcher case arrived at about the same time. For the next thirty minutes or so our entire crew watched the young medical graduate from the Fort Bragg dog lab work out. He was terrific.

The medic needlessly told me to get a medical evacuation chopper in there, and I sincerely tried. In about thirty minutes one was on the way, much to my surprise, considering the closing darkness. The victim—thanks to the American medic—was still alive, and I watched underneath a hooch by the glow of a Coleman lantern as the SF medic administered blood plasma as fast as his patient could take it; because of internal bleeding from a nicked aorta, that was fast. The medic had opened the chest and was trying to repair the aorta or at least keep it closed enough to slow the bleeding.

Nudged by Captain Biggs, the indigenous commander cleared the center of the abandoned village for a landing zone for the medevac Huey that was en route. I did not believe the WIA would make it, but as always, I was impressed with the enlisted medical specialist, who never stopped trying.

The Huey helicopter landed and the stretcher and the SF medic were aboard in an instant. We now had only one qualified U.S. medical specialist on the operation, a concern to me. I didn't approve, but no solution came to mind. The rest of the night was uneventful. The operation went smoothly and without contact. I was impressed with the Cambodian GIs, and with their leadership as well. When Captain Biggs needed advice, he asked for it. We got along very well, considering I had no prior familiarity with any of my U.S. comrades.

On the fifth morning, all of the rifle companies were to come together at point X. The area planned for the meeting had to be secured before the fourth evening was over. It was around 1300 and we had just finished our field rations. Why we had waited so long to assign this operation, I did not understand. After Biggs explained it to the Cambodian colonel and me, he waited. The colonel did his thing, quickly assigning two platoons of the 2nd Company to accomplish the task. I looked at my watch and asked Biggs who of his U.S. resources he was going to send with them. Once again he acted stumped before he replied, "I'll ask for volunteers. Whoever volunteers will have to be in excellent physical shape. In order to be there and secure the layout before dark will damn near mean double-timing all the way."

I looked at my map and calculated the known distance to the objective. "You're right, sir. We'd better get moving. All

SF people are supposed to be in excellent shape so I don't think that's a consideration."

Biggs's PRC-25 radio sounded off to all units, but came up with the executive officer as the only volunteer. I should have been surprised, but I wasn't. I should have kept my big mouth shut also, but I didn't: "Hell, I thought all those kids that wore their hair long and used their OD handkerchiefs as headbands were tough, sir!"

The statement did nothing for Biggs, so I thought for a minute before speaking up again. I was only forty-four years old and in excellent shape. Why not? "I'll go with him, sir. I'll be ready whenever the lieutenant arrives." My rucksack was on my back in ten, and my weapon was in my hand just as quickly.

The Cambodian contingent was waiting for the skinny XO and the interpreter. When the first lieutenant showed, he grinned after shaking my hand. "You're a little old for this speed marching, ain't you, Top?"

Captain Biggs had observed me humping for three days and knew the youngster was full of shit.

"You make me feel better, Lieutenant," I said. "I was worried about you." The XO, myself, a Cambodian medic, an interpreter, and the RTO composed the command group. The first platoon led off at 1400, with the command party following closely; the second platoon deployed tactically while bringing up the rear. I had the distance figured on straight line as very close to sixteen miles as a stupid crow flies. Tactically, meaning checking out danger zones such as river crossings and abandoned built-up places, it would be much farther. I hoped we would be in our night location by 1730, because darkness would be upon us by seven P.M., or 1900. We had been on the move since 0700 that morning, so we were going to earn our money before it was over.

The pace was unbelievable for a tactical foray. The now very somber, six-foot-two-inch officer and I filled our canteens at every chance, but still we were constantly short of water. Our first break was at 1600, and I flopped heavily. My officer counterpart did the same; he no longer had a grin on his face. Despite his age advantage, the young man appeared in a hurt from the forced march. I attempted to cheer him up, but damn if I know why. I took a long swig of water and used my OD neckerchief to wipe away the sweat after the delight.

"We can't have much more, so hang in there, sir." I was watching his face closely, and for a damn good reason. My sweating had—in only five minutes—ceased; his had not. Malaria kept flashing on and off in my computer, and my mouth never could keep a secret. "You have been taking your malaria pills, haven't you, sir?"

I never got an answer, but a nod from the Cambodian CO said we needed to move out smartly. I had not even smoked a cigarette, but I stood my wringing-wet cammies upright and hoisted my rucksack. It took the XO a little longer, but I had no time to worry about a man twenty years my junior not being able to keep up. In an hour of speedy zigzagging we stopped in a tree line, and I knew by the mountains to my front and the large rice paddy that separated us from the alps that we had reached Nirvana. I was hurting, physically, but in thirty minutes I felt back to normal; not so my country cousin. To satisfy my curiosity, I asked the Cambodian medic to take his temperature and pulse. He obeyed. The lieutenant's 105 temperature got my attention.

I asked once again about a problem I'd run into in Vietnam in the past: "Have you been taking your chloroquine preventative tablets each week, sir?" No answer confirmed my diagnosis. The hippy had carried his war against authority a little too far. I threw up my hands in bewilderment, but not for long. "You're on your way to the hospital, sir!" That the medic agreed with me through the interpreter only made me more determined. The RTO, by this time, had the U.S. team leader's command party on the telephone line. I ignored the last feeble plea from my XO before speaking to Honcho One over the PRC-25.

Biggs agreed, but spoke his thoughts sincerely. "I agree to the evacuation, Top, but that leaves you all alone, U.S.-wise."

"I'll be okay," I told him.

I notified base camp and gave our location. They countered with a medevac arrival time of 1815 and an order to use smoke to identify the landing zone. I concurred and went over to the prostrate officer, relaying the future events. He protested feebly but I consoled him as best I could. I would be alone with only third-country nationals, but except for J. B. Miller's companionship, that's the way I'd felt the entire tour.

A Huey helicopter with the red cross in the center circled the paddy only once before my red smoke curled toward him. After landing, the Cambodians loaded the stretcher quickly and my partner was gone. The medic, interpreter, and I went back to the tree line, ate field rations and prepared our sleeping quarters. I took the first watch until 2400, and woke the interpreter at that time. He woke me at two and I took it till four. I was up at reveille and eating fruit cocktail from a can. The interpreter made small talk while he was eating indigenous rations. He promised to find about the ETA of the main body of troops after his meal.

CHAPTER 25

The expected time of arrival would be just before noon, so I studied the map for a while and wondered about the disposition of the sick XO. I dozed under the trees before being awakened by the interpreter. He motioned to Captain Biggs and his crew, approaching. I rose and shook hands with a grinning, panting Biggs. When he took off his rucksack and lit up, I clued him on the evacuation. He told me, as I thought he would, that I could have gone with the lieutenant.

"I've been in this situation before, sir. I saw no problem."

The battalion CO, Biggs, I, and my mouthpiece inspected the hasty perimeter and were satisfied with the results. After a brief field-ration meal we saddled up and headed for Chi Lang and a hot meal. As usual, the pace to the home port was fast, and we closed at 1730 or thereabouts. Unknown to me, the good times at Chi Lang were drawing to a close.

Nothing out of the ordinary happened on the speed march to the house. I was pleased to report to Sergeant Major Miller that I believed the Cambodians could take care of themselves if and when it was warranted. The top soldier took my word for it.

In July 1971 the static electricity surrounding Major Engineer and Sergeant Major Miller turned into a shocking conclusion.

Command Sergeant Major Bowser, formerly the 5th SF Group CSM, was now working for Abrams. He honored us with a visit. I saw the old Okinawan hand and spoke, but he didn't act as though he had time for me. I didn't attach anything to the show of force by MACV. But unknown to Miller or me, the situation at the other Individual Training Support Camp at Long Hai, near Vung Tau, was having some internal problems very similar to the Miller–Major Engineer fiasco we had at Chi Lang. A few days after Bowser's departure, Miller told me he'd received his marching orders. I was shocked, but let Johnnie get it off his chest.

Miller departed Chi Lang a very bitter person, I thought. That night, all alone in that squad tent, I mentally reviewed what I knew about the problems and MACV's apparent solution. Sergeant Major Miller had as much experience as any NCO I had come in contact with in my twenty years, and his judgment was impeccable. Major Engineer knew whose side I was on. How much time did I have left at Chi Lang? It's your move, asshole!

Sergeant Major Hillman, tall at six-two, and a lean 195 pounds, was also an old Special Forces hand. That was possibly his undoing as well. General Abrams must have been having a field day. I heard through the SF field lines that Hillman and a Major Artillery had problems. I guess Hillman and I would get along great; if I wasn't next, that is. Hillman showed up the next day, but he wisely moved into another tent, leaving me by my lonesome. Three or four days later I was transferred to Long Hai.

So what else is new? I would be the NCO in charge of a convoy taking surplus equipment to Bien Hoa before moving on to Long Hai. The resort city was located near Vung Tau on the coast of Vietnam, southeast of Saigon. It was obvious to me that I had, along with Miller and Hillman, become the enemy. Special Forces, in my mind at least, had gone the way of the rest of the Army. I left something in Chi Lang—my respect for the greatest unit I had ever been a part of: United States Army Special Forces. It would take many years to change my mind.

Except for a three-quarter-ton and my jeep, we dropped off the trucks in Bien Hoa and enjoyed a good night's rest. The next day's trip to plushy Long Hai proved what I had already stated. The war was over in South Vietnam. During the Tet Offensive years of 1968–69, if I'd ridden the modern, paved highway from Bien Hoa to the coastal region near Vung Tau, there would have been sad singing and slow walking in Lawton, Oklahoma. But in July 1971 not a mouse was stirring. Our convoy had no natives for a defense force, and consisted of me, a Viet SF jeep driver, and a specialist four driving the three-quarter.

We arrived at the destination before 1700 in the afternoon and turned in the vehicles before being escorted to our new quarters. The camp was near the beach and consisted of tents with wood flooring and compartments. Very plush, to say the least. I was informed that Vietnamese maids would keep the compartment clean and do my laundry after making the bed. War is hell! Depositing my gear, I was informed by my new sergeant major, J. B. Miller, that I would be briefed in the morning. I went to the mess hall by my lonesome, walking along a sandy street that featured tentage over wooden frames for offices and living quarters. Who needed sandbags, now that the war was over? At that point they really did have internal R&R in war-torn Vietnam.

The mess hall served to confirm my findings. The E8s and E9s, or "supergrades," had their own table. I didn't know any of the team sergeants, or Operations sergeants from Panama or Germany, so I carted my delicious tray right on by the unknown superstars until I spotted a table with a lonely specialist five eating his evening dues. Spec. Five Shanahan nodded when I took the seat opposite him. I ate a few bites and studied the individual before starting the conversation. The good-looking young Caucasian boy shared many features of my high school running mate, Harry Shanahan, and Harry's older brother, Pat—both former Lawton High School football stars. Though Pat was before my time, I was acquainted with him.

"Where're you from in the States, Spec. Five Shanahan?"

Shanahan seemed startled that an E8 would speak to a common soldier, but dutifully replied. "I'm from Des Moines, Iowa, Top!"

Because I knew that Pat Shanahan was working for the railroad in Des Moines, I said, "I'm Master Sergeant Bill Craig. What's your first name, soldier boy?"

"William, or Bill, just like yours, Top."

I continued eating and talking, practically simultaneously. "You know, Bill, I've always been like my mother in a way, a little bit psychic, especially in relation to some people."

"Yeah, Top? Hell, try me, then."

"Okay," I replied, "I will." I pretended to meditate into the unknown while putting away the needed vitamins.

"Okay," I finally began. "You have a grandmother named Toy." (Harry Shanahan's mother.)

I thought the kid would have a cardiac. "How in the hell did you know that?" he gasped.

Now that I knew my hunch was correct, I continued to march. "You have an uncle named Harry and an aunt named Jane. Your grandfather is named John and is a retired GI living in Lawton, Oklahoma."

At the mention of my dad's old first sergeant, the kid damn near flipped out. We were attracting undue attention, so we quieted down for a few minutes. "I was a staff sergeant in the 1st Air Cavalry," he told me, "but got busted to specialist five. Hell, I guess you even know why I was busted?"

When I got through laughing, I said, "You're a Shanahan, so you musta got busted for fighting." I guessed correctly before I told him how I knew his relatives from the Oklahoma hills. He was impressed. We strolled from the mess hall to his billet across the street next to the boardwalk. I had made a friend and had one of the few laughs I'd had during my tour. I shook his hand before going to my billets, but I made one thing perfectly clear to the young soldier. "If I can ever be of any assistance, regardless of the problem, let me know!"

The next day I began my tour at Long Hai, being introduced to Major Artillery by Miller, for a starter. Neither of us was too thrilled. About all I got out of the meeting was the mission. We were to train Viet Special Forces (LLDB) and other indigenous NCOs in tactics, map reading, and weapons. Miller and I went back to the office, where I received my assignment. The training headquarters had been established without much administrative expertise. Despite getting the job done otherwise, they just weren't prepared for an inspector general's inspection. I thought I'd heard the sergeant major incorrectly, and asked him to repeat the last statement.

"Yeah, Bill, you heard me right. We're having an IG inspection in a combat zone. Weird?"

"No, not really. This place and these personnel, except for a few, have never heard a shot fired in anger. The bastards deserve it."

"I want you to try to get that damn headquarters, especially the training shop, ready for the inspection by MACV. Can do?"

"In other words, you want me to save Major Artillery's ass while he's looking down his nose at us. I have no choice, but I don't have to like it, Johnnie."

The assignment kept me busy for the three weeks before the IG showdown. I'd just come off two years or so of garrison duty, so IGs were old hat to me. But still, the scheduled inspection would be my first in a combat zone. Somebody must have thought of Long Hai the way I did: combat, it wasn't!

With the blessings of a young Operations officer, a young specialist five and I set out to arrange the files the way the Special Regulations demanded. We studied the regulation before we changed anything. The specialist typed the new folder labels and placed them on the folders, while I went through the system and placed documents in the correct folder. In two weeks we even had a classified-documents file cabinet. Locked, no less. In the inspection, we got a Satisfactory, much to the surprise of the old crew. I wasn't given any time to celebrate; I got a somber message from the reliable American Red Cross.

"Your wife has given birth to a daughter at Fort Sill's Reynolds Community Hospital. The baby is not expected to live. Your presence is required this location."

CHAPTER 26

The message came from Saigon on the night of Sunday, August 29, 1971. I was immediately given a thirty-day emergency leave. My only Class A uniform was in Nha Trang so the next morning found me in Saigon's Tan Son Nhut International Airport in camouflage fatigues, jump boots, and beret. I was placed on the first available aircraft with a load of GIs who had completed one-year tours in Vietnam. I stood out like a sore thumb, but when the happy soldiers saw my somber attitude, they refrained from adverse comments. Thank God.

When the line to the plush civilian jet airliner got to the pretty stewardess, my solemn look brought some remarks from her smiling face. "Why so glum, Sergeant? You're going home. Cheer up!" When I handed her a copy of my emergency leave papers, she returned them and she nodded, unsmiling, permission to load. During the entire trip to Travis Air Force Base the troops were jubilant, and I certainly couldn't fault that. But the fact remained, I was not.

The 707 jet landed at San Francisco International Airport early Tuesday morning the second day of September 1971. I looked rather strange in the odd field uniform, but the MPs on duty at the terminal just looked at my emergency leave papers and waved me on. In two hours I was en route to Oklahoma City on a 747.

As soon as I was off the airliner with both feet on the ground, I called my home. My mother sadly told me that Jacklin Jean Craig had died at eleven o'clock that morning.

Hatsuko was fine but was still in the hospital. Jacklin Jean had lived two days, dying of spinal meningitis.

After the bus ride home, dressed in cammies, I went to see Hatsuko just before the supper meal. She was heartbroken as well. The next day I arranged for the funeral, to be held at Becker's Funeral Home in Lawton, and the burial at Fort Sill in the same cemetery as my father. The funeral was on the fifth of September, but my mother was ill with pneumonia and had to be admitted to a hospital in Lawton. Hatsuko was out of the Fort Sill facility, and the funeral was attended by my family and friends. It was a sad affair, and we left Kathy and Jimmy with friends.

A few days after the funeral, my stepfather had a stroke. In disbelief, I called the ambulance. He went to the same hospital as my mother, in a separate room.

Hatsuko busied herself taking care of the house and getting the kids off to the nearby elementary school. I called my brother Peter in New York City and my sister Pauline in Phoenix and asked them to come home. They both agreed, but before they could arrive, my mother died on the morning of September 10, 1971, unexpectedly, just before I reached the hospital. I was allowed to view the body before departing, in total shock.

Our immediate family, Peter (Buzz), Pauline, Jean, and Joe Bob, were all at home for the first time since our childhood. It was unfortunate that it took such an event to accomplish the feat. For the second time in that short period, I attended a funeral and burial—this time in a civilian cemetery on the outskirts of Lawton. Afterward, Peter Craig and Pauline Snapp departed for New York City and Phoenix, respectively.

In about a week I completed the administrative chores of my mother's death by turning the remaining paperwork over to a local lawyer friend of my childhood days. My youngest brother, a local schoolteacher, assumed responsibility for the care of our stepfather. John had by this time been transferred to a nursing home to recover, if that was to be. My youngest sister, Jean, whose husband was first sergeant of the Fort Sill Military Police Company, agreed to see that Hatsuko had transportation and whatever support she and the children might need while I finished my tour in Vietnam.

By that time it was around the twentieth of September, and I had to prepare for whatever the Army had in store. Off to Fort Sill I went in my stepfather's automobile. As I entered the Personnel office, my camouflage fatigues and beret received plenty of attention, and that was just what I wanted for a change. I was escorted to the office of the Personnel sergeant major, Smoky Stover, who also laid out the red carpet. I explained my situation in detail to the thin, tall Stover, who had about the same time in the Army as I did. I then asked what he thought would happen to a master sergeant with ten consecutive years overseas.

"Due to your family situation, I believe the Army will transfer you back to the States ASAP," he replied, "and for many other reasons besides your family being here. Special Forces is being cut back in Bragg and eliminated on Okinawa, Sarge. So your chances of remaining in Group are slim to none. When those assigned to MACV Individual Training Teams rotate, I doubt if any of them will stay in Special Forces, if that will make you feel any better."

"No," I replied, "it doesn't. But I still can't believe that Special Forces will throw away all that experience, Top."

"Try to believe it, Bill," Smoky said. "Special Forces' days are numbered. I can't say how bad the cut will be, but it will be substantial. Hell, your old unit, the 1st, has already gone by the boards."

That statement by itself brought me to my senses. "You may be right, Sergeant Major. I'm ready for some advice from an old soldier. Shoot!"

"Okay! Why not Fort Sill? There's jobs here for an airborne soldier with a 11F MOS. Believe it!" Stover said.

"Like what?" I asked.

"How well do you know Fort Sill?" he inquired.

I grinned before replying. "I was born here, Top. I'm a Lawton–Fort Sill baby-san. How's that?"

"Okay. The 4th Battalion of the 31st Infantry is right down the road a piece. Start there and see what they say before we go any further. Okay?"

"Okay, then what?"

"Report back here, and let us know what they say, and what you think." I was gone, but only after a handshake and my sincere thanks to Sgt. Major Smoky Stover.

I encountered no problems finding the home of the 4/31st Infantry Polar Bears. Randolph Road, Fort Sill's main thoroughfare, runs east and west through the heart of the Old Post area. Once past the Fort Sill fire station, I parked in the lot at Randolph and Bateman roads. The sign that featured the drawing of a polar bear assured me I was at the right location. The stucco three-story barracks ran north and south along Bateman and faced the west. The two-story headquarters layout at the intersection was of the same construction. I gingerly approached the wooden porch and entered a building built before WWII by the WPA.

A small hall led me to a hallway that went in three different directions. The sign explained everything I needed to know. If I proceeded ahead, I would climb a flight of stairs to the Operations shop; to my right a swinging door led to the S-1 Personnel office. I turned left down a hallway that led to the offices of the sergeant major and the battalion commander.

A left turn and a few steps in my jungle boots found me knocking on the E9's door. He answered and I entered. A master sergeant with dark, graying hair greeted me in awe. I answered in a less profound manner. When I finished my recitation, the leg E8 still looked confused. What the hell am I getting into? I asked myself. The E8 in the military interrupted my disgust.

"A sergeant major has been assigned top, and should be here soon. I'm just filling in until then. I'll see if Lieutenant

Colonel Becker will see you. Hold on a minute. . . . The colonel will see you, Top!"

I was shaking my head as I entered and reported to a well-built white male. He was shaking his head after returning the salute and eyeing my Special Forces airborne getup. These legs were driving me to distraction.

"What can I do for you, soldier?" he asked.

I handed him a copy of my orders and presented him a short résumé. He didn't appear impressed as I ended my spiel: "Would you give me an assignment if I am assigned to Fort Sill?"

"If you're by chance transferred here, we'd sure think about it, Sergeant." I'd been dismissed, and was goddamn glad of it. If D.A. assigned me, he wouldn't have a goddamn thing to say about it. The big dummy!

The meeting left me in a quandary. I fretted on my way home, uncertain as to what my next move would, or should, be. I was determined to retire if ever given another assignment where a slot did not exist or I was not wanted.

Before noon of the next day, after observing the goings-on around my old home, I was assured that Hatsuko, with her neighbors' and my relatives' assistance, would be fine until I returned from 'Nam. I was off to the Inspector General Office at Post Headquarters located in McNair Hall at Sill.

After explaining my situation to the IG representative, I was assured the matter would be settled with the Department of the Army. "Your place of assignment will be up to D.A.," the warrant officer said. I was satisfied and returned to the Post Personnel powerhouse. Sergeant Major Stover was on leave by then and unavailable, so I conferred with a warrant officer. He presented me an option that I'd been unaware of. In fact, the alternative left me in a state of doubt and confusion once again.

"Don't go back to 'Nam," he said. "Sign in here and you'll be assigned by D.A. shortly."

I had my doubts about the legality of such a move, but on

the other hand, the warrant officer made his living dealing with such matters. I thanked him and departed for the house to ponder the latest skinny. In two days nearing the end of September 1971, I came to my conclusion. I was going back to finish my tour in playland, Vietnam. I boarded an aircraft in Oklahoma City in the same uniform I had arrived in, and was in Travis before nightfall. I only stayed there one night before catching a jet back to Saigon via Hawaii and Alaska. Again the aircraft was filled with youngsters from other Army units still in-country. In other words, I was alone to ponder the past month of unbelievable sadness. I arrived alone and lonely in busy Tan Son Nhut International. Rather than ride to Long Hai—a short distance away—by vehicle, I bummed a helicopter ride and was in camp before suppertime. After signing in, I conferred with Sergeant Major Miller about the events in the States. He was as incredulous as I was. He ended the bull session with the same prediction as the Personnel officer at Fort Sill: "You won't be here long, Bill. You'll get a compassionate transfer to the States ASAP. Bet on it!"

I went back to work in the Operations shop, but not for long. The Individual Training Group HQ at Nha Trang ordered me back to their Nha Trang HQ to await a compassionate transfer to the land of the big PX. Except for bidding farewell to Miller, I lost no sleep over leaving. Maybe I would end up in Fort Bragg after all.

At Nha Trang, Darcy et al. treated me graciously, giving me a room to my lonesome. Sergeant Major Darcy wasted little time on a briefing. "Sorry about your family, Bill. The American Red Cross and Department of the Army believe it would serve a better purpose if you were home with your wife and kids at times such at this. Where you're going in the States, I have no idea. It shouldn't be long before we find out, though, so hang around."

With no job and nothing constructive to do, the time dragged. Three or four days of that placed me in a worse mental state than I was already in. I brought the situation to a head the fifth night, in the old SF clubhouse, over a few beers. Darcy and I started the conversation in a civilized manner, but I soon got around to what was on my mind. My part of the small talk could be summarized as being unhappy with his personnel people. His side of it didn't take much longer: "They are doing all they can do."

My "Bullshit!" got the job done; in two days I was standing in Darcy's office.

"Here's your orders, Sergeant Craig. You're no longer in Special Forces, you're Fort Sill, Oklahoma, bound."

"Why Fort Sill, and not Fort Bragg, Sergeant Major?"

"You'd have to ask D.A. that, Bill. I can only repeat what the rumor mill says. SF is being cut back, and General Emerson has said that those people overseas will not come back to Group. I doubt if any people from the USARV Training Teams get SF assignments."

"That's a stupid way to cut back Special Forces, Top, eliminating the people with the experience," I said, walking to the door with my orders in my hand. At the door I turned and bid farewell to a unit I had been in for twelve years and two months. "Well, it's a helluva way to say good-bye, but with the likes of the Army today, I'm better off a leg."

Red-faced, Darcy just had to have the last word. "Get outta my office!" he screamed.

I was on my way back to where it all started, with a reporting date of November 20, 1971.

CHAPTER 27

The out-processing at Cam Ranh Bay was routine in most respects. However, baggage and personal effects were searched meticulously. I was mildly surprised when the issue camouflage fatigues were confiscated, and I complained, but to no avail. The people in charge were very busy and could only offer "Not authorized" before moving me on down the line. It hacked me off for every bit of five minutes. Who needed souvenirs? My body alone had enough of Vietnam's offerings.

In two days and one night I was in a khaki uniform with bloused jump boots and wearing the green beanie on a 707 with another planeload of GIs who had completed twelve-month tours. I didn't strike up any long conversations, but was secretly pleased that I'd only completed seven months of mine. The only thing I regretted was the manner that brought about the reduction of time spent in Vietnam.

I still couldn't believe I was no longer assigned to Special Forces. Even when the airliner approached the Golden Gate Bridge, I was not convinced. While my teammates cheered, I took out a copy of my orders and read my assignment one more time.

FOR THE INDIVIDUAL: Assigned to: US Army Training Center (FA), Fort Sill, OK 73503. Leave data: Thirty (30) DDALV. Reporting date: 20 Nov 71. Scty Clearance: Top Secret.

I folded the orders and placed them in my back pocket, still unconvinced. As the large mode of transportation neared the runway in San Francisco, the date was October 12, 1971. I ended the flight murmuring to myself, and cared less what my plane pals thought about it. "I've got twenty-one years for retirement and twenty-two years for pay purposes. Screw the Army!"

In Oklahoma things were progressing despite my short absence. The kids were up to their delight—elementary school—and Hatsuko was taking driving lessons. None of their routines were interrupted by my arrival, allowing me a month to get myself and my career organized or terminated. Hatsuko and I began by organizing our homelife.

We moved into what had been my mother and stepfather's bedroom, allowing Kathy and Jimmy each to have a room to themselves. The large television set I'd bought and paid for years before was still operative, and my curiosity drew me to the set just about every night. I got to watch my old Korean War pal Dan Blocker on *Bonanza*. After all those years, I still got a kick out of "Hoss Cartwright," as did the rest of the family.

Visiting friends and neighbors took up my daylight hours. It wasn't long before I purchased a used four-door 1968 Chevy Impala, making sure the shift was automatic so Hatsuko could drive the car using her newly acquired Oklahoma State driver's license. She passed her exam in our "new" auto; I didn't fare as well.

I possessed an Okinawa driver's license that had to be useless in the USA. I was told by the Oklahoma Highway Patrol that I had thirty days to obtain a state driving permit by taking and passing a written and performance test. I was aghast; pissed off, too! "Why?" I inquired. "I've had an Oklahoma driver's license for many years."

"When was your last license dated?" the patrolman said. "We have no record of it, so it must have been a while ago!"

The matter wasn't important enough for me to make a big

fuss over. After all, I'd been driving for twenty-seven years, so how could I flunk a driving exam? It was just part of my stateside orientation. The large patrolman gave me an appointment for the next day to take both tests before I drove to the house where Hatsuko greeted me with her first driver's license ever. She passed the course and received her rewards on the final day of the course. I was happy for her, and it still never entered my mind that an old driving expert would have any problem.

Admittedly, I had driven very little on four-lane roads in ten or eleven years, but I still foresaw no problem. The day of the test started well when I maxed the written portion. The performance part was fine until we arrived back at the patrol station on Second and Gore Boulevard. I was on a one-way, two-lane street when the officer told me turn left into the station parking lot. I was in the right-hand lane and didn't hesitate to do as ordered: I turned left—from the right-hand lane, no less. All his writing and the verbal abuse from the Oklahoma Highway Patrolman told me the results before he handed me my copy. I had flunked. I didn't want to believe it, but did have the presence of mind before departing to reschedule the driving portion for the next week.

Never lacking for nerve, I proceeded home and told my wife and kids that I'd flunked the driving test. Hatsuko, a rank amateur as a driver, gained a ton of confidence in her achievement, so I gained something from the boo-boo. Despite my success the very next week, I heard about my failure from the kids for two or three years. The moral of the story was that, due to my exit in 1961, I had a lot to learn about my new country.

On or about November 15, 1971, I signed in at Fort Sill and asked if I'd been assigned as yet. I was informed by Sergeant Major Stover to jack up the infantry battalion once again. I attempted to but the sergeant major's office was still empty. I returned to Personnel and told Smoky to give up the ghost. "Hell, they don't want me or they'd already have called. What else, Sergeant Major?" He directed me to go to the Field Artillery Training Center the very next day.

I approached the WWII wooden headquarters building dressed in greens, jump boots bloused, and an overseas cap with the glider airborne patch on the front. After some preliminaries I was ushered into the office of a black sergeant major and greeted warmly by the Operations sergeant. He smiled and fielded my question after reading my orders. "Sure, Sergeant, we have jobs for people with your expertise, and tell Stove I said so." The visit was over and I was back in Post Personnel in quick time.

There was a shocking surprise. I waited for a specialist fifth class to finish reading my 201 file, and then he called his buddies over to stare at it as well. I turned to get out of the limelight and spotted the short, squat, powerfully built command sergeant major just before he spotted me. He walked toward me like he'd known me all his life. I was not unaware of the glider patch on his overseas cap, nor did the 173rd Airborne Brigade patch on his right shoulder escape my stare. When he stood directly to my front, I almost came to attention before he sounded off in an airborne whisper that could be heard downtown.

"Quit playing games, Craig," CSM Gergen said. "Finish inprocessing and get your ass to the 4th of the 31st Infantry Headquarters, where you damn well belong." He was gone and into Stover's room behind a slammed door before my mouth could rebut.

The spec. five quit showing my records to everyone on post and asked me one final question. "Where do you want the ten thousand dollars you have in the overseas savings to go, Top? You need to fill out the paperwork as to its destination."

While I filled out the certificate that would place my overseas savings in a Lawton bank, CSM Gergen slammed Stover's door. He gave me a dirty look for a farewell gift. Stover was out the door and heading in my direction with a similar look on his skinny face. Well, what the hell! I wanted to be wanted, but did it have to come all at once? Stover stopped, and I ceased the processing when he spoke.

"You're now in the infantry battalion. When do you want to end your leave?"

"I did yesterday, Top. Want me to report over there when I finish here?"

"Yeah, you'd better, before we both get killed. Good luck, Bill. That's a mean ol' bastard!"

"I know, Sergeant Major, but don't sweat the small shit. Hell, I'm used to it!"

I parked my Impala in the infantry parking lot and, with my record jacket in hand, approached the local puzzle palace. A guard mount was in progress to the side of the large building. I spotted Gergen before he spotted me, but not by much. CSM Gergen was inspecting the guard mount, no less.

I was shocked, but damn if I know why, with what I'd seen in the Army the last six months. Gergen saw me strolling on his sidewalk and could probably read my mind as well. "An E9 inspecting the guard. It's come to that, I guess." I also saw his Combat Infantry Badge with a star (second award), and Master Jump wings, before he brought me out of my daze in a loud, profane manner.

"Get your ass in my office, Sergeant Craig. I'll be there shortly!"

I heard him but I doubt if he heard me, mumbling though I was: "They need an E9 to inspect a guard mount. Where are the NCOs—or the officers, for that matter. It's no use; I've got my twenty, hell, I'm gone."

I placed my 201 file on the boss's desk, seated myself and waited, but not for long. As was characteristic of Gergen, he came in loud and clear. I stood until he seated himself and began eyeing the 201 record jacket. He scanned the story of my military life, and me as well from time to time. I was observing Gergen in a critical but admiring manner. He had more jump status time than I did, and I admired that to start off with. He was approximately five feet ten inches tall, and weighed in around 185 pounds, with no flab that I could detect. Like my own, his khaki uniform perfectly fit his wide shoulders. His polished brass belt buckle shined and met the seam formed by his pants and tucked-in shirt. I had already eyed his jump boots, and was pleased I had him beat in one respect. I knew he'd noticed the shining fact as well. His blue eyes grabbed mine momentarily but released me back to my analysis and resumed reading the Army's version of my last ten years of run, dodge, and jump. His rugged features finally rose from his chore and he spoke to the second highest ranking man in the room.

"Very good, Sergeant Craig. Now that you're off jump status and a leg, like myself, what do you have planned?"

"I appreciate the trouble you've gone to, to get me over here, old soldier, but I think I'll hang it up. Hell, I've got my twenty! I'm fed up with it all."

"I don't agree. But tell me your problems before I say anything else," Gergen came back.

I did, and he did, as promised. "Again I don't agree with you, Bill. I'm sorry as hell about your mother and baby girl, but life must go on. Special Forces is cutting back, and someone hadda go. Believe me, you're not by your lonesome. Hell, I've been on jump status longer than you, and just left the 173rd Airborne Brigade. Think that didn't piss me off?

"What you're overlooking is the fact that the Army needs us now like they haven't for a long time. For my part, I'm gonna straighten out this outfit if I have to throw out everybody in it. I need your help."

My mouth fell open, but CSM Gergen held up his hand and closed it. "The Army is cleaning up its act now, I think. No longer can the first sergeant and the commander select their NCOs as they see fit. Past performance and achievements will be one's key to the so-called supergrades [E8, E9]. Let's help our profession make a comeback." Gergen paused.

"It's Thursday, so sign in at Personnel and come back Monday ready to take over as Operations sergeant. Okay?"

The long speech caused me to forget what I did to bring it on. I rose so as to close the one-way debate. "In duty uniform, Top?"

"Yes, Sergeant Craig, fatigues, jump boots, and that OD baseball cap we all love so well. Cabler will be glad to see you!"

I left the premises, but while driving home the name Cabler rang a bell. An SFC Cabler had been in I Corps Special Forces during the Tet Offensive in 1968. I recalled hearing his name over the voice radio, in addition to other NCOs speaking of him after my return from the hospital. Well, whatcha know? Maybe I wasn't going into this unit blind. There was another SF Group NCO who would be by my side.

Over the weekend I talked to my spouse and came to the conclusion that staying in the Army, even at Fort Sill, might be the best way to go. I could retire when I had nothing else to do. With an outstanding boss, such as Gergen surely was, I might even enjoy the experience. I would report in Monday to stick out my hitch, which still had two years before completion.

I reported in after work call at 0730 and saw that my jump boots gave off a better airborne glow than Gergen's. He noted it, too, so the day started off in a positive manner. Gergen asked me what I'd decided, and I gave him my conclusions. He told me to be seated, that he wanted me to meet the new colonel who had arrived about the same time I had. Gergen returned and told me I'd meet him later in the day. "I'm gonna turn you over to Cabler and he'll brief you and square you away, jobwise. Remember, Bill, my office is always open, for whatever the reason!"

We went up the stairs to a hallway that ran east to west. Two offices that fronted the south side of the hall belonged to the Operations officer, Major Waddell, and his assistant, Captain Paul Ingle. We turned right, and a few feet from the stairwell we swung through the swinging doors that led into a spacious Operations Center. SFC Cabler, small at five-eight and 140 pounds, paused from cleaning out his former desk to welcome us. The CSM introduced us, although we knew each other better than he thought. When Gergen departed we got with the program. Cabler surprised me after we talked briefly about our whereabouts during the Tet Offensive. He was also from Oklahoma, and not too far from our present location. His small hometown nestled near Chickasha, only fifty-two miles from the Lawton–Fort Sill area. It was my turn to surprise Cabler, but I waited until we were seated at my new throne before I did so.

"You were what?" Cabler asked loudly.

"Not so loud Bill," I ordered. "Gergen doesn't know it, so let's keep it among ourselves. But yes, I was in the 522nd Infantry Battalion (Separate) in 1954 and 'fifty-five, doing the same thing this battalion is doing now, except I was a demolition man then. If nothing else, it'll keep the briefing time down. Start it off with a unit breakdown, if you don't mind."

"Okay, Top. That's changed since your time here. The unit has a head and head company composed of the staff sections, a motor pool, and one honor platoon that attends designated funerals and post ceremonies, when needed. The Post Operations directs and schedules those thirty or so people, so we don't get into it. There's a large motor pool section because we have Armored Personnel Carriers. We are the 4th of the 31st Infantry Battalion, Mechanized.

"We have two letter companies, A and B, and they stay full despite Gergen kicking every dud he can outta the Army. Alpha Company has around 180 personnel at this time. Bravo, or B Company, has an Armored Personnel Carrier platoon in addition to three rifle platoons and a heavy weapons platoon equipped with 81 mortars. That's the Table of Organization and Equipment that we have to get the job done with." Cabler paused, but I had nothing to say.

"You still know the mission, I'm sure," he said.

"Yeah, Sarge, I haven't been gone that long. We furnish infantry support for the Field Artillery School's Student Training Requirements. I doubt if any of the problems have changed much. Gimme a rundown on the Operations shop and I'll let you get back to work, William!"

The job boiled down to shuffling paperwork, in the main, and producing training schedules wrapped around post requirements. One thing was different from the bad ol' days, and it tickled me pinko: no Saturdays were classified as work-days, and any unit that wanted to labor on the sixth day of the week had to get permission from Post Headquarters. When I was informed, I had a few comments that brought a smile of agreement from Cabler.

"It's about time. Garrison troops never accomplished any-thing on Saturdays, nohow, but drink coffee and listen to the chaplain from time to time. It'll make the mess sergeant delirious and save the Army at least a few million in coffee money."

"Yeah," Cabler chimed in, "and the preacher can go back to work on Sunday. We have two people on your side, Top, besides me, both spec. fours. Johnson and Kirby have been here for at least four months or more. Both can type and try to stay outta trouble as best they can." The briefing ended on this note, and had established my routine for the next twenty months.

I would be at work at 0730 and knock off around four o'clock for my daily run, when possible. If I had to work late, I would do the exercise in a park close to my home. The route to the downtown track was near a drinking establishment called the Mug, which furnished motivation I really didn't need. On days that my wife needed the car, I graciously al-lowed her to take me to work; she could also pick me up at 1630 for the trip home. Given the relaxed schedule, with no extra duty, I often wondered if I would really get paid for it. But each and every payday the money continued to arrive.

A number of events over the next year and eight months kept me entertained. They were few enough that I can list them all in quick time. Someone made a typo on a letter that went out of the Operations shop to a line company. No big deal except the CSM caught the boo-boo and called me to his castle. I listened to the ass-chewing and inherited another paper-pushing function. Effective instantly every piece of correspondence that originated in our shop had to go over my desk before departure. One day while I was doing just that, two desks down from my very own, Spec. Four Johnson was checking out the *Army Times*.

"What's your middle initial, Top?"

"Johnson, I'm busy. Knock off the comedy!"

"I'm serious as a heartbeat, Top. William what Craig?"

"William T. will get you there."

"I know," Johnson said, "it got you there. You're number 898 on the Department of the Army's sergeant majors' list. Congratulations, Sergeant Major."

For myself, I thought the joke to be in poor taste. Hell, I'd only been in grade four years, with barely twenty-two years in the Army. The quotation had Captain Ingle, Spec. Four Kirby, and SFC Cabler converging on Johnson throughout the shop. Apparently, I was the only one who wasn't taking the joke too seriously. But Captain Ingle's remark got my mind in gear.

"Congratulations, Sergeant Major Craig. I wonder how long it will take for that number to come up?"

I stood up in disbelief and strolled to the desk where the crowd had assembled. "If you're bullshitting, Johnson, I'm gonna find something constructive for you to do!"

The crowd parted while Johnson remained seated. I eyed the list and there it was. Number 898. "Well, I'll be goddamn. How come the *Army Times* knows that shit when neither I nor my unit knows a damn thing about it?" I asked.

"A damn good question, Top," Ingle agreed. "I think you ought to find out the answer."

I borrowed Johnson's rag and was in CSM Gergen's office fast!

"First I heard of it," Gergen said. "Are you bullshitting me?" Glancing at the list and confirming the number, Gergen was on the phone, but I didn't stick around. I returned Johnson's paper and resumed my own paper drill. Gergen soon learned that Post Personnel received only the people who were currently being promoted. After work I bought my own *Army Times* as proof of my promotion number. Of course, with a number like 898 I could show and tell for the better part of a year before it came up. I would remain elated until February 13, 1973, the date of rank for my promotion to superman. Everything has drawbacks, and the 898 was no exception.

If I accepted the promotion, I was obligated to serve two more years. Did I want that obligation? Did I need that? Living the life of an ordinary working person from nine to five helped me come to a decision quicker than it did for Gergen to eat out Post Personnel's ass. I fell for it. I'd secretly always wanted to be all I could be, and that opportunity lay in number 898.

The end of 1972 was approaching before I realized that making E9 had other aspects besides a two-year obligation; like a slot or opening for an 11F E9 Operations sergeant. I began looking for a slot close to home because the infantry battalion had only one open E9 slot, and that was command sergeant major. I would be a staff sergeant major so I was not eligible.

Cameron College, located on Lawton's west side, had Reserve Officer Training Corps (ROTC), but the E9 slot was occupied. The sergeant major assigned to the location directed me to East Central State University at Ada, Oklahoma. I called the institution and was invited to come the ninety miles east of Lawton for an interview. With Gergen's permission, I made the trip and the interview in one day, dressed in my Army greens, and was back home in time for one of my wife's delicious meals. A few days later I was called and accepted by the ROTC commander of East Central. I, in turn, called 4th Army in San Antonio, Texas, and confirmed the assignment. They had no objections and informed me that when I was promoted, my orders to Ada, Oklahoma, would follow. Things were going my way, so I took a leave and accomplished the next step on my own.

My children were up to their necks in swimming at the local YMCA. Being a native son, I knew that Byng, a small town a few miles from Ada, had an indoor pool and sponsored competitive swimming. I went to Ada and found a realtor who showed me homes in Byng. I selected a house on a one-acre lot at a location near the one and only school. The price was reasonable, so I took my wife on the next trip in order to sign the paperwork with the bank that financed the $21,000 home after I made a minimal down payment. All I needed to complete the coup was for 898 to come up on the promotion list and we were gone. Unknown to me, not everyone was in accord with my well-laid plans. The last part of 1972, the shit began to roll downhill . . again.

Gergen, the best command sergeant major in the U.S. Army, inadvertently threw the first monkey wrench into the works. To Lt. Col. Raymond Cooke's disgust, he was ordered to Fort McPherson, Georgia, ASAP, to fill the vacant command sergeant major slot of the 3rd Army. The U.S. Army was finally showing me something. In quick time Gergen called the first sergeants of HHC, A and B companies, and me, into his office. Every E8 in the 4/31st Infantry (Mech) was seated in the small cubicle before Gergen began his summation and solution thereof.

"You'll know I'm leaving, so I won't rehash that. What I'm going to do now is to select the acting CSM until one is assigned from D.A." For some reason I stiffened, and possibly the first sergeants reacted similarly, before he continued.

"A little background music first. Fort Sill had graciously offered to loan us a staff sergeant major until an infantry CSM arrives."

I spoke up amid the grumbling among my peers. "Never happen, GI. The way it is, the artillery shits on us every time they get a chance. With one of those assholes, we'd be deactivated in a year. No thank you!"

"That's very close to what I told Colonel Cooke, and he agreed with me, and you. He specified that he wanted an E9 with an infantry background or he'd stick with one of his E8s." He eyed each one in the room with the last statement but spoke directly to me in his next breath.

"I have selected the soon-to-be E9 among you to take my place. I don't need your acceptances, but I do hope you agree with me. Master Sergeant Craig has the most time in the Army, for one thing. For another, he's a native son, and knows Fort Sill better than he'll admit. Also, the temporary fulfillment will not disrupt any of the units you other people are first sergeants of."

My concurrence did not enter into the discussion, and when the meeting dissolved, I had been presented with my first command sergeant slot ever—or E9 slot, for that matter. I wanted to object, but deep in my heart I knew it would be excellent training for me. I handed the Operations reins back to the previous owner, Cabler, and went to on-the-job training ASAP, but only after one other important accomplishment. I had a one-hour conference with Lieutenant Colonel Cooke that was icing on the cake. I had his complete backing, enabling me not to worry about minor mistakes in judgment. The first ten days Gergen hovered, so any mistakes still would have been his. After his departure, I was on my own.

What does the CSM job consist of? Still, to this day, a very good question. A year or so later at the Sergeants Major Academy, this question came up time and time again. Out of twelve test papers, no two papers held the same answers. This was my game plan: (1) Assist the commander in the accomplishment of the mission. The CSM normally has more time in service than the CO, and problems that may loom large in the commander's eyes may well be easily solved by the more experienced NCO. (2) Look out for and assist the NCO Corps and be their representative on high. How about looking out for the privates? The NCOs had damn well better be looking out for them. My job description was very general, but it's what I had in mind when I reported in, and I never ran head-on with any situation that changed my mind.

My first encounter of a controversial nature occurred quickly. I had just completed my first duty roster since Camp Polk in 1950. I laid the Battalion Staff Duty Roster aside with a sigh of relief and lit up, only to be interrupted by a knock on my sacred door. The warrant officer entered with such a stern look on his face that I damn near forgot who was in charge, but not quite.

"What can I help you with, sir?"

"Sergeant Major," the warrant officer answered. "Sergeant First Class Shore has too many motor pool duties to be pulling Staff Duty NCO! I want him ED'd." Excused from duty.

"That sounds familiar, sir," I replied. "I've just finished my first roster and I can't accept your opinion as valid enough to excuse him, sir."

The WO, an old soldier who should have known better, persisted. "I'm saying he should be ED'd from your roster. I insist!" he said, raising his voice.

"Sir," I said emphatically, "I will not ED the man on that basis. You're talking to the wrong person; I'm not in your chain of command."

I rose and walked out the door to the colonel's door, knocked and opened Cooke's door before I spoke. The colonel asked what I wanted, and I said, "Sir, there is someone here to see you." I then turned to the WO. "If Colonel Cooke agrees with you, I'll change the roster, but not for anyone else." I had said something I'm sure every CSM in the Army that's worth his salt will agree with: "I only have one boss and cannot please every second lieutenant in the Army." The case was closed with a deserved ass-chewing, much to my satisfaction.

The CSM assigns NCOs in the battalion in any unit I'd been in, and the 4/31st Infantry Battalion (Mechanized) was no exception. I had no problems with this arrangement because I stayed abreast of the personnel in each unit. I interviewed each NCO before the Personnel shop cut internal assignment orders.

Colonel Cooke, a Georgia boy, and I got along very well. I assisted him doing a few inspections of the billets and personnel, taking pains to see that the NCOs corrected the deficiencies. The road to number 898 was rolling smoothly when a former captain then working in the Pentagon threw some shit in the game.

CHAPTER 28

The first time Hugo called, around 1600, I was making my daily physical training run. Colonel Cooke said Brigadier General Victor Hugo had called from the Pentagon and wanted to talk to me. "He said he would call back tomorrow sometime, Sergeant Craig. He also expressed amazement that you were taking PT on your own." Cooke grinned. "Who is he, Sergeant Major?"

"Sir, he was my A-detachment team leader in Buon Mi Ga, South Vietnam, in 1964. He was a good one, I might add. The last time I saw him on Okinawa, he was a major, so he musta had a lower number than I did."

The colonel grinned and closed the conversation on this sunny day in January 1973. The next day, in my opinion, was not so sunny before its conclusion. I just wasn't ready for a phone call that would, or could, change my entire life along with that of my family's.

Sure 'nuff, at 1400 I was summoned from my office to that of Lieutenant Colonel Cooke's. "General Hugo's on the line," Cooke said when he handed me the phone. I knew it was my ol' team leader when he addressed me as Ho Chi Minh, just the way he did at Buon Mi Ga in 1964. It did not go unnoted that Cooke was monitoring the conversation. After congratulations on my promotion, the newbie general got to the crux of it all.

"Where do you want to be assigned when you leave Fort Sill, Ho?"

I explained the assignment I had received to East Central State at Ada, Oklahoma. General Hugo was less than impressed. "I hate to spoil your plans, Ho, but I have an excellent assignment for you. The Sergeants Major Academy at Fort Bliss, Texas, has just begun its first class and they're hurting for cadre. You have a college degree, so I think the assignment is made for you. Whatcha think?" Hugo had struck fear in my heart, but my answer tried to disguise it.

"I wish you'd called a few months ago, sir," I lied. "I've already bought a house near Ada, sir. I can't back out now, Captain! I'm sorry to have to disappoint you." I grinned at my humor while the Pentagon and Lieutenant Colonel Cooke frowned at it.

"It's General Hugo, Sergeant Major! You were too hasty, Ho. You'll have to fall back and regroup. We believe you belong in Fort Bliss, and I'd hoped you would agree."

I played my last hole card. "I'm sorry, sir, but 4th Army has already approved the assignment, so you're outta luck. As soon as the CSM arrives here from Korea, I'm gone."

"No, Ho, I'm sorry 'bout that. We outrank 4th Army a tad. If you think we're going to allow an E9 with a college degree to go to some school and give basic training to thirty or forty kids, you're out in left field, hardhead. Let me speak to your commander, Sergeant Major."

"Okay, Captain!" In a pissed-off frame of mind, I handed the phone to Cooke. Red-faced, I watched in anger and dismay as Hugo put my CO in a brace from nine hundred miles away. It was the first time I'd ever seen a light colonel sit at attention with only his mouth moving. All I could get from the lopsided conversation was my boss's, "Yes, sir. Yes, sir." When he hung up the phone, I allowed him to do all the talking.

"Sergeant Major Craig," said a tight-lipped, red-faced commander, "you almost got us both reduced in grade, among other things. Do you always address generals as 'Captain'?" I never got a chance to answer the question.

"I want you to go home, load up your wife and children, and report to the Sergeants Major Academy for an interview, scheduled by you know who." I opened my jaws to speak, but closed them at the colonel's raised hand signal. "Take a three-day pass. Your interview is Tuesday at 1000 hours. If it takes longer than three days to complete, don't sweat it. Be back here when you're finished. Any questions?"

I knew better than to say anything; my mouth had us in enough trouble. It was a Friday, allowing a couple of days to prepare for the long journey to El Paso, Texas, and Fort Bliss. To my surprise, the wife and kids were thrilled by the upcoming travel time. Kathy and Jimmy were out of school and my wife wanted to see her new country just as much as the youngsters. I was the only stick-in-the-mud of the bunch. Therefore, the packing and preparation took little time to complete.

I carefully prepared a khaki uniform for an interview that I really didn't desire. I kept asking myself what I was going to do with a house in Byng, Oklahoma, six hundred miles from El Paso. Maybe the academy would not accept me because of my excessive time in Special Forces! But the way General Hugo had carried on, locking my commander's heels, I really doubted that.

After another family conference, we decided to start the five-hundred-mile trip on Sunday. If we tired before reaching our destination, we could always stop at Midland, Texas, and move on come Monday. Early Sunday morning, after church, we were on Highway 277 to Wichita Falls, Texas. Around suppertime we were in Midland, Texas. We stayed in a motel that night and rested up, but only after Jimmy and Kathy wore out the swimming pool. The next day we were on the desert drive to our destination. After we left Amarillo, the scenery was flat, sandy, and monotonous. It's been called Texas's answer to the Sahara Desert. I'll buy that.

Monday afternoon we checked into the guest house at Fort Bliss proper. Depositing our luggage, we adjourned to the nearby Post Exchange, which was huge in comparison to Fort Sill's facility. In lieu of supper, we devoured snacks before driving to recon the academy, which was located on what had been Biggs Army Air Field. We exited the Fort Bliss gate that paralleled Highway 54 and spotted the main gate and the Biggs designator at the same time. The gate was unmanned. We traveled the main road that ran by the family housing on the right and administrative buildings on the left that bordered the abandoned airstrips. I turned left and spotted the Sergeants Major Academy Headquarters, classroom buildings, theater, and Post Exchange. I made a U-turn and slowly repeated the maneuver, checking the building numbers to see where my interview would be. The number coincided with the head-quarters, and we stopped at 1800 hours to look it over without leaving the vehicle. The school structures were WWII-era one-story wooden buildings that had wings connected by shel-tered walkways. Nothing fancy, but it would keep out the weather.

I met Command Sergeant Major Bill Bainbridge at approxi-mately 0945 the next day, while the wife, Kathy, and Jimmy continued their sight-seeing. In my khaki uniform with all awards and decorations, and the hated low quarter shoes, I was escorted by the future sergeant major of the Army to a room three doors down from his and Colonel Morton's offices. Two lieutenant colonels were seated at a long table, and Bainbridge seated himself between them. I sat opposite the pair of officers and handed Bainbridge my records, or at least what Sill would release of my records. While Lieutenant Colonel Piland checked my qualifications, the other two kept a conversation going. Lt. Col. George R. Stotser, a thin, short-cropped, brown-haired individual, asked the only question that made me pause for the cause, in addition to giving me an opportunity to rip my drawers.

"You have a ton of civilian schooling, Top, but except for the Special Forces Qualification Course and a message-center

school in 1950, you have very little military schooling. Why?"
It was not the first time that question had come up.

"Tough to say, sir. Always been too busy, or my unit
wouldn't see fit to send me." I was thinking that they should
send me through the Sergeants Major Academy beforehand.

Stotser only nodded, and after about twenty minutes of
question and answer, Bainbridge called a break. I went outside
in the dry heat of El Paso city while the three decided my fate.
Frankly, I wasn't too interested. In ten minutes I was seated in
front of Bainbridge. Much to my relief, his sidekicks had
departed. He wasted little time concluding the interview.

"We think you will do fine as an enlisted faculty group
member. The academy is looking forward to the day when all
small group instructors are sergeant majors. When would you
be available, Sergeant Major?"

"A month or so ought to do it, Top. I want the kids moved in
and ready for school before September."

"Okay, Bill, the orders will be down to your unit in a
month or so. Good luck," Bainbridge concluded. I, with a
wife and two kids, had a routing slip to the home of the Air
Defense Center, the Sergeants Major Academy, and Fort
Bliss, Texas.

I set my feelings aside on the trip home to Oklahoma. My
wife helped a ton by saying, "General Hugo would do nothing
to harm you or your Army career." But that truth finally
soaked in by the time we reached 2820 G Avenue, in Lawton.

The arrival of the CSM from Korea on or about June 1,
1973, turned on the green light. With Lieutenant Colonel
Cooke's blessings, the first soldiers and I organized and led the
4/31st Infantry (Mech) in an NCO parade in honor of our new
NCO in charge. The tall, thin, well-mannered CSM appreciated our efforts. I, in turn, notified the 4th Army and the
Sergeants Major Academy. Orders for Fort Bliss were in my
hands in two weeks. We, as a family, attacked the obstacle
course by the last of June 1973.

Post Transportation arranged to have what little furniture

we had at Lawton packed on the date we requested. In addition, they notified the household storage facility to deliver the goods we'd stored in Okinawa to Fort Bliss ASAP. Our personal items would go with us in the automobile. I arranged with my relatives to rent and renovate the home in Lawton. Our last problem before departure was in Byng, Oklahoma. The real-estate agent who sold us the property agreed to rent it until he could find a buyer. In the meantime, we were stuck with the monthly payments plus the payments for the home in Lawton. For a family that didn't yet have a place to stay, we owned a lot of houses.

Exactly as rehearsed for the interview, we boarded the Chevrolet for our new home of assignment. The kids were eager for the PCS move, but my bride and I were less than enthusiastic; we were resigned to the change. We started early, and because of Texas's liberal definition of speed limits, we were in the Fort Bliss guest house that very night. Because my travel time would cover it, I skipped the signing-in ritual for that night.

I signed in the next day in uniform at the Bliss Personnel shop and was treated to VIP status. This being an E9 was gonna be all right. Then I was shipped to Biggs Army Air Field, and got back to the real world. Piland, the black lieutenant colonel who sat on my interview board, would be my boss for the in-processing. He said, "If you have any trouble moving in, let me know, maybe I can be of assistance. If not, I'll see you when you're finished. You new faculty group members have some things to accomplish before Class Number Two begins. Any questions?"

I agreed to rush the processing, which consisted, in the main, of being assigned quarters on-post and unloading our household goods. The furniture from Okinawa would be in addition to what we had packed and shipped from Fort Sill. In only three days we were assigned quarters at 3430 Hero Avenue in the Logan Heights area of Fort Bliss proper. The duplex was an exact duplicate of our quarters in Okinawa, but we were unable to get into the driveway because of all the pickup trucks that obviously belonged to working-class civilians. Nevertheless, we parked on the curb and approached our new home.

It turned out that the quarters were being renovated, to include painting the interior, and would be ready for occupancy by the next week. At the kids' insistance, we were given directions to Logan Heights Elementary School, two and a half blocks away.

We received some pleasant surprises upon our arrival at the large, one-story facility. The first surprise was the distance, which told us our youngsters could walk to and from school in a relatively safe environment. When we moved onto the large ball park and playground, I was mildly taken aback by one of the coaches of the boys' baseball team. The large, well-built redhead saw me, and we grinned and waved at about the same instant.

Master Sergeant E8, at the time, Charles Telfair had been a member of the Individual Training Detachment at Long Hai. Despite my short stay at that pleasure resort, I remembered him and I could see that he recalled me as well. We greeted each other and filled in the last two years since our departure from Vietnam. Telfair had been promoted a little bit sooner than I. Jimmy, my nine-year-old, broke into the military chit-chat; rather loudly, I thought. "Daddy, Daddy, I wanta play ball!"

"Okay, just hold your horses. This is a Little League team, isn't it, Charley?"

"Yeah, Bill," he answered while eyeing Jim's diminutive stature. "How old is he?"

I told him, in addition to assuring him that the kid could play well enough. Charley took him over and introduced him to the coach and to his own son. Hatsuko and Kathy shook their heads, clearly wanting to get away from the jocks and back to the guest house. I could only grin. By the time Telfair and Jim came back, my son felt more at home at Fort Bliss than the rest of us. "When are we gonna unpack, Dad?" Jimmy blurted out. "I need my glove and baseball shoes."

"Next week, Jimmy. We'll move in and you can play with 'em then." He didn't like the delay, but what the hell.

Hatsuko and Kathy wanted to motor, so I gave them the car keys after Telfair promised Jim and me that he would transport us back to the guest house after practice. I readily agreed, as I wanted to get another viewpoint on my assignment from a person who had already been exposed. By the time the females had defected for the guest house, Jimmy had bummed a glove and was earning his turn at bat chasing the batted baseballs. For myself, I got down to business with my ex-teamy.

He'd been there only a few months and was now a faculty group member (FGM) in Class One. I was all ears, mentally speaking, and urged him to continue to march on the same parade field. I would only interrupt when I had inquiries.

Telfair started the session informing me about the multiple field grades (major and above) that I had seen since my arrival. They were faculty advisers, but due to the shortage of sergeant majors, many of them were being used as faculty group members. I asked him to explain the difference. "The FGM is the classroom honcho and guides the class to its objectives," he said. "He also evaluates each student at the end of the six weeks or so." The last statement stumped me because I'd been led to believe the course was six months in length.

"Yes, the course's entirety is six months, but the students stay in only one classroom and under one FGM for approximately six weeks before moving to another group."

"How big are the classes, Charley?"

"Approximately twelve people and no more than thirteen," Telfair said. "Let me start from the beginning to simplify the process for you. Okay? The academy is modeled after the War College in Fort Leavenworth, Kansas, for field-grade officers, and utilizes the small-group instruction process. In this method, most classes, but not all, are presented by the students. Their presentations are evaluated by the FGM, as is each student's participation at the end of the six to eight weeks. However, the FGMs do present instruction in subjects such as Speech, Tactics, English, and some classes in Leadership and Management. It's my first go-round, but I've had no trouble with it. Do you have any other questions about the assignment?"

"No, I guess not, Charley. I should have my family settled in soon. What will I do during the break between Class One and Class Two?"

"We'll all be busy, Bill. You have two short, forty-hour courses to attend. The Methods of Instruction class will be given for newbies at Fort Bliss by one of the Air Defense School instructors. The other forty-hour jobby will be given at the academy. It's called the Small Group Workshop, and you should find it very enlightening. After that, we'll all be sponsoring the new students and their families who will be moving on-post!"

I was aghast at the last statement, and my disbelief was obvious by my facial expression. "Students, E8s and E9s, bringing their families on a six-month school assignment. You've gotta be shittin' me, Charley!"

"I figured that would surprise you, but you may change your mind before you're through with your first class. The students are encouraged to bring their families for several reasons. First of all, they have their next assignments before they get here. And the second reason is that the academy wants the wives to get involved in their hubbys' career."

"Such as?"

"Well, so far I've seen cooking classes, sewing classes, and they even help plan the dining-outs."

"What the hell is a dining-out, Charley?"

"A dining-out is a formal outing that features speeches, food, and entertainment. They don't say they're mandatory but I haven't seen many students or FGMs miss one yet. If they did, it might well reflect adversely on their evaluations. A dining-in is a formal affair also, but it's stag. There is one of each for each class, so get your blues or whites ready, Freddy."

I owned not a set of the Army's blue formal wear but, for a change, I decided I wouldn't fight the problem and made a mental note to purchase a set as soon as we got settled. By this time, baseball practice was over and Jimmy and Charley Junior came over laughing as the sweat rolled down their faces.

The head coach told me he'd be happy to have Jim play on the club. He gave us the times and dates, and Jimmy had his work cut out for him during the summer months. Sergeant Major Telfair had my son and me back at the guest house in time for our informal dining-out. I'd been impressed by Telfair's minibriefing.

As promised, several days later Telfair helped hang the curtain rods for the new home. After our move was completed, I reported to Lieutenant Colonel Piland and he put me to work, as he'd promised. I was presented orders to attend a one-week methods-of-instruction course in a classroom near Post Headquarters at Fort Bliss.

Before reporting in on a Monday morning in August 1973, I thought about my first chore from several viewpoints: as an NCO instructor who had taught at the Special Forces Training Group at Fort Bragg; an NCO who began and wrote, with some assistance, the combat orientation course in Nha Trang, South Vietnam in 1968; an NCO who had taught thousands of indigenous in Laos, South Vietnam, and Taiwan, I was now going to school to learn methods of instruction. Rather than start off my new assignment with a negative outlook, I thought back to Lieutenant Colonel Stotser's remark about the lack of military schooling in my 201 file. The course would go on my record and in my jacket file, certificate and all. My six hours of college speech courses would help get me over my nonexistent shyness; besides, I could use the spare time to get settled in at Logan Heights. That was my frame of mind during the refresher training, and the way it turned out, I was thankful for the proper mental outlook.

The class was composed of ten NCOs of lesser rank from units scattered thoughout Fort Bliss. The instructor was an Air Defense captain who appeared pleased that I was one of his charges. We were required to introduce ourselves and to give periodic oral presentations before the final, which would consist of a twenty-minute class on a military subject. I presented my final on Priming of Military Explosives. I wasn't worried about being technically inefficient; in fact, I was the only one in the room who knew what the hell I was talking about. I escaped with honors and received a certificate that read, "Instructor Training Course, Special Class (40-hour equivalency) 13 to 17 August 1973."

The small group workshop began just after the graduation of Class One. The two hundred or so grads went into the history books, being the first ever to receive diplomas from the enlisted man's highest military school. My wife and I attended the ceremony in the Biggs Theater, and the members of Class One went to their next assignments shortly thereafter.

I attended the small group workshop along with Sergeant Majors Spore, Kaplan, Foreman, McLaughlin, and several others I can't recall. The class was filled by many of the same field-grade officers who had been subbing as FGMs due to the lack of sergeant majors in Class One. The imparted information was very beneficial to all concerned, including me. The central teaching point, in the opinion of the students who had instructed previously, was that the students, E8s and E9s, were going to do eighty percent of the instructing. I liked that. The class training schedule would designate what was to be covered and the reference material where the information was contained. The FGM, using the class roster, appointed the principal instructor, who would select his assistant or assistants, as the case might be. It was not unusual for the entire class to be involved, as that was one of the guiding lights of the small-group method. The new FGMs would be no better off in their first course, Class Two, than the students, in that they would have to stay up with the class in order to evaluate it at its conclusion. I was ready and able at the start of Class Two in September 1973. My kids were in school, and my wife, under the able guidance and tutelage of Mrs. Bill Bainbridge, was involved in several of the wives' clubs, sewing being her forte.

I spent the next six months keeping one step ahead of my class. The afternoon study halls and studying at night kept me abreast of my subjects, if not my students. Physical training was an on-your-honor affair, and I proved I had some, despite the hot, dry El Paso sunshine. I jogged and walked every afternoon, though the high altitude and thin air took some getting used to. However, the self-inflicted punishment did not affect my eyesight. I noted that some of the students—and cadre—were not quite as honest. It would be Class Three before I voiced my disapproval about the lack of participation, or about any of the regimentation. The season of the year dictated the Class A uniform that the transients and the cadre wore to school; khakis in the summer and Army greens in the winter, what little winter was available in the southern tip of Texas.

Busy, busy, busy was my password for Class Two. Much busier than I would be for classes three, four, and five. Admittedly, in many of the subjects some of the members were more knowledgeable than I. My pride being what it is, I didn't take to that. Thus, the long tedious hours at the study lamp. The six months went by very swiftly for all involved, including the families.

Mrs. Bill Bainbridge helped my wife with her initial sewing club, which met three times a week, Hatsuko learning more from the American wives than they did from her—in my opinion. The old Japanese adage that placed the wives on the lower rung slowly went by the boards. Much to my surprise, Hatsuko began questioning some matters pertaining to our domestic routine. She even became involved in paying bills and writing checks on our dual checking account. Shame on you, Mrs. Bainbridge! In other words, much to my disgust, my wife, who already knew El Paso better than I did, was becoming Americanized. Thank God I was too wrapped up in my schoolwork to really appreciate these future advantages.

What classes did I enjoy and learn the most from? A tough question that required some thought. It always narrowed down to three or four that should be interesting. Management? Because of the role of leadership in the Armed Forces, management takes a backseat. But should it? Management is the supervising of something, such as a business, to accomplish an end. Leadership is leading people in order to accomplish a mission. You cannot manage people! Or can you? Civilians apparently think so. I, like most of my classmates, thought otherwise. This phase of the management class brought about many heated discussions, but the majority of us never changed our beliefs on the subject.

Despite all the experience in the student body, we learned some things through the discussions. What is more important, facts or opinions? That question was asked at the beginning of a videotape by a professor from Purdue University. Most management experts will blow this one. I would stop the tape at the conclusion of the easy question and poll the class for their answer. Invariably, we would end up about 50/50 in our responses. I would start the tape and we would all learn something. The prof would continue with his enlightment. "Opinions are the most important! If I have an opinion, I can drum up all the facts I need to support my contention!" Regardless of the experience factor, we all learned something from the classes.

In the leadership classes, due to their grass-roots exposure, the entire student body would, and did, in my opinion, put the War College students to shame. And I am the first to admit that they blew away some of my misconceptions in the process. For instance, despite having Marine Corps, quartermaster, ordnance, naval, or field artillery backgrounds, their well-thought-out solutions varied little, if any. There went my Special Forces and infantry leadership superiority theory out the classroom window.

Another class that rattled my cage to the maximum was Listening! Yes, Listening. I didn't need this four hours, either! Did I? The faculty group member speaks to the class to start the block of instruction. "We all believe that we have come to a void in our Ultima [the academy motto] training! Am I right or Amarillo?" The class grins before the FGM concludes his opening remarks. "That was my conclusion the first time I gave or received this instruction. I've changed my mind. But will you?"

The FGM at this point appoints three students to go into the hallways. They are instructed not to talk to one another during their short stay. The FGM goes on with the class for approximately five minutes before he recalls his charges, one by one. He asks the first student what he had said in his opening statement. After the student finishes his recital, the FGM would recall the second student for a repeat performance, and then the third. After hearing the three screwed-up versions of the opening remarks, you would be convinced, just as we all were. Yes, everyone needs a class on listening, unless you're one of the very damn few who keeps an open mind at all times, and possesses good recall that is not clouded with your own troubles and misconceptions. If you're listening to a lecture, for instance, but are mentally putting down the lecturer, you're not listening. If you're carrying on a conversation and your mind is thinking of an answer or a retort, you're not listening. I was so impressed with the instruction on this subject that to this day I believe it should be given in all high schools and colleges throughout the land, in addition to workshops for companies with more than three or four employees. We all learned something in the short demonstration.

The speech class was the FGM's baby. One of the students talked to me after the orientation. His request surprised me: "Sergeant Major, I'm just not all that confident in this subject. I think I can meet all the requirements but the final speech. I could probably meet that if you would agree not to videotape it for rerun purposes. Whatcha think?"

I presented one of my better speeches to see if I could tighten up his sagging confidence: "No one is a born speaker, Johnson. Self-confidence will come with practice. You're fortunate in that your audience is pulling for you all the way. You'll be ready for television by your last talk. I can't grant your no-taping request, but believe me when I say you won't need it."

In the small-group class method, the students criticized every delivery, but as I'd said in my sermon to Johnson, they all had their classmates' interests at heart. After Johnson's first, short, introductory speech, his fellow students knew what I knew: all Johnson needed was practice. Because I could read my classes by that time, I didn't worry. The class came down hard in their criticism of the more polished speakers, but lightened up on those not as proficient. The students knew what they were doing, and I seldom interfered.

Johnson was as ready for his final taped speech as most of his classmates. When I ran the qualifying speech he'd projected on our portable TV, I couldn't help but notice the smile or two Johnson exhibited upon seeing his image. I was just as proud of him as he was. Before graduation, Johnson came by and thanked me for not allowing him to renege on his final. His thanks was, to me, one of the joys of teaching. What I didn't tell him was that many of my leaders had made me do things I didn't want to do, and I was a much better person because of it.

CHAPTER 29

Class Three alone had fifty-four guest speakers, celebrities who managed or attempted to keep us abreast of everything from the state of the Armed Forces to politics in El Paso, Texas. Here's a sampling of the guest speakers we enjoyed and/or tolerated in 1974: Brigadier General Mildred C. Bailey, Director of Women's Army Corps (WACs); Brigadier General Benjamin Davis, U.S. Air Force, Military Personnel Center, Pentagon; Command Sergeant Major Thomas N. Barnes, U.S. Air Force; Sergeant Major Clinton A. Puckett, Sergeant Major of the U.S. Marine Corps; Major General C. J. Le Van, Commander, Fort Bliss, Texas; and finally, Brigadier General Michael D. Healy, Commander, JFK Center for Military Assistance at Fort Bragg, North Carolina.

Yes, the former Colonel Healy who, in many GIs' opinions, sold Special Forces down the tube to Abrams and MACV in Vietnam in 1969. The colonel who took over the 5th SF Group (Abn) when Colonel Rheault was relieved in the infamous "Green Beret Murder Case." General Healy gave an excellent speech on the method the JFK Center employed to help everyone, except the country that most needed it, South Vietnam. The powers that be in the waste plant (Pentagon) had decided to abandon our former allies in Southeast Asia in order to be hip—politically. Special Forces, the JFK Center's only real asset, was mentioned sparingly by Healy, so I wasn't too alert to his garbage. I was alerted, however, after the question-and-answer period, to the fact that there would be a happy hour that very Friday night at the American Legion Club. All former members of Special Forces were invited, with Healy being the guest of honor. The party, as we understood it, was arranged by former members of the 10th SF Group in Bad Tolz, Germany. Apparently, he was an old head in that SF unit I had never been a member of. Yeah, I'd go! Anything for the academy; besides, I'd get to indulge myself in a pastime I still enjoyed. Married life had never altered that part of my personality.

The stag affair was held in a large meeting hall of the legion just off Dyer Street. It started off friendly enough. The only people I could honestly say I knew at the bash were FGMs Foreman, McLaughlin, and Hale—none of whom were hardcore Southeast Asia hands. Therefore, I had never run my mouth off to them about my feelings for "Iron Mike."

I finished one beer while watching the goings-on. Still observing the crowd of people around Healy, I spotted his Second John aide sitting at a table by himself at the far end of the room, which was fronted by a bar. I got a couple of beers and headed for his table in a friendly manner. He smiled and we shook hands after I introduced myself. I was sympathetic with the young man, while thanking God I'd never been paid to kiss a general's ass from morning till night. I did reveal a few facts to him before we changed the subject from why I wasn't getting with the program. He grinned.

When the aide's grin was replaced with a solemn expression, I felt a presence behind me even before Healy moved to the side of our chairs and spoke in a slurred manner. "What are you telling him, Sergeant Major? Special Forces doesn't repeat our business to outsiders," he said aggressively.

I gritted my teeth and silently thanked God that I had only two beers to motivate my mouth. "Sir," I said acidly, "I'll talk to anyone I goddamn well please, and say whatever I please."

Healy's mouth fell open in disbelief. He stuttered, but finally managed, "Well . . ." He turned and was back with his cohorts, the innocent lieutenant in hot pursuit. I felt the evening was not completely wasted. I went to speak to FGMs Foreman and McLaughlin before exiting the American Legion with a general-grade (O-9!) smile on my face for the first time that evening.

I was not at all worried about repercussions while driving home. Get serious.

Healy had, I hoped, learned something every NCO should know by the time he makes buck sergeant. Once you're drinking liquor of the intoxicating variety, watch your conduct around troops—regardless of rank. Of course, you don't give orders and expect them to be heeded, nor do you make remarks that can be interpreted as critical. However, if by chance you do and your rectum feels distorted the next day, there may be a reason for it. You may have had one of your remarks shoved up your ass sideways, or one of your requests ignored and accompanied by laughter, if you're lucky.

Faculty group members covered three different groups of students in every six-month course. The students were reassigned to different groups and FGMs at the end of the seven-week period. For the losing FGM it was individual-evaluation time. My first stint in Class Two proved to be an afternoon chore that ate up the entire week. Like any task, the first time around would be the most trying and the most beneficial for the future. I devised my own system, one I deviated from only slightly in the groups yet to come.

I used the following guidelines for every student: leadership, participation in classes not assigned and school activities, general attitude, personal appearance, organizational ability, management, and physical condition. If appropriate, I would list the strongest traits first followed by the lesser, and which trait gave me the most trouble. Because of an inability to test physical conditioning, evaluation of that characteristic was very difficult. After three evaluation drills in Class Two, my mind went back in time to Okinawa and Colonel Rheault's solution in 1969.

The physical training test for those over forty years of age was now being administered in the U.S. Army, if not the entire Armed Forces. Before the beginning of Class Three, I did the best I could, considering my status. During an FGM meeting with Bill Bainbridge, I said: "We make statements on our evaluations about a student's conditioning, statements we can't prove or disprove under the present system. I run and walk every afternoon, and there are students—and FGMs—I seldom if ever set eyes on. I suggest we give the students a PT test upon entry and one before graduation, Sergeant Major."

Bainbridge, as well as a few FGMs, was shocked and didn't hide it very well. "We can't do that, Sergeant Craig," the boss said.

"Why not, Top? I'll take the test with 'em. At least we would know what we're writing about."

"We're not here to embarrass anyone, Craig."

I had tried, but it would only be after the future Sergeant Major of the Army and I had departed the establishment that a conditioning program was instituted. Except for that burr under my saddle, I rode the evaluation route smoother and smoother through Classes Three, Four, and Five.

The graduation of Class Two was a huge success, and for many reasons besides a full auditorium of well-wishers. I'm sure many thoughts went through the students' and FGMs' skulls before, during, and after the ceremony. My thoughts even returned to General Victor Hugo, though I hated to admit I was wrong. If I ever get a chance, I thought out loud, I will tell him that he had coerced me into the finest, most rewarding assignment I'd ever had in twenty-four years of active duty in the U.S. Army.

My family was no less pleased with the assignment than I. The kids were A students in the elementary school that was within walking distance. Air Defense Command Sergeant Major Tubbs lived on our right, and our families—husbands, wives, and children—got along famously. The Copellos occupied the other half of the duplex, and we often went out together on the weekends. Sergeant Major Stover, the former Personnel sergeant from Fort Sill, lived down the road a piece and visited us from time to time. When Hatsuko had some problems with her academy-related activities, she leaned on CSM Bainbridge's wife, Hazel, and never failed to receive the advice or help she needed.

Financially, the paychecks of an E9 with over twenty-four years would keep us from harm's way. When the oil crisis of the times hit the fan, I joined FGMs Spore, Parsons, and Stover in a car pool and continued to march. I only had a few more highlights before moving on to higher ground. Bainbridge and I also had a few more adventures before this great event occurred. Despite the PT test loss, I had never given up and was still determined to win one, regardless of the odds. My next opportunity was not long in coming.

A group of E8s and E9s sprinkled with field grades from the Artillery Center at Fort Sill, Oklahoma, was scheduled for a tour of the academy. CSM Bainbridge summoned me to his office for my part in the stage play. I was subsequently informed that I would give the orientation briefing to the Artillery supergrades and their escorts. The one-hour, classroom-type affair was relatively routine, but my selection left me confused.

"Why me, Sergeant Major?" I said. "I'm not a redleg. In fact, I couldn't even get along with the bastards when I was in an infantry unit at Sill. Get Spore or one of those high-angle FGMs to welcome the assholes."

After the boss's color came back to normal, he said, "It's your turn, Bill. You're not briefing them on the 155 howitzer, damn it."

"Okay, Top, but they won't appreciate a Special Forces, infantry, engineer soldier being their briefer."

My CSM just wasn't impressed with my weaseling. "I picked you because you know more about Fort Sill than anybody at the academy, or who will be in the audience, for that matter. I know you were born there. Get with it, Okie!" Bainbridge grinned.

"How in the hell? Who shot off his mouth?" I mumbled as I walked out of the main head shed. "I can't seem to win one, but I ain't giving up."

I only had to rehearse the briefing once to get it down pat. I even had my attention-getter formulated for the redlegs north of the Red River. The affair was to take place in the school portion of the academy, the first classroom on the right from the entry. I was even grinning as I faced the audience. I deliberately kept my glance from the CSM, who was seated in the back row. After introducing myself, I attempted to grab 'em where they came from.

"Normally," I began, "the briefer will have a similar military background to his audience. Today, that will not be the case." At the very least, I knew I had one person who was now giving me his undivided attention.

"I have an infantry, engineer, Special Forces background, but still I was selected for this task. The reason I was selected, according to CSM Bainbridge, was because I was born at Fort Sill Station Hospital." The remark got some grins and laughs of disbelief. Bainbridge must have gotten a charge out of it because his face sure was red. I had their attention, and the remainder of the proceedings went off without a hitch. Afterward, CSM Tom Haughney and the Fort Sill crew were laughing and joking with me about my hometown and vicinity. Bainbridge was conspicuous by his absence.

It was during Class Three that the Special Forces students and FGMs received some unexpected attention. The guest speaker was none other than the Chief of Staff of the U.S. Army, Creighton W. Abrams. Along with FGMs Foreman, Telfair, Hale, and McLaughlin, I attempted to keep an open mind to the ranking man in the Army. The speaker was very sharp and made the troops feel at ease, despite the absence of questions at the conclusion. His last statement before departing the stage was a bit startling.

"I would like to see all Special Forces students and cadre in the lobby at the conclusion. Thank you for your attention."

The gathering in the lobby was around thirty personnel. The general's dog-robber called attention, and the chief gave us "At ease" before he began his short spiel. "There is some talk going around the Army that I have it in for Special Forces. I've called you here to put a stop to that type of malarkey. I have all the respect in the world for your unit and wouldn't harm it for the world. Are there any questions?"

After a forever of silence, he nodded at his aide, who placed us in a respectful stance and followed the head man away. We mumbled around for a few minutes before we followed his lead. Did we believe him? Well, the mumbling needs some interpretation, and the interpretation can be broken down into one word: BULLSHIT!

Class Five was going to be a revelation, not only to me, but to William Bainbridge as well. The class would not graduate until June 19, 1975, and we continued on our busy schedule. We were into our second-group runaround when the announcement came from the head shed in far away D.C. CSM Bainbridge was to become the fourth Sergeant Major of the Army.

Yes, my arguing partner would replace SMA Leon L. Van Autreve about the same time that Class Five was to hit the road. Most people were not too surprised; jealous perhaps, but not surprised. In the opinion of many NCOs, he'd been selected for the most prestigious slot in the Noncommissioned Officer Corps. I was happy for Bainbridge, as was my wife because of her adoration of his wife, Hazel. Then came the invitations to his going-away fest. It was to be held at the Fort Bliss O Club! I was shocked, and complained about it until my wife became very annoyed.

Yes sir! CSM—soon to be SMA—Bainbridge's going-away party was to be held in the Fort Bliss Officers' Club! My teammates were not as torn up about that as I. My complaints came to a head one afternoon in the hallway of my favorite institution. I, SMA-select Bill, and a few others were discussing the "farewell" when my boss got it out of my closet.

"Just what is your complaint, Bill?" Bainbridge asked.

"My complaint, Sergeant Major, is that I do not like to socialize with officers. I don't go to their clubs, and I don't want them in mine. I thought that was part of the caste system we've had for lo these last two thousand years."

"Your attitude toward the Officers' Corps is going to hurt your career someday, Bill!" he replied.

"It's a little late for them to do anything now, Sergeant Major; unless they add E10 to the enlisted ranks."

Infection of both ears made it medically unsound for me to attend the fourth Sergeant Major of the Army's going-away party. My wife attended while I baby-sat at the house. Once the infections were cleared up, the doctor passed along some good news about my constant ear problems.

"You have very bad perforations of both eardrums. We now have a skin graft procedure that will close both perforations."

"Will that improve my hearing, sir?"

"It will, to an extent, Sergeant. But the most important accomplishment will be the cessation of your chronic infections."

Nearing the end of Class Five, the major performed the operation. I stayed in William Beaumont Army Medical Center for three or four days and was back to work in ten days. I was very impressed with the surgeon and the facility. Located on the outskirts of northwest El Paso, the ten-story facility was as proficient as any I'd ever been associated with in the military.

After Bainbridge's departure, a temporary CSM moved in under the cover of darkness. Because of my recent medical problems, I was not assigned to a group in Class Six. I was goofing off rewriting current lesson plans and subbing for FGMs when I appeared on the command sergeant major list in August 1975. Making the list did not faze me in the least.

Making a decision in regards to the appointment was a different matter entirely. I did not have to accept the appointment to E9 command sergeant major; I could have turned it down and suffered no recriminations from the Army. I did not want to air the subject with anyone presently on assignment to the academy, leaving me only one other source—my family. This was the corner I had to turn in August 1975.

My family was settled in at Bliss/El Paso. My children, Kathy and Jimmy, were now members of the Fort Bliss swim team. The competitive activity kept them busy with two-a-day workouts and competitive meets on most weekends in El Paso or vicinity. None of us had any disagreements with the Fort Bliss school system, but if I accepted a CSM appointment, a new assignment would be forthcoming. And where was anyone's guess. If we moved to another place, it would mark the children's fourth new school in only six years.

The appointment would leave me, unlike the general-grade officers, with no increase in pay, only an increase in responsibility and prestige. I would still be pay grade E9, an obvious flaw in the system that has not been corrected to this day. Sergeant Major of the Army, where were you when we needed you?

With those drawbacks, why I considered the appointment at all was tough to explain to my wife, but I gave it a go. The refusal rate in 1975 was almost beyond belief, and we had one FGM who had already turned it down, but continued doing a superb job as an FGM. The question of accepting or refusing the appointment invariably came up in the Academy Leadership and Management classes, with surprising results. In a word, the student majority believed that personnel appointed to CSM should be required to take over a battalion or higher command. I agreed! Because under the voluntary procedure, the Army was not able to appoint the best personnel for the available slots. If fifty were selected and twenty turned the offer down, you then had to select twenty (or more) personnel who you did not believe were the better people in the first selection. Vulgarly put, the system sucked!

After three days of talking to my spouse and going through mental gyrations, I decided to accept the appointment. In the commander's office in late August, my primary MOS was changed to 00Z5S, or CSM, Special Forces qualified, with date of rank of September 1, 1975. My assignment followed very closely. That also pleased me no end.

CHAPTER 30

Orders were delivered around the middle of September 1975, assigning me to a unit that did not then exist. According to the directive, the briefing would be held at Building 6808, Logan Heights, Fort Bliss, Texas, located only a mile from my quarters. I could find that.

The Logan Heights area consisted of family housing where I resided, in addition to a cantonment area that was west of my family quarters. The area was WWII-era wooden buildings that I was very familiar with thanks to duty at Forts Bragg, Sill, Gordon, and Campbell and Camp Polk. The briefing was held in the wooden headquarters of the new unit, which was still being renovated. A group of NCOs and administrative people listened to CSM James R. Tubbs. Yes, my next-door neighbor, Tubbs, would be the brigade CSM of the new unit. He had informed me a week before, and I was eager to get the skinny on my new unit.

"By direction of the U.S. Army Training and Doctrine Command, Fort Monroe, Virginia," Tubbs said, "the U.S. Army Air Defense Basic Combat Training Brigade will be activated on October first, 1975, at Logan Heights, Fort Bliss, Texas. The BCT brigade will be organized with a headquarters battery, two basic combat training battalions, a committee group and U.S. Army Reception Station, Fort Bliss. The BCT brigade permanent party organization will consist of sixty officers, 474 enlisted men, and thirty civilians. A restoration project has been initiated to restore barracks, mess halls, and training facilities in the Logan Heights area, as you can see.

"We are fortunate to have with us today the two command sergeant majors who will run the BCT battalions," Tubbs went on. "Command Sergeant Major Craig came from the Sergeants Major Academy." Tubbs pointed. The sparse crowd of enlisted men clapped, and I waved in response. "He will honcho the 1st BCT Battalion. He has an infantry, engineer, and Special Forces background with over twenty-four years in the Army." Again I waved as Tubbs moved on.

"The command sergeant major of the 2nd BCT Battalion will be CSM James Boyle!" A young E9 rose four chairs down from my position, clad in a sharp fatigue uniform with spit-shined boots. The dark-haired Irishman, five-foot-nine and 175 pounds, started to reclaim his folding chair before Tubbs spoke again.

"If you don't mind, Jim," Tubbs said, "you could give us some background on yourself, as I only received your orders a couple of days ago."

"My name is CSM Boyle and I just came from Santa Fe, New Mexico, with my wife and three children," Boyle said. "I have been in Air Defense units practically my entire Army career. Like CSM Craig, I was just appointed to my present rank. I'm looking forward to the Air Defense branch having its own basic training at Fort Bliss. In this manner, the trainees will move from BCT to advanced individual training here at Fort Bliss. That's the way the Infantry, Artillery, and Engineer trainees do!"

After Boyle was seated, and before Tubbs began anew, I knew I'd learned something. The young CSM was correct. An Artillery recruit at Fort Sill finished his basic in seven weeks and moved just down the road in order to complete advanced individual training. Until this moment the move to AIT had meant a permanent change of station elsewhere for the Air Defense recruit. Thank you, CSM! A smoke break outside, and Tubbs was at the podium once again.

"Before we take our bus tour, I will give you a rundown on the only officers I have orders on at this time," Tubbs said. "Colonel Merle D. Starr will be the first-ever brigade commander. He went to Officers' Candidate School at Fort Sill after three years' enlisted service. He has commanded a number of batteries as well as an advanced individual training battalion and a basic combat training battalion with the Infantry Training Center at Ford Ord, California. He has seen action in Vietnam, and served in Greenland and Germany. He has also served in several high-level staff positions. His last assignment was as special assistant to the deputy commander here at Fort Bliss. He holds the Legion of Merit, Bronze Star Medal, Air Medal, Army Commendation Medal with three oak leaf clusters, and the Combat Infantryman Badge." Tubbs looked my way and smiled at the mention of the coveted award. I was bored and didn't return the favor.

"The 1st Basic Training Battalion commander is now en route to Fort Bliss, but I have very little information on him, Command Sergeant Major Craig. But Lieutenant Colonel Martin G. Olson has the Combat Infantryman's Badge also." He grinned. "Your XO will be Major R. B. Wilkie, who is stationed here at Bliss." The remainder of Tubbs's scenario concerned the 2nd BCT Battalion CO, Lt. Col. Ernest Tobin, and had CSM Boyle hanging onto his chair. As for me, I was already ready for the facilities tour and didn't give a damn who knew it.

We left our vehicles in the brigade parking lot and moved as a group in a shiny thirty-passenger olive-drab bus. We didn't move far, however. Just across the busy thoroughfare of Dyer Street was a small road and a shabby guard shack, one that I hoped was going to benefit from the refurbishing project. A few hundred yards away on both sides of one long, paved street lay the facilities of the working folks.

We started on the east end, at what would soon be the consolidated mess hall, or the "dining facility," as the young soldiers called it. It was of stucco construction and large enough to feed the anticipated five hundred trainees. The civilian contract labor was working even while we gawked. Across the street was the orderly room of A Battery and the living quarters facing the orderly room and battery headquarters. All of the line units were adjacent to one another, and their layouts did not vary, all the way to the mess hall of the 2nd BCT on the west end of the facilities. We moved on foot, in the heat, on up the line.

The next wooden structure was oblong with a hall running down the center. At the east end of the hallway were two offices, one for the CO and one for the XO. Apparently, the CSM didn't rate too high in the scheme of things. I inquired of a civilian honcho, and was proved wrong for a change. Another office was under way on the west end of the 1st Battalion Headquarters. The south side of the hallway was the administrative room for the S-1 (Personnel) shop. The west end belonged to the S-2 and S-3 (Training) officers. The work was moving along smartly, and we moved along as well.

We moved to a permanent stucco building that looked quite modern in comparison to the rest of the layout. The single-story building was the Post Exchange, and it was also undergoing "renewal."

We continued on to the future home of the 2nd BCT area, and it varied not. The area orientation tour was soon finished. On the bus ride back to our brigade parking lot, the brigade dispensary was pointed out by our tour guide. We were told that any serious medical problems would be dispatched to the William Beaumont Hospital. All we had to look forward to after the tour was the arrival of enough permanent party to get the show on the road.

CSM Boyle and I combined our talents each morning to give our people physical training topped off with a run. To my surprise, Boyle was in top shape despite being in his late thirties. When Colonel Olson came on the scene, we moved to our new home on the hill with what few stragglers we had at the time. It was amid the hammer-and-nail construction that the colonel and I had our first heart-to-heart. It was more of a learning session than anything else. I found out a ton of facts and figures about the quiet Swede. He was a graduate electrical engineer, married, without dependent children. He had experience on Battalion and higher staff but had not had any command time lately, and proved it, emphasizing needlessly that his door would always be open to me. I should hope so, I thought. I'd hate to have to pay for the damn thing after breaking it down. When he finished, he asked me what my philosophies concerning CSMs might be. Being immodest, I raved on and on.

My first point was that I was to be the final determination when it came to NCOs. He had no quarrel with that. Point two: no enlisted personnel would be in his office, for whatever reason, without going through me or my representative. And three: my enlisted representative or I would be present at all Battalion Article 15s (unit-level "nonjudicial" punishment) proceedings, remembering that a battery (company-level) Article 15 contains lesser fines and restrictions. If the battery CO has administered punishment and cannot detect improvement, he will, and can, recommend an Article 15 by the battalion commander. I knew the colonel knew that I knew he had everything to gain and that I had nothing to lose. A CSM cannot be promoted, but most LTCs (0-5s) are looking for full-bull (0-6) colonel. The talk concluded, but in reality went on until the day we parted.

After three months of arrivals and preparation, the U.S. Army Reception Station, Fort Bliss, began receiving trainees, on December 29, 1975. By that time, the 1st and 2nd basic training battalions were in excellent shape, NCO-wise. First sergeants running the units were Greenwood; J. E. Hammond, a neighbor of mine on Hero Avenue; C. G. Shipley; and R. A. Jones. Only a few meetings and we were all on the same wavelength in regards to discipline and training. We were very fortunate to have such outstanding personnel to start the ball rolling. In the battalion headquarters section, we had an ace in the hole in one

Sergeant First Class D. A. Smith. In my opinion the tall, skinny Smith was a Personnel NCO without peer. I consulted him at every turn to keep me abreast of the Army's infamous paper drill. He never let us down.

The first seven-week cycle of training was initiated on January 9, 1976, in A Battery, 1st BCT Battalion. My routine changed a tad on that date as well. After scanning the incoming paperwork SFC Smith had stacked on my desk and placing it in the proper dissemination box, I would talk with Lieutenant Colonel Olson, if needed, then move out to the line units. After a visit with the battery first sergeant, I would observe training for a short while before moving on to the next line unit. This morning chore would take two to three hours. One activity caused this routine to waffle from time to time. The trainees lived at McGregor Range in H-type stucco barracks during their third through fifth weeks of training. From McGregor they would move by foot to Myer Range and live in two-man pup tents while qualifying with the M-16 rifle during day and night firing. Other field training consisted of live grenade throws, the M-60 machine guns, claymore mines, M-203 grenade launcher, hand grenade assault course, and fire and defensive courses. This cyclic event would find me or Colonel Olson on our way to the range at least two or three times a week. The jeep ride to the ranges that lay east-northeast of Fort Bliss and El Paso proper took up damn near an hour.

That sums up my first CSM assignment, and the duty varied little until September 1976. This does not imply that I didn't have some exciting highlights during my first year tour. Fact is, one of them made me infamous, in and around Fort Bliss, Texas.

In December 1975, just before our first cycle began, Olson, Boyle, Lieutenant Colonel Tobin, and I were on temporary duty orders to Camp Polk, Louisiana, for a one-week period. Olson was smiling when he handed me a few copies of the asinine travel orders.

"Who dreamed this shit up?" I said. "I need to go back to Camp Polk like I need a hole in the head."

Olson not only wiped the smile off his face, he attempted to justify the action of higher headquarters; to no avail, of course. "But Sergeant Major, we need to see basic training in the flesh. Camp Polk is supposedly one of the best basic combat training centers in the Army. We'll get to see the hands-on training."

"Sir, I've given basic to two thousand Montagnards in Vietnam and Laos," I said exaggerating only a little. "They ain't gonna teach me zilch. I'll probably teach them more than they teach me!"

Lieutenant Colonel Olson walked away muttering instructions to me or himself, I never knew which. "Be here Monday morning at 0530. Our plane leaves at eight."

I had no choice, but in the last few years I had become a concerned father of the first water. Now that I was home for a change, I enjoyed helping my wife with the "bringing up the children" chores. I consoled myself with the fact that Jim Boyle would be with us, so I'd have a beer-drinking partner in humid Louisiana.

Monday began with a short flight to Cajun country and being put up in the Bachelor Enlisted Quarters and BOQs at Camp Polk. We were to meet with our commanders the next morning in the Post Headquarters and be greeted by the commanding general and command sergeant major. This protocol stuff was hell. Boyle and I drank beer in the NCO Club after supper and learned more about Polk than we really wanted to know. After breakfast the next morning, we were in Post Headquarters with our bosses. We met the post sergeant major, and he said the ol' man was busy on the phone and would see us shortly. "What did you say the commanding general's name was, Sergeant Major?" I asked.

"General Charles E. Spragins," he said, pointing to the nameplate over his door. Colonel Olson was watching me closely, for some damn reason.

"General Spragins was a captain when he commanded the 10th Ranger Company during the Korean War, wasn't he, Sergeant Major?" I inquired.

"Yeah, Sergeant Major, I believe he was. How'd you know that?" Olson seemed to relax a little, so I had to do something. I raised my volume just a tad.

"I was one of the Four-five boys during the Korean War. Hell, I bet he doesn't remember T-Bone Brooks, Bill Jordan, Gene Gower, Buster Cape, Carl Stevens, or any of them other Okies."

"Send that damn man in here at once, Sergeant Major!" General Spragins shouted.

The post sergeant major only nodded in my direction and I was gone, grinning all the way to the post commander's throne. He came out from behind his desk and disregarded my salute in a most unmilitary manner. I was still grinning when he shook my hand and sat my ass down. He wouldn't own up to knowing me, so I told him that I was in the Pioneer & Ammunition Platoon, 2nd Battalion, 179th Regimental Combat Team, and knew most of the 10th Rangers before I entered active duty in 1950. He inquired about each one from my area of operations, and we managed to blow about fifteen minutes while Olson and crew stewed with the top NCO of the camp, post, and station before Spragins called a halt.

"I'd better welcome your people, Top. I'm supposed to be a busy man." The outsiders came in and looked at me like I wasn't playing with a full deck. Spragins cut it short and sweet and we were gone. Our tour of the ranges would start the next day. I kidded Olson and Boyle about taking over the post sergeant major's job before we were dumped at the NCO Club close to our billets.

Live hand grenade training on the range is possibly the most dangerous task in basic training and anywhere else it is undertaken with young soldier boys. But it was there on the range at Camp Polk that I won one from my brand-spanking-new commander. After observing a few rounds of trainees throwing live grenades downrange, I started the conversation with the sergeant in charge. Olson merely observed.

"What kinda problems do you have with grenade training, Sarge?" I asked.

"The usual, Sergeant Major! Scared trainees not putting the live rounds out far enough from their foxholes. Plus, once in a while we get a case or two of bad grenades."

"Yeah, I know," I said, "and what do you do about that?"

"There's nothing legal we can do about it. God only knows we report it and complain, but to no avail."

"Wrong!" My one-word reply got his attention as well as Colonel Olson's. "Wrong!"

His head came up sharply at the reply. "You must know something I don't know, Top," he said.

"Try this, Sarge. It comes right outta the regulations. Take the box or boxes of grenades and turn a few of them upside down. If they have come this way, they must be turned in. It's a fact, Jack!"

"That's in the book, Top?" I nodded before he continued. "I'll check out the regulation, Sergeant Major, and do just that." He grinned.

I waved at the NCO in charge while we strolled to the rifle range. I noted that my boss now had a new estimation of his enlisted chief. The trip back to Bliss proved uneventful.

A few weeks into our first BCT class, we were honored with a visit from the brigade CO, Colonel Starr, and the Assistant Commandant of the U.S. Army Air Defense School at Fort Bliss. Brigadier General Oblinger, a senior parachutist, was a West Point graduate, and a very impressive one at that. It was unfortunate that I couldn't accompany my CO on the tour, but I had other priorities and had no time for it. CSM James Tubbs, the brigade CSM, wasn't along, so I sweated it not. When they arrived at the battalion HQ building, a screaming clerk from B Battery charged my office and got my immediate attention.

"Sergeant Major, Sergeant Major," he shouted. "Gonzales is on top of the orderly room roof, naked, and won't come down."

I exited the office at a dead run and stared at the trainee nudist a few seconds before my mouth and my temper took over. "Gonzales," I shouted, "get your goddamn ass off that roof and get some goddamn clothes on, ASAP!"

Much to my relief, Gonzales reacted as he should have. "Yes, Sergeant Major," he meekly replied before beginning his descent. Two drill sergeants awaited his reentry to the real world.

I turned and walked by Starr, Olson, and the general, muttering to myself as I saluted. The salute was returned, but Oblinger said, "I haven't seen many NCOs like that." I continued to my office, but sincerely hoped he was correct. My language had been atrocious, but I'd communicated, and that's what it's all about.

I was seated only seconds before I began my soliloquy to the first soldier of Battery B; this time I omitted most of the foul language, but not all of it. "Yeah, Top. I want him at William Beaumont Hospital ASAP. I'll grease the skids with the sergeant major of the facility and make sure we'll see no more of that basket case." Gonzales didn't know it, but his Army days were severely numbered. He was not competent to be a soldier boy. I wasn't too damn sure the civilian populace would appreciate our returning their gift, but I had no time to worry about it. To confirm our relations with William Beaumont Hospital facilities, I used my jeep and Olson's driver to visit the sergeant major there. In addition to Gonzales, I also had a side issue to discuss.

After a serious talk with the head enlisted man of the hospital, I picked up my wife's records. In thirty minutes I was talking to a very serious, middle-aged physician in the orthopedic section. He only glanced at the medical records, which did not contain the X rays of my wife's hip that were taken at least six years earlier at Camp Kue Army Hospital in Okinawa.

"Yes, the Army has approved of hip and knee replacements, Sergeant," he told me. "We are relatively new at it, but the best trained in the Armed Forces. I must warn you of one conflict that has come up several times since we have begun the process. We do not operate on someone just because they think they need it. The joint must be damaged to the extent that it cannot be repaired otherwise. We'll have to see your wife's X rays before we can okay the replacement. I want no misunderstanding about that."

"You got it, Doc." I was not worried about the joint's being damaged enough to need replacement. I vividly remembered the X rays from Okinawa. The thigh bone, or femur, of the left leg had penetrated the joint through and through. How she had endured such a childhood injury for almost forty years was far beyond my imagination. I believed all that was needed was her permission to get the show on the road.

After supper we sat in the kitchen and talked while Kathy and Jimmy flipped the dials on the television. Despite her being overjoyed at the prospect, Hatsuko arrived at a decision only after an hour of discussion. "Regardless of whether the new joint removes the limp from my walk or not," she said, "if it eliminates the constant pain I endure from day to day, it will be well worth it." I agreed with her decision, but first we had to get "Doctor Joint" to agree.

After the physician examined the pictures the next week, he conferred with his associates and agreed that the operation was necessary to maintain my wife's mobility for the years ahead. The operation was scheduled for ten days hence, which permitted us some preparation time.

Freida Boyle, wife of CSM Jim Boyle, lived a block down the street from our quarters. She agreed to keep Kathy and Jimmy until supper each day, allowing me to take over after I returned from work.

According to Doctor Joint, the operation went off without a

hitch. The third day after the operation, Hatsuko met the three of us in the hospital lobby in her wheelchair. William Beaumont had done something right, for she was happy to see us, and her smiling face proved that.

Unlike the good old days when the medics waited until you lost motion in your limbs before allowing you to be up and about, in two weeks' time she was assigned to physical therapy. In three weeks the stitches came out, and a week later she was home. Except for her exams and therapy, our lives were back to normal. Hatsuko still had a slight limp, possibly out of habit, but the pain no longer existed. The transformation was brought home to me on a Saturday morning when I accompanied her to her physical therapy session. I was watching as she rode a stationary bicycle when I noted tears on her cheeks. "You look like you're doing okay, hon," I said. "Why the tears?"

She grinned. "I'm happy because I'd always wanted to ride a bike like the other kids when I was a little girl. I couldn't do so because of my hip, and now I can!"

In six weeks Hatsuko was back to her daily grind. Whatever the Army might have owed me had been more than repaid. I was once again proud of my profession.

Our first year of BCT at Fort Bliss had another memorable event that would stay with me throughout my lifetime. The new Sergeant Major of the Army was coming to Fort Bliss, Texas! When I heard the news, I knew damn well that my former boss was just dying to see me, or trap me, or whatever. Needless to say, I was correct. He was still determined to win one, regardless of the cost. We'd see. CSM Tubbs confirmed my suspicions a few days later, informing me that Bainbridge would tour the BCT area and would stop to see and talk to our unit. At least he hadn't asked to meet me in the Officers' Club.

The summer was approaching in 1976 when SMA Bill Bainbridge confirmed his visit. I knew in my heart that we had many things in common. One item I was sure of: he thought he was breaking in a new CSM, and I thought I was breaking in a new SMA. The battleground would be First Sergeant Greenwood's A Battery at 1400 hours on a bright, sunshiny day. Bainbridge, and a local CSM tagalong, would inspect the trainees before a short presentation. Olson nervously counseled me about the meeting, despite knowing it wouldn't do a damn bit of good.

The trainees, with the drill sergeants firmly in charge, were "at ease" in a four-platoon battery formation. First Soldier Greenwood and I made small talk while standing in front of the formation in our fatigues and bloused boots. We watched as three olive-drab sedans made their last turn and headed our way. "I'll go greet him by the orderly room, Greenwood," I said to the large, black topkick. He grinned and went about his business.

I stood at rest on the curb while the vehicles parked bumper-to-bumper. Noncommissioned officers dressed in Class A Army greens with black, low-quarter shoes unassed the first vehicle. I was rewarded by the sight of Post Sergeant Major Jones, of African descent, and Sergeant Major of the Army Bainbridge, exiting. Both men were approximately the same size, a stocky five feet eight inches. I shook both men's hands before I turned and led them to the formation in front of B Battery's orderly room. I declined an offer to accompany them through the open ranks of recruits. Greenwood did the honors. It was over in ten minutes, and Greenwood closed ranks and turned them over to the Sergeant Major of the Army.

About all I took away from his short presentation was that he was looking out for their welfare in the puzzle palace. He then rattled my cage the way he often had at the Sergeants Major Academy. "Are there any questions, or complaints?" he asked. To say I went into shock would be an understatement personified. *I* knew the trainees were not being mistreated, but the SMA apparently didn't trust the NCO Corps. To top off the blunder, a trainee sounded off. We weren't ready for that, either.

"The dayroom is never open, Sergeant Major. We never get

to play pool!" Naturally, Bainbridge referred the question to me, and I passed the buck to Greenwood, who replied in the negative.

"Open the dayroom, Bill!" Bainbridge commanded. I nodded at Greenwood, who flipped the key to an orderly, who sprinted to the Army's version of a pool hall.

When there were no further inquiries, SMA Bainbridge and a grinning post sergeant major shook my hand and told me what a fine job we were doing. While the sedans moved away I cursed softly under my breath. "You ain't gonna win 'em all, assholes." I lollygagged around while the trainees moved back to the classrooms before speaking to Greenwood. "When do you people open the dayroom, Top?"

"When the drill sergeants ask for it to be opened," Greenwood said. "We're not here to teach billiards. They'll have to wait until they get to advanced individual training to enjoy themselves."

"It's our unit, Sarge. Lock the goddamn thing. If he wants to run this outfit, he'll have to move closer to El Paso." Greenwood smiled, handed the keys back to the orderly, and the episode was over. Except for my report to Lieutenant Colonel Olson.

When I finished that chore in its entirety, he went into shock, as usual. I lost no sleep over it, as he'd always recovered before. There were other serious problems to face before my career was over.

CHAPTER 31

The officers and NCOs of the 1st BCT Battalion had a problem caused by someone aloft, a problem we could not solve but never gave up on. Never since our inception had Battery C had a supply sergeant. The unit struggled along with assistance from various sources. Supply personnel from our other units assisted when able, and drill sergeants who were on restricted duty due to medical problems sometimes chipped in. The problem worsened before it got better. Gracious Fort Bliss finally sent us a specialist four with a supply job title (MOS), and things smoothed out some, but not much. Why did it bother me more than the other members of our staff? I guess because I knew from the past that a new unit seldom suffers from lack of key personnel. By that I mean that the Department of the Army normally sends the new units the key NCOs to operate with from the beginning. So where in the hell was our damn supply sergeant? You can bet your bottom dollar that he was somewhere in the vicinity of Fort Bliss, Texas. You don't think that Post Headquarters would shortstop one of our people, do you? Yeah, I did, too.

In the summer of 1976 the post inspector general's office announced that an inspection of the BCT brigade would be forthcoming. Except for the supply problem, we didn't sweat it too much; the officers had more to lose than the NCOs from a poor performance. My only objection was that I believed it to be too early, 'as we were only seven months old as an operational unit. But hell, the bastards in those jobs had to have something to do.

After the three-day affair, we were seated in the briefing room at battalion HQ waiting for the results. I was not too optimistic but wished, for Olson's sake, that we would come out with our colors still flying. We did, except for one glaring deficiency: the supply section of C Battery received an Unsatisfactory, the only one. While Olson just appeared stunned, I was furious, and my red face reflected the fact. At the conclusion, we were asked if we had any comments concerning the outcome. I waited for Olson to rise, but when he did not, I couldn't let us go down without a murmur.

"We have never had a full complement of NCOs since our inception less than a year ago," I said. "The unit that did not meet the standards in the supply field has never had a supply sergeant. The fault lies, therefore, with a headquarters much higher than ours!" I seated myself and looked at the inspectors, awaiting their rebuke or apology. I received nothing for my troubles. The critique was officially over in minutes. I made a mental resolution: I'd get a supply sergeant for that unit, and find out who had diverted him for a year, or there ain't a cow in Texas!

I began working on the resolution that night at the NCO Club. Friday night was boss's night at the club, and I told Olson I would be there, with or without him. His answer escapes me but it was obviously negatory; he did not appear for the monthly postwide event in the main NCO Club. Clad in duty uniform, I drank a few beers. I chatted with CSM Boyle and a few acquaintances from the academy before I got down to brass knucks. I spoke at length to Colonel Lutz, a former SF officer and then commander of the Air Cavalry unit on-post. I inquired about the CSM of the unit, John McLaughlin, who was also conspicuous by his absence. I then sat at a long picnic table affair opposite a former FGM who now ran some rear-echelon unit on-post. The conversation started off friendly enough until I brought the slime out in the open, using the infamous WAG (wild-ass guess) system.

"Mac, why don't you give me one of those two supply sergeants you're over?"

McCarthy suddenly turned solemn and sour, surprising me with his answer. "Why don't you mind your own goddamn business, Bill?"

I couldn't believe he'd said that. I started out in a low tone that grew louder with each word of my tirade. Suddenly, Colonel Lutz was by my side. He guided me to the bar and ordered a round before one remark of his brought me to my senses; it might have even transported me back to Fort Bliss from the rowdy days at Fort Bragg. We stood at the bar when the Special Forces veteran made the statement.

"Bill, you're not in SF anymore. You can't do that sort of thing. It just isn't expected of us. *Relax!*"

I did as I was told, but I vowed again that I would solve the supply assignment problem if I had to jail everyone in the Air Defense chain of command. I began in earnest bright and early Monday morning at the Post S-1 (Personnel) shop with a young, slim E9 who obliged my request for a briefing on troop strength of units stationed at Fort Bliss. He had all of his chain of command charts handy and gave an excellent and very thorough briefing. When it was over, I was convinced of one thing if nothing else: Fort Bliss big shots were undermining D. A. assignments.

"Why don't you shift some people to units that are understrength and balance the units on post?" I asked innocently.

"I work for the post sergeant major, Top," the young man said, "not for you!"

I was back in my office after lunch contemplating my next move. The Training and Doctrine Command was in charge of training centers such as Sill and Bliss. I had met TRADOC CSM Lavoy (not his real name), several times at Bliss while at the academy as well as in my present position. Maybe he could persuade Post CSM Jones to balance the unit strengths.

CSM Tubbs, the brigade CSM, hadn't, or was unaware of it. Hell, why not? I placed a call to TRADOC and in minutes was speaking to CSM Lavoy. The conversation didn't go as planned.

"If you're short cadre, Craig, talk to the post CSM."

"I've been in the Army all day, Sarge. I went to everyone on post, so I called you," I said.

"You don't want to talk to me, Craig. Sounds like you need to talk to the TRADOC inspector general."

I knew he was bluffing and I certainly wasn't in the mood for that. "Hell, if you think that's the way to go, put the sonofabitch on the line," I growled. Now I was bluffing.

A major somebody introduced himself, and any thought of backing down was over. I told him my complaint and he informed me that it had been recorded. I was off the phone at precisely 1400. The shit was in the fire. At 1600 that very afternoon, some of the manure had rolled from Fort Monroe, Virginia, back to El Paso, Texas.

CSM Jim Boyle had my attention on the telephone line. He was hard to understand between all the laughter and sobs of joy, but I finally began to receive his transmission. "I was in a jeep with Post Command Sergeant Major Jones, on the way back from McGregor Range, when he received a phone call from Post Headquarters. They told him that one of his CSMs turned him in to the TRADOC IG. When they mentioned your name, he almost turned white," Boyle roared.

I felt obliged to say something. "No mean feat, in his case!"

"If you wanted to stir up the Army, you done good," Boyle said. "You'll be busy tomorrow, however."

"I doubt it, Jim. Tomorrow I'm gonna do what you did today. I'm going to McGregor Range, but not with Jones, probably with Olson." I explained what it was all about, and Boyle's laughter drove me into hanging up and moving on down to the commander's cubicle. I didn't need to take Olson any further into shock than necessary.

* * *

"You did what?" Colonel Olson screamed.

After I explained the entire scenario to my boss, his blood pressure came back down. I think. At least he didn't puncture my one and only eardrum.

"So what happens now, Sergeant Major?"

"For one thing, sir, we'll probably be over in supply people shortly," I said. "Maybe TRADOC will straighten out Fort Bliss, but don't bet on it."

About thirty minutes after quitting time, Tubbs called from Brigade. I'd been waiting for that.

"Say again, Jim," I asked.

"The post sergeant major wants you in his office tomorrow at 0900 hours. What did you do now, Bill?"

Much to his surprise, I detailed my actions before I declined the appointment with Jones. Tubbs couldn't believe what I'd said, so I repeated it. He ended his portion before I got in the last word, for a change.

"You'd better be there at nine, Bill!"

"Sorry, Top. I can't make it. I do work for Colonel Olson, not Jones. In fact, he may not believe this, but he and I are the same rank. I'll be at McGregor Range if you need me. 'Bye!"

We were almost at McGregor Range before Olson was informed about the nine o'clock appointment. By a mere coincidence, the time was 0900. I told him what I'd told Tubbs. "Ain't no sweat, sir!" His head-shaking was becoming a habit.

From the unit's point of view, the results of the adventure were mostly positive. Except for Jim Boyle almost dying from laughter, I enjoyed it immensely. In three days C Battery had an SFC (E7) supply sergeant. That Fort Bliss, according to the TRADOC IG, was over by twenty-eight Supply personnel, was not broadcast by me. In ten days I met Lavoy and Jones at the McGregor Range facility. Fortunately, we were walking head-on so the conversation was curt. Jones stared straight ahead and ignored me, but not so Lavoy. He smiled and nodded before he spoke, never slowing his pace.

"Did you get that supply sergeant, Sergeant Major?"

"You got that right," I said loudly. Although events would prove me wrong, as far as I was concerned, the matter was concluded. Our unit needed no more notoriety.

CSM Jim Boyle had a surprise of his own making in the summer of 1976. He'd decided to retire September 1, 1976. "Why?" was all I asked.

"I'll have my twenty years in then, Bill, and will only be thirty-eight years old," the intelligent young soldier said. "I'm gonna start a second career before I get like you old farts."

"Thanks, Jim. Let me know how you make out. I'll have twenty-six years in pretty soon my own damn self, and one never knows."

Like the person I'd figured him for, Boyle's success story was not long in the making. He had many job interviews after he'd put in his retirement papers. He dwelt on his successful conclusion with a question.

"Have you ever heard of one H. Ross Perot? Well, he's a former naval officer who now owns a computer outfit named Electronic Data Systems, EDS. He's been very successful. This outfit is now based in the Dallas-Plano area."

"Don't let me interrupt you," I said, "but what the hell do we know about computers?"

"There are jobs in EDS for people without that type of experience, Bill. Security, recruiting, and so forth. Let me tell you something you will like about the outfit." Boyle pulled his chair closer to my desk, lowered his voice, and continued to march. "If you work for EDS, you cannot be a hippy; you must present a decent appearance on and off the job. That means a haircut, no beards, and appropriate civilian attire. He's particular who he hires, and favors veterans. Draft dodgers and the like are a no-no. I was hired and EDS will send me to computer school in Dallas before I'm assigned. Not bad, huh? Getting paid to go to school, Bill?"

I filed the information while Boyle was busy preparing for his first retirement and second career. In August 1976 I received orders assigning me to an artillery battalion in West

Germany. I was given sixty days to accept the permanent change of station or retire to a life I knew little about.

I objected to the assignment because I had no background in the field artillery, except for having been born at Fort Sill, Oklahoma. My children, eleven and twelve now, had already been in three school systems. And lastly, because of my Far East assignments, I had a thing about duty in the European Theater of Operations. While I was mulling over the pros and cons, I received a letter from the artillery battalion commander in Germany asking me when I would arrive. I couldn't answer the query because I didn't know. I did try a few other ploys before I threw up my hands.

Meanwhile, CSM Jim Tubbs was transferred to White Sands Missile Range, New Mexico, to take over that post. My replacement arrived and I became the brigade sergeant major. The position only proved to me that the problems were at the grassroots level, not at the higher commands. Colonel Starr and I got along very well, and nothing exciting came from the temporary duty assignment.

I explored another avenue before deciding the issue of my future with the Army. I'd heard through my Special Forces associates that my old CSM from I Corps in Vietnam had retired, leaving the CSM of Special Forces–Europe wide-open. Hell, I thought, it's worth a shot. Despite having to slave away as Brigade CSM, I called the assignment branch at the Pentagon and talked to the head enlisted sergeant major. Upon hearing my request, he asked me what qualifications I had for the assignment. After answering that asinine question, he made my shit hot again. "Admittedly," he conceded, "you're qualified, however, it's not up to us to fill that slot. The general-in-charge would have to select you."

"If the generals are making the assignments, what the hell do we need with you and your people?" A few moments of silence followed before we wrote each other off and hung up the phone. If the young assignment enlisted expert had done nothing else, he'd helped me make up my mind. If choice assignments were handled by the general-grade officers, I had no more chance for one than a snowball in hell. My active-duty days were over, and my retirement papers followed shortly afterward. My retirement ceremony would be on October 31, 1976. Beginning November 1, 1976, I would be a civilian, whatever the hell that was.

In spite of resolving the toughest decision we'd faced since our marriage, my wife and I still had a few more to go before the fateful date. We did just that! On one of our several visits to see an old retired SF sergeant major, John T. Lockhart, and his Okinawan wife and daughter, we got the big one out of the way. We believed, and Lockhart agreed, that if you couldn't find a job in the Dallas/Fort Worth, Texas, area you probably wouldn't find one, at least in that time frame. Therefore, on one of our excursions, we purchased a new three-bedroom, brick home on one acre near Springtown, Texas. To top off the country home, we purchased the adjoining five acres as well. With a nice place to live in countryside surroundings, all that was left before our move was the retirement ceremony.

The retirement ceremony is not a requirement, but I was of a mind that attendance should be required for all retirees, regardless of rank. Within three days of the auspicious occasion everything but our suitcases, clothing, and Kathy's puppy dog, Lady, was on its way to Springtown, Texas.

While driving to the post guest house, in the heart of Bliss near the puzzle palace, I had my final brilliant idea before leaving my past life and friends behind. Generals were afforded VIP quarters in the guest house. Why weren't command sergeant majors? They, like the generals, had reached the height of their profession. I didn't want Kathy, Jimmy, and Hatsuko to endure cramped living conditions during their last few days in the Army environment. Hell, it was worth a shot. I decided to keep my idea a surprise until it was attained.

The pretty lady who awaited our arrival was unaware of the intent as well, but I let 'em all in on it quickly. "No, lady, I'm a command sergeant major, I want VIP quarters like all the other big shots," I said. My wife and kids only stared at me.

"I can't do that, Sergeant Major. I'd have to call the post sergeant major about that."

"Do whatever is necessary, lady!" I paid little attention to her as she dialed the phone. I did notice that her face reddened considerably at one phase of the operation. She was still blushing when she hung up. "Well, young lady, what did he say?"

She continued shuffling through the card file during her reply. "I'll tell you as soon as I find your VIP quarters' number."

She handed me the lodging key, and I passed it on to Hatsuko, who began the short trip to the elevator with the kids while I awaited a reply to my question.

"Here's what he told me, Sergeant Major. 'Give that SOB anything he wants, just get him off this post!' "

We were in and out of the elevator and in our spacious quarters in quick time. When the wife and kids saw the layout, they were pleased to no end. "How did you manage this, Daddy?" Hatsuko asked.

"It's easy, honey, when you've got friends!"

INDEX

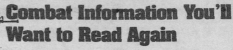